Victoria Vanstone is the host of *Sober Awkward*, a popular comedy podcast that tracks two former party animals as they navigate life without booze. Victoria started writing on the day she gave up alcohol and became a renowned over-sharer on her blog drunkmummysobermummy.com. The reformed 'party girl' is now on a mission to help others stuck in a pattern of normalised social binge drinking. Originally from Reading in the UK, Victoria now lives on the Sunshine Coast in Queensland with her brood of uncontrollable children, a rather confused dog, and a very patient husband.

If you're enjoying *A Thousand Wasted Sundays*, please tag me (@soberawkward) in your posts and share your Sunday! #1000sundays

A THOUSAND WASTED SUNDAYS

VICTORIA VANSTONE

PANTERA PRESS

PANTERA PRESS

The information in this book is published in good faith and for general information purposes only. Although the author and publisher believe at the time of going to press that the information is correct, they do not assume and hereby disclaim any liability to any party for any loss, damage or disruption caused by errors or omissions, whether they result from negligence, accident or any other cause.

First published in 2024 by Pantera Press Pty Limited
www.PanteraPress.com

Text copyright © Victoria Vanstone, 2024
Victoria Vanstone has asserted her moral rights to be identified as the author of this work.

Design and typography copyright © Pantera Press Pty Limited, 2024
® Pantera Press, three-slashes colophon device, and sparking imagination, conversation & change are registered trademarks of Pantera Press Pty Limited. Lost the Plot is a trademark of Pantera Press Pty Limited.

This book is copyright, and all rights are reserved.
We welcome your support of the author's rights, so please only buy authorised editions.

Without the publisher's prior written permission, and without limiting the rights reserved under copyright, none of this book may be scanned, reproduced, stored in, uploaded to or introduced into a retrieval or distribution system, including the internet, or transmitted, copied or made available in any form or by any means (including digital, electronic, mechanical, photocopying, sound or audio recording, and text-to-voice). This book is sold subject to the condition that it shall not, by way of trade or otherwise, be lent, re-sold, hired out, or otherwise circulated in any form of binding or cover other than that in which it is published and without a similar condition being imposed on the subsequent recipient.

Please send all permission queries to:
Pantera Press, P.O. Box 1989, Neutral Bay, NSW, Australia 2089 or info@PanteraPress.com

A Cataloguing-in-Publication entry for this book is available from the National Library of Australia.

ISBN 978-0-6457579-4-1 (Paperback)
ISBN 978-0-6457579-3-4 (eBook)

Cover Design: Hazel Lam
Cover Images: Paul Craft/Shutterstock.com
Publisher: Katherine Hassett
Project Editor: LinLi Wan
Copyeditor: Sarina Rowell
Proofreader: Pam Dunne
Author Photo: Carly Head
Typesetting: Kirby Jones

Printed and bound in Australia by McPherson's Printing Group

MIX
Paper | Supporting responsible forestry
FSC® C001695
www.fsc.org

The paper this book is printed on is certified against the Forest Stewardship Council® Standards. McPherson's Printing Group holds FSC® chain of custody certification SA-COC-005379. FSC® promotes environmentally responsible, socially beneficial and economically viable management of the world's forests.

*For my husband, John, and my children,
George, Nell and Fred.*

*As far as I can remember,
all of this is true.*

I decided to stop drinking while it was still my idea.
Billy Connolly

Contents

Prologue	1
The Kid with Big Eyes	5
Raising Sea Monkeys	18
Champion Napkin Folder	25
Piles and Placentas	32
Labouring Cow Vaginas	41
Pretty Scandinavians	50
'If I Do This Well, I Will Always Have Friends'	53
Delirious with Happiness and Painkillers	60
Cigarettes and Alcohol	67
'Sorry About My Tit'	75
Little Knotted Bracelets	84
Snot and Free Cake	87
Jim Morrison is Angry with Me	92
Mum Shorts	98
Big Fish, Little Fish, Cardboard Box	103
Fluffy Jumpers and Tupperware	109
Dry Humping Care Bears	116
Hungover	123
Free Beer Here	124
Sour Milk	131
'You Are Under Arrest'	133
A Conga Line of Broken Promises	138
Overdosing with Big Bird	141
Home by 10 pm	152
Good Old-Fashioned Brainwashing!	157

Invisible	168
The Stump	174
Operation Wombfill	188
A Tsunami	193
A Life Vest	204
International Sex Machine	206
A Blue-Eyed Baby Girl	215
Poor Drunken Choices	220
A Bit of Leprechaun Magic	228
The Shits and India	232
Beneath Lies and Lager	239
Everything You See I Owe to Spaghetti	248
Am I a Weirdo?	256
Camembert and Warm Beer	261
Rainy Days and Mondays with Dianne	266
Lady Lumps and Prune Juice	271
Irresponsibly Responsible	276
Can I Have My Toothbrush and Dignity Back, Please?	291
To Me, with Love	299
A Thousand Wasted Sundays	306
Epilogue	315
A Note to those Reconsidering Alcohol	319
Thanks	321

Prologue

I woke up and couldn't breathe.

Something was around my neck.

I reached up.

I was wearing a small bow tie, like a ventriloquist's dummy. I had no idea where I got it. I dug my fingers under the tight ribbon, ripped it off and threw it across my bedroom.

Shame gave my conscience a nudge. My heart raced.

I peered under the sheets, not knowing what I was going to see. I scanned my body and found my sequinned dress clumped up around my waist, like a deflated rubber ring. I had scratches on my knees, a black toenail covered in dark, congealed blood, and dancefloor dirt scuffed up my shins. Remnants of an unknown adventure mapped out in blotches over my pasty skin.

Maybe if I stayed in bed and didn't move my pounding head, I could stop this hangover from forging its way into my body. Maybe if I lay still, my hangover wouldn't notice me.

I squeezed my eyes shut, hoping to sleep off the worst of it.

But sleep didn't come, only questions.

Where the bloody hell did I end up?
Who was I with?

How did I get home?

I sat up, switched on the lamp next to my bed, downed a glass of stale water and tried to piece together my night. Vague memories rose and fell like bubbles in a flute of champagne.

Dancing on a bar; Sambuca shots. A sweaty, red-faced bouncer saying, 'I think you've had enough, love,' as he shoved me towards a fire exit. Then just flash cards of a night out. Strange places, faces moving away, stumbling in the rain, hands reaching down to pick me up, the bright lights of a restaurant, mayonnaise dripping onto waxy paper, the room spinning, then strands of hair dipping into the toilet water below me. The only sound I remembered was my moans reverberating deep inside the enamel auditorium. My insides hurt as I heaved; nothing was coming out, just air and the rancid smell of the Abra Kebabra takeaway.

Then, total blackout.

I yanked the quilt back up over my cold shoulders. *Thank fuck it's Sunday.*

I didn't have any plans. I could wallow in my squishy pit of discontent until this stonking hangover pissed off. I plumped my pillow and lay down.

But noises from the land beyond my bedroom invaded.

Cupboards banging, the sticky sound of the fridge door being opened, the annoying *clang* of a single coin being flung around in the dryer.

Then something high pitched, like a cat being strangled.

What's that?

It must be the TV.

'Can you turn that down?' I shouted through a hole in the duvet.

But the noise got louder.

My door was pushed open. A warm light from the hallway seeped into the bedroom and my husband's silhouette filled the space.

'You'll have to get up, Vicky. George needs feeding.'
'What?'
'The baby's hungry!'
Oh, yeah.
Shit.
The Baby.

The Kid with Big Eyes
Reading, UK, early 1980s

'Hasn't she got big eyes. Is she all right?'

'Yes, she has lovely big brown eyes ... What do you mean by "Is she all right?"'

We were waiting in the queue at the post office when a dribbly lipped old lady tapped Mum on the shoulder.

'Well, you know what big eyes mean, don't you, dear? Big eyes – small brain. You know, a bit slow.'

I hung onto Mum's long flowery skirt as the old bat tried to convince my poor mother her daughter was backwards.

'She's fine. Mind your own bloody business!' Mum grabbed my little hand and tugged me. I stuck out my tongue as I was pulled through the open door.

'Come on, Victoria. Don't worry, your eyes are beautiful. Let's just go home and eat tomato soup and watch *The Sullivans*.'

A seatbelt was pulled across my chest and clipped into the black and red socket in the centre of the car. As I sat watching Mum get in the front seat without her big hair getting squashed, I thought, *My big eyes mean I'm not normal!*

I'd always felt a bit off. Thanks to the meddlesome lady at the local post office, I now had an explanation. I wasn't catching up with my siblings due to an unfortunate genetic disposition.

I was half relieved to know what I'd been thinking was true. I was half pissed off because no one in my family had bothered to tell me.

When we got home, I ran upstairs to the bathroom and locked the door. I stepped on my little green stool and stared at myself in the mirror. At first, I squinted to make my eyes narrower. It made me look like a Bond villain. I leaned closer and, with my nose squashed against the glass, used my thumb and index finger to stretch one eye open wide. My eyeball looked like the inside of a Scotch egg, all white and slimy. I don't know what I was looking for. I blinked and stepped down onto the damp bathroom mat. I clenched my fists by my sides and stood there holding my breath, squeezing my eyes shut, hoping to shrink them to a more socially acceptable size.

Thinking I had an undiagnosed syndrome of some sort was not the best start in life. I felt separated from the world very early on. Life seemed to go on above me, like in a *Tom and Jerry* cartoon. I liaised with the bottom parts of people's legs that strode around me and got on with life. Trapped in a forest of loose-fitting tights and mucky Adidas trainers, in a world below the knee. I spent my days getting a glimpse of what was going on higher up, forever on my tiptoes peeking over things, using all my strength to pull my chin over tabletops and brick walls. I scrambled onto laps when I could, desperate to be more involved, to get a better view of the grown-up world and not feel so ... abnormal.

*

My world was Reading, in the south of England. A leafy town within stumbling distance of heaps of cosy pubs. I was born at the Royal Berkshire Hospital, not quite in a crossfire hurricane – it was more of a slight sideways drizzle that dribbled down the plate glass windowpanes of the Georgian building. When Mum pushed me out, Dad was still at the office, busy selling barcode scanning machines to men in grey suits that smelled of cheap coffee. Mum got the job done on her own, and was home in time for a Jaffa Cake and celebratory glass of Babycham.

She said the best thing about having a baby was the hot shower afterwards, but she wasn't the sentimental type. For the hallway, she favoured pictures of crying clowns over grinning school portraits and had sold all our family heirlooms at local carboot sales for 50p each.

'It's just a load of old tat,' she would say as she packed faux mink coats, gold-framed paintings and colourful glass vases into boxes in the back of her car.

'What day of the week was I born, Mum? Am I full of grace or woe?'

'All I know, Victoria, is my false eyelashes ended up halfway down my face and you had a massive head, a bit like you do now.'

I was a Friday child – loving and giving. The final member of our party of six. I had a brother and two sisters. Making me the last parcel of shit and tears to join the clan.

*

For the first few years before my inevitable introduction to alcohol, I slurped milk from a bottle and downed orange squash by the gallon. I saved mooching around in a pair of stained tracksuit pants, and necking paracetamol over a dish-cluttered sink, until my teens. There was at least some innocence before the chaos.

When I was a kid, I often heard the term 'a bit of a handful' up there in the adult realm. I was a pest with a penchant for eating playdough, doing rainbow dumps and smearing the technicolour slop in my nappy onto walls. I stuck beads up my nose, gobbled slugs from the garden and spent my afternoons throwing rocks at windows. I was that kid. The one with the dirty knees and snotty nose. The one who ate fish food when no one was looking. I stole the shavings out of a metal tin that sat next to the aquarium and placed the large, salty flakes on my tongue. One by one, they melted like snowflakes.

'Stop eating fish food, Victoria. There'll be none left for Steely Dan.'

Steely Dan was my brother's fish. He won him at the local fair and brought him home in a transparent sandwich bag filled with water. When looking after me, Neale, a lanky Bowie fan, danced around the lounge room singing 'Starman' and quaffed whisky from bottles hidden under the stairs. His Bauhaus t-shirt slipped off his shoulder as he climbed over the sofa, screeching into a hairbrush. When he wasn't all punky, throwing eggs at telephone boxes, spraying his hair green, he was inflicting painful punishments upon me. They all had names:

Camel Bites — a sharp knee grab.

The Typewriter — jabbing his finger into my chest.

Motorbikes — revving my ears like the throttle of a Triumph.

The Dutch Oven — holding my head under the quilt after a massive guff.

The Death Grip — shoulder blade squeeze.

The Fish Grip — under-chin pinch.

And, of course, the classic: the Chinese Burn — twisting the skin on my wrist in opposite directions. This one had me on my knees, begging for my life, while he rummaged in my pocket for my last Rolo.

But I idolised my brother, so forgave most of his affectionate torture.

*

My parents had both been married before. Neale and my oldest sister, Louise, were my half-siblings. I was too young to understand how this dynamic affected our daily life. All I knew was when they were with us, I loved them, and when they were with their mum, I missed them.

Louise was 13 years older than me, a teenager by the time I was born, and her life was enthralling. She was cool and aloof, always heading out the door to meet friends. When my sister *was* home, she stayed in her room, hunched over her bed, scribbling in a diary that had a tiny padlock. She read me a few lines once. I sat on the old piano stool with my hands tucked under my thighs, swinging my legs. I was eager to get an insight into the mystical world of boys.

She undid the padlock with a tiny key and flipped the diary open.

'"Wednesday",' she declared. '"Today was the ending of the most beautiful thing in my life. At lunchtime, Steve told me he didn't love me and is now going out with Camilla."'

She then flicked over a page.

'"Thursday — Still the living torment!"'

Her week at school was as dramatic as an episode of *Dallas*. It meant her diary was much more interesting than mine.

The only noteworthy entry from my own teenage jottings was: *Today I had toad in the hole for lunch and then saw a squashed frog on the road. Overall, a rather amphibious day!*

When Louise finished reading, I looked over her shoulder at the biro-filled pages. Pink love hearts surrounded boys' names. Steve was crossed out. But the names of Matt, Kevin and Tim, still objects of her affection, were written in big, bubbly handwriting with smiley faces in the Os.

There were also snog lists, and tatty little notes sellotaped to the hinge of each page.

'Whose telephone number is that?' I asked after noticing a row of numbers written in thick gold glitter pen.

'That's Danny Simpson's. He likes me. I know because Clare told me, and Clare knows his sister and she said he thinks I'm pretty.'

'Right,' I said.

Lou was madly in love one day, and the next promising to kick them in the gonads. Romances were dramatic and her heartbreaks painful. After ten plays of 'Tainted Love', some theatrical crying and intense winding of the telephone wire around her finger, her heart was repaired. Then she topped up her lip gloss and went down the park to snog the face off her next obsession. I watched her pull the front door closed with her hand inside the letterbox.

'See ya!'

Standing in the kitchen, I dreamed of the day I could go with her.

My other sister, Sarah, four years my senior, often got stuck with the 'handful' that was me. She was less affectionate than my other siblings, but as long as my toes never touched hers and I didn't interfere with her sticker collection (especially the ones with googly eyes, and the scratch and sniffs), we got on pretty well. Even though she would eventually be shorter than me, I looked up to her. Everything she did was cool and trendy. If she wore a rah-rah skirt or beadle boppers, and played *Viva Hate* at full volume, I did too. On Sundays, Sarah religiously recorded the Top 40. I sat next to her, picking mud from under my fingernails, as she simultaneously pushed the play and record buttons on her stereo. Sometimes the cassettes got mangled. It was my job to manually rewind them, by sticking a biro in one of the holes and spinning it around my head like a clacker at a football match. Once our favourite songs were recorded, we shared our utter disgust that Renée and Renato's 'Save Your Love' still hogged the top spot. We used felt-tip pens to decorate the tape boxes until it was time for teeth and bed.

When I wasn't annoying Sarah in her bedroom, I was pacing behind her, asking stupid questions.

'Where do sausages grow, sis?'

'Why does grated cheese taste better than sliced?'

'Do pigs have teeth?'

'Why can't dogs speak?'

'Because it's a bloody dog,' she'd say. 'Now, go and clean up my bedroom.'

I found it infuriating, though, that our dog Mitzie couldn't hold a decent conversation.

'Now's the time, Mitzie,' I'd whisper to her. 'I won't tell anyone. Say something, girl. Give me a sign!'

Mitzie tipped her little head to one side and looked at me with her shining black eyes.

'Come on, answer me,' I begged.

Then, one day, it happened!

Not really. Unfortunately, this isn't a tale about talking Yorkshire Terriers.

I think Mitzie was upset after I squeezed her into a Cabbage Patch Kid's dress and hurt her back leg.

Being the baby of the family meant I was destined to feel a bit left behind. I watched on from afar as my siblings rebelled. I desperately wanted to catch up, and soaked up some tactics for when my time came. I studied how to dodge chores, slam bedroom doors when told off, and avoid getting caught when stealing custard creams. Minor offences kept me entertained. Putting hair from Mum's brush in the bottom of hot cups of tea, changing around all the stickers on the Rubik's Cube, carefully undoing the clear tape from the Cadbury Roses tin, and scoffing all the Caramel Kegs.

On playdates, I was mischievous too. I pulled buttons off TVs, knocked over ornaments and punched my friends. I was as irritating as I could be without getting arrested or put up for adoption. I had a reputation for destroying everything in my path and ended up getting banned from people's houses.

'I'm sorry, Maureen. We can't have Victoria round here again. She's too disruptive.'

I *had* poked all the little plastic windows out of a brand-new doll house. Then I was caught in the dining room, with a cheeky smile plastered across my face, having picked the corners of the freshly laid wallpaper and torn it off in reams, floor to ceiling. Mum was horrified. From then on, she and I stayed home, lots.

Instead of hanging out with friends, we baked cupcakes, polished the silverware, and sat together on the brown sofa, singing 'Round and Round the Garden' as she traced circles around my palm.

'One step, two step, tickle-y under there.'

The inevitable tickle never ceased to surprise me, and she always added a big squeeze at the end.

'Again, again!'

'You cuddle those children too much,' said my gran, peering over the top of her paper.

'And doesn't Victoria look like that stocky rugby player, Will something? You know, the one that was on the telly last night?'

'Oh, stop it, Dora,' Mum hissed.

Gran's barb hurt my tubby heart, but I succumbed to a cheek kiss when she rolled down the window of her green Peugeot and handed me a flamboyantly signed three-pound cheque.

'Spend it wisely,' she said and clunked the gearstick into reverse, disappearing out of the drive. I ran upstairs and slid the rolled-up cheque into the slot of my piggy bank, saving it for a Slush Puppie at St Martins, the used-bandaid-infested local swimming pool.

*

Dad took me swimming most Saturday mornings. The pool smelled of wee. I had to wade through abandoned verucca socks and creep past naked ladies with big bushes to get to the showers. Once in the pool, I used Dad's body like it was a diving board. He cupped his hands beneath my foot and propelled me high into the air. It was magic. Once my fingertips were sufficiently turned into prunes, he treated me to a paper cone of chips covered in tomato sauce from the greasy spoon next door. The chips were so hot, I had to hang my mouth open and breathe some cold air in over the top of them.

I called Dad 'The Silver Back' because he had a line of grey hair that ran from his neck all the way down his spine, and he ambled like an ape, legs far apart and arms bent at the elbows, perpendicular to his body. His mother said his legs were bowed because she'd carried him on her hip.

'You'll never stop a pig in an alley,' she said every time he wore shorts.

Dad always had a ball of blue fluff in his belly button. He used to pick it out as we watched *Grandstand* on Saturday afternoons, his round gut on display as he ate a steak and kidney pie.

He didn't cuddle much, not like Mum, he had more important stuff to do, Dad jobs. He sat on a dining room chair and trimmed his toenails, fixed the taps, mowed the lawn, and continually searched for socks, wallets and keys. Dad was away a lot, working, but when he came home from business trips, he always brought us mini Dairy Milks or giant bars of Toblerone. I hated it when he was away, but his black leather briefcase of chocolates and our trips to the pool made up for the time apart. One of my fondest memories of Dad is the time we went to London Zoo, and he chucked a Chewit in the chimpanzee enclosure. An inquisitive baby chimp, after a brief inspection, threw it into its mouth with the wrapper still on. When the chimp started to choke, Dad grabbed Sarah and me by the hands and whispered, 'Run.'

We legged it towards the ornate Art Deco gates, with a man shouting, 'Didn't you read the sign? Come back 'ere!' My dad hadn't run that quickly since the Surrey County Athletic Association's 100-metre dash in 1957.

With the zoo no longer an option, our monthly visit to the dump became my favourite excursion with him. We bonded over bin bags and demolition. We sang all the way there, with the car windows wound down.

'To the dump, to the dump, to the dump, dump, dump.'

When we arrived, I clambered over the back seat and handed crumpled notes to the scruffy bloke who operated the boom gate. As Dad emptied the boot, I threw bricks at sheets of glass and watched them shatter. I always fell asleep on the way home, spread along the back seat with seatbelt buckles digging into my ribs.

I liked to stay very close to Dad whenever we had guests over, because I never wanted to miss out on his hilarious, underhanded comments. They were said quietly, subtle remarks that weren't for everyone's ears. Often crude and distasteful, but always funny. I thought my dad was the wittiest person in the world, and was proud he was so offensive.

Some afternoons, I joined him next to his record player, listening to old recordings of Derek and Clive, and Spike Milligan. I sat at his feet, laughing when he laughed, copying his movements, mimicking his posture. His whole body jiggled when he chuckled, and as his head tipped backwards, I could see up his hairy nostrils. It wasn't the jokes that made me happy, it was the sight of Dad wiping tears of joy from his eyes.

Those long, hot summers of the early 1980s all rolled into one long, sunny day, spent getting grubby, making muddy concoctions, and mixing putrid-smelling perfumes out of twigs and rose petals. I stepped in dog shit a lot and forever dragged my plimsolls along kerbs, trying to remove the offensive canine paste from the thin lines in the soles. I played kiss chase, climbed trees. I also loved to kick the inflatable silver inserts from wine boxes left over from my parents' parties. I heard liquid splashing inside. By pressing hard on the plastic button on the little tap, I let out the vinegary fumes. It smelled delicious. Those space-age wine bags are one of my first memories of alcohol. I understood there was wine inside and I wasn't allowed to drink it.

I'd seen booze; it was around me from a young age. It was piled up in the garage or sticking out of a silver ice bucket. But I had no interest in it then. I was too busy being a kid. A kid watching on, learning from afar. Waiting.

Our house was chaotic at times. There was shouting, arguments, tears and tantrums, all of which were soaked up with kisses, bedtime stories and lots of 'I love you's.

I was lucky, happy. I loved my crazy family to Swindon and back.

*

Before I started school, my mum dragged me to the hairdresser and I got the most dreadful cut. Nowadays, if this haircut existed, the authorities would step in. Hair-massacre day is wedged in my memory like a doorstop. The cold, sharp scissors scratching across my forehead, the rancid breath of the lady as she cut a perfect line from one ear to the other, the locks of lovely long hair dropping on the ground around me. My new fringe was as straight as the top of a page, with the back section spiked up with a gel like the slime out of Ghostbusters. When I looked in the mirror, I burst into tears. I went from a pretty (wide-eyed, large-headed, rugby-player-faced) girl to an unattractive boy. My fingernails dug into my palms, my bottom lip folded over, and I bowed my head, chin touching the silky gown tied around my neck. Mum put her hand on the back of my neck and said, 'Don't worry, Victoria, the bog-brush look is all the rage.'

I glanced sideways and saw my sisters hide giggles behind their *Bunty* Annuals.

As fireworks went off in the dark sky above our house, I began the new year as an overweight, bug-eyed, straight-fringed lad. The comments about me quickly changed focus from the eyes to 'Gosh, isn't he a handsome little fella.' And accompanied by a painful cheek pinch.

The haircut was the first time I ever hated something about myself. No matter how much I tried to flatten the spike and part the fringe, I looked ugly. Resembling a petrified hedgehog caused me to retreat behind Mum's long skirt, where I felt safe, where the world couldn't see me. I was too young to know any feelings of self-doubt could be drowned out by bucketloads of booze. Until I made that discovery, I withdrew into my little world where I was happiest – below the knee, with the ants, the flowers and the tic-tac-toe.

Raising Sea Monkeys

It said on the packet to hold the white stick in the stream of urine for 30 seconds. Until that moment, I believed I knew where wee comes from. Turned out I didn't. It was like chasing a pig. When I thought I had it, off it trotted in the opposite direction. Where the stick went, the wee didn't.

The box came with two tests. I drank a pint of water, washed my hands, and prepared for round two. This time, relaxed, I held the stick in position. My plan was to hold it in one location, and hope for the best. I felt the stick fill with the weight of liquid flowing over it. There was no way this stick was getting 30 seconds. I brought the test up to eye level when I was done. It was damp in all the right places. Score.

The instructions said to wait five minutes for the results. I balanced the stick on top of the toilet roll holder, and waited, my knickers and trousers around my ankles. It was a funny way to approach a life-altering moment – my bum hanging in a toilet. It wasn't like getting a handshake after passing my driving test or a rosette pinned to my jumper after winning a donkey derby (the Newbury Show, 1987).

I stared at the stick next to me. *One line or two?* I wondered.

Parenting or freedom? Stuck at home singing silly songs about mashed potatoes or bumming around the world like I'd been doing for the past ten years?

I leaned uncomfortably towards the latter.

The timer on my phone chimed.

I stood, pulled up my trousers and knickers in one tug, picked up the stick and took a casual glance at the result.

I expected myself to be saying, 'Thank fuck for that.' Then chucking it in the bin and carrying on with my life.

But there were two lines: positive.

'I'm going to have a baby, for God's sake!'

I felt faint and held onto the wall for support.

Come to think of it, I was more tired than usual, but put it down to a monumental two-day hangover. It *had* been a huge weekend. A pre-wedding get-together. My usual spectacular bout of alcohol poisoning in all its bruised-knee, lost-wallet glory. I had few memories of the sordid affair, apart from being on all fours, shouting, 'Human Podium!' Then allowing everybody in the nightclub to climb onto my back for a dance. A tray of dropped shots. Waking up on the floor of a mate's spare room, wedged between the bed and a wardrobe, with sore boobs, dirty hands, and footprints on the back of my tank top.

I must be getting old, I thought as I downed a pint of water. I had hoped to sleep off the worst of it, but my reckless drinks-mixing rumbled in my gut.

I can't be pregnant ... Can I?

I looked at the stick again. The lines got clearer by the second. Two bright blue bars.

I flicked the stick, shook it to see if it might change its mind.

The packet had been sliding around the bottom of the bathroom drawer for a while. I bought it at Woolies the previous year after a scare (also known as an '"Oh, fuck it" moment'), so perhaps it was out of date? I picked the wrapper out of the rubbish basket and scanned it. I squinted at the numbers on the plastic seam but, without my glasses on, I could only make out the year: 2013. It hadn't expired. I flipped it over and read the back, hoping there was such a thing as a false positive. Maybe I had eaten too many eggs and that was mucking about with the result. The front read *First Response – The early result. Over 99 per cent accurate.*

I walked into the kitchen, perched half my bum on a stool, took a deep breath, and cried. Big, blobby tears streamed down my face. I didn't know if I was crying from sadness or happiness. It was overwhelming.

A mother, a parent. Me?

Ridiculous.

I blew my nose and tried to pull myself together. In highly emotional moments like these, I usually reached for wine but this was more of a cheese-and-pickle moment. I went to the fridge and grabbed the Red Leicester and the jar of Branston pickle. My knife tapped the side of the glass jar as I lifted the sweet chutney out towards a slice of buttered white bread, the noise making a question enter my head: *Can you eat pickle when you're pregnant?* It was the first time I had ever questioned my pickle consumption.

I carried my plate out onto the deck to get some fresh air. The sound of the ocean breeze passing through the gum trees soothed my world of worry. I sat and watched boats chug across the bay, hulls cutting through the dark, flat water. I pondered if my journey was going to be plain sailing too.

People have babies all the time, I thought. *I'll be fine.*

I wanted this, I wanted a bit of normality, but I had no idea if I'd be a good mum. All I'd ever done was party.

I sat on the deck all afternoon, rubbing my forehead with my thumb and forefinger, a nervous habit. It made me look like someone who might have just scrawled *Mummy never loved me* on the bathroom wall in their own excrement.

I went over everything that needed to change.

We'd have to move house, earn more money, get a cot, a baby monitor, nappies, one of those toys that goes *ping* and makes babies laugh. We'd have to look like we knew what we were doing, be organised, remember to feed it, make sure it slept, and didn't choke on sliced apple. We'd have to teach it to behave, not swear at strangers or bite its friends at day care. We'd have to attend birthday parties, talk to other parents about football training and ballet, sing nursery rhymes and push swings. We'd have to be the sort of human beings people look up to. Currently, I only looked up to people when they reached down to retrieve me from the gutter.

What sort of mum would I be? Stressed? Laid-back? A mum who smoked ciggies and talked too loudly in shopping centres? Like the Pied Piper, followed by a line of feral brats? Perhaps an Earth Mother, who excreted bliss balls, wore a felt floppy hat, recycled toilet paper, sipped kombucha from a jam jar? A mum who posted pictures on Instagram of her family, all smiling, wearing matching pyjamas? Or a gym-junkie mum doing lunges as she wiped kale-flavoured vomit off her Lorna Jane leggings? I had so many options.

What about the wedding? I was getting married in three months' time. How on earth was I getting married without drinking champagne?

Surely a couple of cheeky wines?

I got up, went inside, and googled *How many glasses of champagne can you have when pregnant?*

The first article stated even a sip of alcohol wasn't advisable. I kept scrolling. There had to be something saying that downing chardonnay once a week was acceptable. My hand on the mouse was clammy. Scroll, click, scroll, click. Nothing. Just loads of articles about the damage to the baby from drinking.

I slapped down the lid of my laptop and promised myself never to search the internet for any pregnancy-related material ever again.

Some bleak months were in store and another 18 years of winging it.

It was going to be hard work, but I was in love with my fiancé and had always wanted to have a family. This baby was made with love; deep down within me, even though I was scared, I knew that was enough.

A mum. Me. Bloody hell!

No matter what, though, this baby wouldn't get in the way of me having fun.

'This baby won't change me,' I said aloud.

I would still dance on speakers, say 'fuck' all the time and down buckets of cheap wine at weekends.

I can do this!

Then the back door slammed.

'Helloooo?'

My smiling future husband bounded into the kitchen.

'Are you all right, Vic? Have you been crying?'

I handed him the pregnancy test.

'We're going to have a baby,' I said with an awkward smile.

His knees buckled, and his eyes brimmed with tears. I hadn't seen him this happy since he found out about hot Ribena. In fact, I'd never in my life seen anyone look so delighted. He put his arms around me, and we both sobbed. He cried with joy, I cried because seeing people cry made me cry.

Then I blurted out, 'I won't be able to get sloshed at our wedding. Maybe we should postpone?'

He laughed, told me not to be so ridiculous, and put the kettle on.

We spent the rest of the evening sitting outside in uncomfortable deckchairs, chatting, as the sun descended behind the scribbly gum trees.

'I'm nervous,' I told him. 'I've never pushed a bowling ball out of my vagina before.'

It wasn't just the bowling ball; I was worried about the pregnancy, and having to raise a human. I wasn't very good at looking after myself, let alone a baby. I'd drop it. Leave frying pan handles within reach. Leave it at home. Accidentally put it in the washing machine.

'Keeping things alive' wasn't my forte. I killed all my stick insects when I was nine. They dried up and their legs fell off. Hamsters never lasted more than a month in my care. They were found stiff, stuck behind the radiator, or, months after going missing, tiny bones were uncovered in the airing cupboard, in a mound of fuzzy rodent hair. Our dog, as I said, had a gammy-trolley leg and I couldn't even keep my shrimp-like sea monkeys alive. The packet had said: *The Easiest Pets to Have*. Ignoring them since Boxing Day had something to do with their sad demise. I discovered them (in June) floating on the surface of the tank, entombed in their novelty aquarium.

'Do children come with instructions ... like sea monkeys?' I asked without thinking.

'What?'

'Oh, nothing.'

I decided not to mention my 'pet hit list' to John. Best not to taint his view of my well-rounded, non-serial-killer-like personality.

'Do you think I'll be a good mum?' I asked him after dinner.

'You'll be amazing,' he said without hesitation. 'But let's just get the pregnant bit out of the way and then worry about the mum bit later.'

'Okay,' I agreed.

We curled up next to each other on the couch, to watch a movie.

'Can you pass me an extra pillow, please?' I asked.

'Here you go.'

'Can you get one for my back too?'

'Here you go, lean forward.'

'Thanks. Can you rub my feet for a bit?'

'Sure.'

'The foot moisturiser is in the bathroom cabinet,' I said, glancing at him.

'Okay.'

'Oh, can you plug my phone in too?'

'Yep.'

'And get my glasses? And I need a drink and a chocolate biscuit.'

'Yes. Anything else, Your Ladyship?'

'Yes. While you're up, can you do the dishwasher, and take the bins out?'

Maybe being pregnant won't be too bad after all.

Champion Napkin Folder

Age 6

'Rogerrr!' Mum shouted Dad's name from the kitchen. 'Can you get the punch ready? And change your shirt, there's a stain on the front.'

'Yes, dear. Doing it now.'

My parents were having a party. Pots bubbled on the stove, and plates were piled on top of the heater trolley. The dining room table was covered in a waxy cloth and nibbles in brown wooden bowls. Standing on my tippy toes, chin on the table, I plucked out a cheese and pineapple stick protruding from a foil-covered orange and grabbed hold of a couple of warm sausage rolls. I kneeled under the table, surrounded by the shapely legs of the mahogany chairs, shoving the snacks into my face. I picked fallen flakes of pastry from deep inside the shagpile carpet, to hide any evidence of my feast.

'Roger, can you put my rollers on when you go upstairs?' I heard Mum shout again. 'And put the nice glasses out. The mayor's coming tonight.'

I was surprised by this news. The last time the mayor paid us a visit, our dog shagged her shin. Our ratty little pooch drilled her crotch against the mayor's wrinkled brown stocking like she was a jackhammer. Dad had to prise her off, paw by paw, and make amends with an awkward apology and a strong Scotch. But my parents' parties were so good that the nice lady mayor had decided to risk another pair of tights and attend. To be on the safe side, I locked the dog in the laundry with a Meaty Chew.

My parents made a great team. Dad was the boss of setting up, Mum oversaw the cooking. He hurried around with stacks of chairs and trays of glasses, while she put sprigs of parsley on chunks of pâté and covered hot dishes in swathes of aluminium foil.

Mum was in her element when in the kitchen. With fogged-up windows, clattering pans, slippery lino floors, she swirled from hob to cupboard to sink, like a ballerina gliding on ice. She wore a shiny plastic apron with a naked female body on the front. It had a clover-leaf flap covering the private parts. I used to get the apron out and show it to my mates when they came over. Mum had got it from Dad for Christmas. We all cheered her on when she slipped the apron on and danced around the living room.

Mum could whip up a meal for 60 guests without an ounce of panic. My three older siblings and I helped, folding napkins into fan shapes, or rolling them up tight to slide into gold rings. We placed plastic parrot-topped stirring sticks in long-stemmed cocktail glasses, sliced up squashy boiled eggs, put peanuts into little bowls, and folded bacon around stumpy cocktail sausages. We took turns popping our heads through the serving hatch for any leftovers, or mixing bowls to lick.

Now I watched on as she leaned over the stove, bending her plastic apron-tits in two, inhaling the smells, then stirring hard with a big wooden spoon. She noticed me and smiled. I smiled too.

Her kitchen smelled of warm soup and garlic bread. There were *pings* from the microwave and the chimes of timers as party pies rose in the oven. Her index finger dragged along the inside edge of huge ceramic mixing bowls, as she tasted her concoctions. She paused for thought as she decided what the dish needed, and then grabbed a giant salt grinder, twisting it over the pot.

'How is it now, Mum?'

She brought the spoon to her lips and nodded.

'Yep! It's bloody cordon bleu, Victoria. I will be awarded five stars in the *Michelin Guide* before long! Now, go and ask Dad to get me a glass of sparkly and tie some balloons to the letterbox. People won't know we're having a party otherwise.'

With everything prepped, she retreated to the bedroom to get ready. I crept in, sat on the bed, waiting for her to finish her hot bath. With a towel wrapped around her midriff and one on her head, folded like she was a Bedouin, she drifted into the bedroom. I liked her face without make-up. Seeing her fresh out of the bath was like seeing her for the first time. Her skin radiated warmth and she smelled of Imperial Leather soap.

At her little dressing table, perched on the low stool, Mum began her transformation. After a twist of the blue top of her Nivea face cream, she spread a dollop under each eye, like Adam Ant with his white stripe, and let it soak into her skin. With her head upside down, she blow-dried her red hair. She was renowned for 'big hair' – it seemed to arrive five minutes before her and skimmed the top of the door frame when she entered a room. Getting it to full volume took time and effort.

Once her hair was dry and fluffy, the hot rollers went in. Mum held the pins in her mouth and, with both hands, collected a chunk of hair and rotated the rollers until the hair caught in its little claws. When secured, using a U-shaped pin from between her lips, she expertly fastened the tuft into place.

While Mum's hair curled, she got a see-through plastic case out of her top drawer and started on her nails. I inhaled the smell of the nail polish remover as she rubbed off the cracked varnish. Each nail was painted bright red, with three swift upward movements. She held her nails near her mouth and blew, up and down, like she was playing a harmonica, until they were dry. She pulled the rollers out, frantically back combing each curled clump.

A flute of champagne sat untouched atop her dresser. Tiny bubbles skimmed the edge of the glass as they floated to the surface.

I moved from my spot on the bed when she grabbed a tall golden can of hairspray. She pushed down with her finger on the white plastic trigger, and her arm moved around the top of her head, spraying until I couldn't see her through the mist. Hair complete, she applied layers of foundation, blue eye shadow and a pair of false eyelashes. With her face stretched and distorted like a Dr Seuss character's, she blinked frantically until the glue dried.

'Can you go into the bottom of my cupboard and find my gold shoes, please, Victoria.'

I crawled into the cupboard and threw shoes from the dark, unidentifiable pile so they landed where she could see them.

'How about these?'

'No, the heel is broken. I'm going to take them back to Marks.'

'These?'

'No, not high enough.'

I dug deeper into the pile, until I found a matching pair. The cupboard was warm and smelled musty like the inside of an old hat. I felt quite comfortable in there, at home almost. A favourite hiding spot, that cupboard reminded me I wouldn't be a kid forever. One day, the shoes would fit me.

Mum put on her black dress with the fringe around the bottom and slipped on the pair of stilettos I selected. They had an opening where her knobbly toes squashed through. She picked up her drink and tottered out of the room in a haze of Chanel No. 5. The heel on her shoes made little holes in our thick white carpet, a trail for me to follow downstairs.

People arrived, bottles were handed over, hands were shaken. I stood near our front door, arms outstretched, collecting the coats. When the pile got too heavy, I dumped them on the bed in the spare room.

When I returned, people were at the nibbles, talking loudly. The men stood close to each other, their brown flares almost touching, and looking like black paper silhouettes against the textured red wallpaper. Standing in a row, they swayed to and fro, heel to toe, discussing cars and computers. My brother talked of his new Commodore 64 and how he managed, after three weeks, to write a program where a weird pixilated mouse danced across the screen. The men were impressed, which made my brother's eyes sparkle. They swilled amber whisky and water in thick tumblers. The wives stood in a circle, sucking Tia Maria through stripy bent straws from tall glasses. I carried my beanbag over to the corner of the room and watched the night unfold.

The 1970s were late leaving Reading and spilled over into my parents living room. The guests swanned around like film stars. The women in floaty dresses, eyelashes like llamas', platform shoes like a glam rocker's, with flicked hair and shimmering lipstick. The men were like members of ABBA, with thick hair, furry sideburns, and huge pointed shirt collars. Some held cigarettes near their mouths, taking strong pulls between sentences. The tobacco burned bright and crackled with each inhale. Lines of white smoke twisted together above heads, and disappeared when more people arrived and the front door let in a gust of cold night air.

Dad appeared in the living room every couple of minutes, carrying bottles or upside-down wine glasses slotted between each of his stubby fingers. His hands reminded me of bunches of small bananas, thick skinned and curved. He handed out the glasses, filled them to the rim, and moved around the guests, topping them up, until the bottle was empty. With a quick trip to the garage, he replenished his stash.

A man I didn't know pushed a high-wheeled silver tray into the centre of the room. Multi-coloured bottles shook and banged into one another as the tray moved along the floor. People gathered around and the man handed out tiny glasses filled with a clear liquid. Lips met glasses, heads snapped back, and bodies quivered as the shots hit their systems. I watched as guests got floppy. Earth, Wind & Fire blared from the huge speakers behind me.

For hours, I flipped through records that leaned against the wall. I pulled waxy discs out of scuffed cardboard sleeves, placed them on the turntable with care, dropping the needle onto the first groove without letting it slip or jump. I played Barbra Streisand, Bread, Simon & Garfunkel and Fleetwood Mac for the happy revellers.

As it got later, the music got louder, and people danced around me. Hands reached down for me to join them. I blushed and shook my head, content to take it all in from the ground. I should have been in bed, tucked up with my Mr. Men books and blanket. I worked out that if I stayed quiet and kept on playing good tunes, no one would notice me. I helped myself to white plastic cups of lemonade, and passed the time pulling apart discarded cocktail umbrellas with mysterious Chinese writing inside.

Drinks kept flowing and, as the clock ticked past midnight, elegance descended into disorder. A big-haired glamazonian vomited into the punch bowl and got carried off for a lie-down. A gatecrasher shoved his hand down Aunty Silvi's diamanté top, and a lady cried in the downstairs toilet.

My arm was yanked when one inebriated partygoer decided it was funny to run around the room with his willy hanging out. It looked like one of the uncooked pork sausages I'd wrapped in bacon earlier in the day, all pasty and droopy. He got shoved out the front door as I was pulled up the stairs and told to go to bed.

I didn't sleep. The music was too loud. I stayed awake for hours, listening. There was laughing, shouting and glasses being smashed. The police arrived; the volume was turned down. The sound from the party moved around the house as people found their coats and passed-out partners. The noise spilled into our stone driveway. I peeked out of my window as guests stumbled into flowerbeds and staggered onto the main road. A group swayed in a huddle, singing *woo woo* from 'Sympathy for the Devil', while a man teetered on the kerb, thumbing for a cab. I turned the handle of my blind to block out the light from the streetlamps and grabbed my teddy.

I can't wait to be a grown-up, I thought before falling asleep.

Piles and Placentas

During my pregnancy, John and I lived on Sydney's Northern Beaches, which they call the insular peninsula. The area doesn't feel like reality; it's more of a coastal complex where the outside world's worries dissolve like raw sugar into a long black. Yoga and quinoa rule, and mums with ponytails bounce along the seafront, holding green juices in one hand and pushing expensive prams with the other. I did my best to fit in, but my yoga shorts had a split in the crack after an over-enthusiastic Downward Dog, and I preferred a builder's brew to a chai. Tea preferences aside, it was a beautiful place to live, with a view of the glittering Pacific Ocean.

The first few months of pregnancy were good. I was missing my usual humungous glasses of wine of an evening but knew that my time would come again. The morning sickness was bearable, and I hadn't stabbed anyone yet … overall, I was doing well.

Antenatal classes were held in an old red-brick building that was on top of a hill and looked a bit like an asylum. I wasn't nervous. I liked meeting new people, as long as they weren't too pretty or had better banter than I did. I hoped to make friends I could roll my eyes and giggle with when the nurse held up gigantic sanitary towels or said the word 'discharge'.

I imagined we'd all look the same, seeing as we were at the same stage of our pregnancies. As I entered the room, I wondered if I was in the wrong ward. Unlike me, the women had tiny bumps, as if they were carrying small rodents in their wombs. Elegant, with blonde bobs and glowing cheeks, they wore stretchy outfits with running shoes, like they were coming from a Pilates class. No sign of fatigue or spotty faces; they were the image of beauty and health.

I made my way through a gap in the chairs, like a blubbery old walrus. Heaving my giant body around the room, tapping sweat from my brow with a hanky, I couldn't hear the other women move. Like they were mice, dainty and quiet. I scraped chairs across the floor and pushed tables out of the way. Being levered into the antenatal ward by a crane, like an elephant delivered to a circus, would have made less of a kerfuffle.

'Lardy bum coming through!' I said, trying to get a laugh.

I found a chair and plonked down my bottom, part of it hanging off the side like the crumbling edge of a meat pie. A daft smile hid my judgement of the bobbed-hair brigade. Then, with a bumper packet of Fizzy Cola Bottle sweets produced from my handbag, I waited for the fun to begin. I saw John cross and uncross his legs a few times, and eye the exit, so I held his hand.

The nurse, a kind-faced lady with dimples, and jet-black hair pulled into a tight bun, appeared. The bobble on top of her head looked like a cherry on a cupcake. As my eyes scanned her body, I noticed she carried a wicked-looking doll under her arm.

'Hello! My name is Susan and I'm going to teach you how to be a mum. Oh, and this is Clive.' She lifted the doll in the air, like Simba at the end of *The Lion King*. 'Just pretend Clive is your baby.'

She used Clive – the devil doll – to demonstrate a baby's various positions inside the womb and help us visualise the journey through the birth canal. Its head protruded upside down from a fake spongy vag, its bright blue eye (the other one had fallen out) locking on to me. When showing us how to swaddle, Susan dropped the doll. Its head twisted unnaturally and its eye glared straight at me. Again.

'Cyclops baby is out to get me,' I mumbled to John.

'Shhh,' he said.

I knew I was supposed to be engaged with the class but instead I daydreamed about Clive coming alive and chasing me with a bloodied knife down a dark alley.

After some inane chat about feeding, which I ignored, we watched part of a birthing video, which was more terrifying than *The Texas Chainsaw Massacre*. There was crying, screaming, chunks of wobbly flesh put in metal trays. I don't know what else there was. I closed my eyes, put my fingers in my ears and hummed *The Wombles*' theme song in my head.

John tapped my arm.

'It's over.'

'God, I need a beer after that.'

'Me too.'

All the partners were called into another room by a male nurse, while the future mothers learned about breathing techniques and afterbirth. Five minutes later, the door opened. The men walked back into the room single file, faces as pale as marble.

Mine sat down next to me.

'What happened? Are you all right?' I whispered.

'That very blunt male nurse just told us that, in the worst-case scenario, you might die, and the baby might die. He said we had to go home and think about that.'

'Well, isn't that just bloody lovely,' I said, shocked. I gave him a brief 'Don't worry, I'm not going to die' arm cuddle and we turned our attention to the class.

It wasn't all doom and gloom. We were inspired by stories of one-hour water births, tales of yogic mothers who had Indian doulas guide babies from their front bums. We watched another video, of a lady looking sweaty in a hospital gown and exhibiting various birthing positions: on all fours, on her back, bouncing on a big red ball, squatting like a sumo wrestler. I swallowed hard, holding back my emotions as I watched men crumble with pride at the bedsides of their warrior wives. It was frightening and lovely all at once.

The climax of the video had the entire room transfixed by a 1970s mega bush that had a watermelon appearing from the curly undergrowth. The intimacy of the shot made a little bit of vomit pop up and say hello in the back of my throat. The shot cut to the woman's face. Her eyes were wide and the veins in her neck protruding. She hung on to the handles of the bed and pushed with all her strength. I couldn't bear to watch, worried she would spontaneously combust. I turned a little in my chair and looked away. I fixed my gaze on the photos stuck on the walls with bronze-coloured drawing pins. New mothers smiled at the camera, with perfect newborns, wearing little knitted hats, resting on their chests. The babies were cute – lovable, almost – the mothers were happy, angelic in some way. The cheesy grins that came at me from the wall gave me a sense of hope. Maybe having a baby would feel nice and wasn't all blood, guts and Clives.

Maybe I would smile afterwards too?

When the video finished, we toured the nearby hospital. Dull chants of 'Om' echoed as we passed the birthing suites. The smell of scented candles wafted through the maternity ward and a beaming new father walked by, pushing a translucent wheeled pod with a tiny baby inside.

'Congratulations!' I said as he passed.

His elated expression made me relax a little. *This is going to be fine*, I thought.

After sightseeing, we reassembled in the antenatal clinic. I sat down, and listened as Susan spoke to us about pain relief options.

'I'm scared,' said a woman as she gripped a piece of screwed-up tissue. 'I'm no good with pain.'

'If it gets too much, sweetie, just ask the midwife for a TENS machine, and if that doesn't work, you'll get a big old shot of pethidine in your thigh that will plonk you on cloud nine. Don't worry, dear, we do this every day. We'll look after you.'

As the lady loosened her grip on the tissue and gave a shy smile, Susan added, 'Oh, and if you have to get a C-section, please don't move during the epidural, otherwise you might be paralysed forever. Now, who wants a leaflet on whooping cough?'

After a little tea break, I reached under the chair, and dug around in my handbag until I found my tissues. I handed the now-trembling lady the whole packet.

Then I heard the howls.

'AhhoooooooOOOOO!'

'That's probably a mother having an episiotomy,' Susan said with a smirk. 'Don't worry, only thirty per cent of women tear.'

When her beeper bleeped, she disappeared from the room.

Tear? What did she mean by tear?

Before I had a chance to think about my snatch ripping in two, and being in so much pain that I howled like a wolf stuck in a bear trap, Susan reappeared, pushing a trolley. She rattled towards us like a flight attendant about to serve dinner.

We gathered around.

'This is a placenta,' she said, as if she was presenting a new puppy.

The red mass resembled what you'd find hanging from a metal hook at the butcher. Mash, onions and gravy wouldn't have looked out of place nestled beside the big glob of red meat.

'If you want to take your placenta home, make sure you fill in the form in the front of your red booklets. It's very high in nutrients. You can whack it in a smoothie, if you like,' Susan said.

I nearly coughed up my Earl Grey. The thought of eating my own rotting insides, whizzed up in a blender with the accompanying piss, blood and shit, wasn't very appealing.

'Mmm, yummy.' I nudged the lady standing next to me.

'I'm going to spread mine on toast,' she said.

I wasn't sure if she was joking.

Apart from the gruesome stuff, and the riveting news that I might pop my clogs during childbirth, I enjoyed the class.

When Susan opened the floor to questions, I couldn't think of anything smart to say. I thought, *Can I bring my own tea bags? Is celebratory champers allowed? Can someone please assist me in removing this small plastic chair from my arse crack when the class is over?*

But one question did spring to mind. One of my main concerns about the birth was John seeing my lady door so … ajar. How would our sex life ever recover?

I plucked up some courage and asked, 'Is it best for our partners to stay at the top end during the birth?'

A husband stuck up his hand.

'I can answer that,' he said.

The room went silent.

He described the birth of his first child, using a beautiful metaphor: 'Seeing the baby come out reminded me of the time my Cornish pasty exploded in the microwave.'

Everybody laughed apart from me.

My vagina, a steaming demolished meat pie.

I turned to John and said firmly, 'You'll be staying up the top end!'

After the laughter and the trauma of the class, everyone in the room connected – the men over the potential deaths of their wives, the women over piles and placentas. I quickly carved out my role in the group by slipping in immature jokes. I planned punchlines when I should have been learning to swaddle and breastfeed. My insatiable need to entertain took precedence over learning how to take care of a baby. By the end, though, I had picked out the women I knew I wanted to see again, the potential 'mum mates', and was glad I had made it without fainting or wetting myself.

*

The last few months of pregnancy were hard, as I battled various ailments. My days were a haze of reflux medication, swollen feet, hospital check-ups and leakages from different orifices. I couldn't have imagined that life's most natural experience could be so, well, unnatural. Every part of my body ached, rubbed and chaffed. I became renowned in our suburb as 'that weird lady who carries a big red chair'. There was no way I could get comfortable in anything apart from that one magical chair. I took it everywhere. I looked batshit crazy as I dragged the huge red beast into waiting rooms and cafés.

Weird, unpredictable stuff happened to my body as my due date got nearer. Sore, scrunched-up fingers, swollen like they were on gorilla-hand ash trays. Skin like E.T. the Extra-Terrestrial's, wrinkled and dry. Legs that resembled kebab meat on turning spits. Hair thinned out and wispy, like I was an ageing sloth. Tits flopped south like windsocks, nipples darkened like slices of black pudding. Even my bottom burps changed – they sneaked out without warning and were louder, like comedy trumpets.

My body was not the only problem, my mind also got bent out of shape. I cried if I stood on an ant, shouted at John if he bought the wrong chocolate (it needed to be Lindt Dark Sea Salt, 70 per cent cacao) and had a meltdown if my poached eggs made the bread soggy. The hormonal changes pulled me in different directions – happy, sad, scared, elated. Old feelings of panic tapped me on the shoulder, but I refused to turn around. I knew the feeling well and had the tools to handle it all. At times, I did consider taking a swig from that bottle of crisp chardonnay banging around in the fridge door. Getting hammered when things got a bit much was appealing but, like one of those grabby machines at a fair, I expertly directed my hand towards the juice carton.

In bed, I was surrounded by a mountain of pillows, a fortress of feathers, jostled and pummelled to support my aching frame. Each night, in a frenzy, I pushed, shoved and bolstered to find a sleeping position. Towards the end of month nine, I slept upright, like a corpse propped up at a Mexican funeral parlour.

I got through pregnancy by ramming chocolate muffins in my face hole and John rubbing my sore feet. I fought through the pain, the piles, morning sickness, and the total hatred of all humankind. I couldn't wait to meet my baby and be done with my bodily malfunctions. I looked forward to being myself again and was about to be blessed with the best excuse to get pissed ever, Motherhood.

*

One night, after a long nine months, a curry and a 'special night-time cuddle' with John, water flooded down my legs.

'It's happening!'

'Get the bag!'

In an absolute panic, we jumped in the car and headed up the hill to the hospital. In the darkness, I placed a hand on my husband's thigh and gave it a little reassuring squeeze.

'Let's still be us,' I said. 'This baby will have to slot into our lives. I won't let it take over. I still want to go out and have fun. I still want to be me, and you to be you.'

But what I didn't know was that my baby would shower me in something I couldn't avoid.

Love.

And it caused all sorts of problems.

Labouring Cow Vaginas
Age 11

'You're going to miss the bus!' Mum directed her screech up the stairs. I scanned my bedroom for my uniform. It wasn't there. I headed downstairs and out the back door into the garden, where a damp pile of clothes sat below my window.

When my bedroom was untidy, my mother had a menopausal tendency to throw its entire contents out the window. My stereo, my CDs, my rubber collection (erasers, not condoms – I didn't collect condoms until I was a teen), all my clothes, my teddies and my Monopoly board. This routine happened so often, most days I got ready for school in the garden, in the drizzle, with the dog eyeballing me.

I stuck my arm into the mass, to the same depth as a vet would into a labouring cow's vagina, and rummaged until I found a shirt and tie. It was better to reach into the epicentre of the pile to get drier clothing. I peeled moist socks from the surface, found a hairbrush and stood in a puddle, brushing my hair.

Once ready, I threw the hairbrush over my shoulder, back onto my walk-out wardrobe, and headed to the kitchen to find breakfast. The thought of eating anything at all made my stomach turn but I knew if I didn't eat, Mum would notice.

On the way, I spewed an elongated good morning to Sarah. She sat on the bottom stair with a piece of toast hanging from her mouth, pulling on a Doc Martens boot.

'Good morning!' she replied. 'Are you feeling a bit under the weather today?'

'No! I'm frigging not,' I said through pursed lips. I chose to ignore her all-knowing glare and pushed past her to the kitchen, banging my bag against her head on purpose.

'What's in my sandwiches? Not shrimp paste again?' I quizzed Mum as milk from my cereal dribbled down my chin.

'No. Garlic and herb cheese spread.'

I gagged.

'It's seven forty-five, you lot!' Dad shouted as he straightened his tie in the hallway mirror. 'You all right, Vicky? You look a bit tired this morning.'

'I'm fine,' I said, looking away. 'I didn't sleep great, had a horrible dream that Zippy the puppet from *Rainbow* was throwing potatoes at me in the shower.'

'Righto. Well, have a good day.' He ruffled my hair, then picked up his black suitcase, kissed Mum on the cheek, grabbed his keys from the bowl and headed out the door.

Without a clue what I had been up to.

I lifted the cereal bowl, slurped the sugary dregs, and packed my homework into my bag. I put my shoes on without undoing the laces, then grabbed my stinking sandwiches from the bread board.

'See you later. Remember you've got tennis after,' my mum announced. 'Love you.'

'Love you too.'

I slammed the front door behind me and ran down the road to meet the bus.

I was more out of breath than usual, panting when I flashed my pass at the driver. He grunted in acknowledgement as I swayed between the rows of tatty seats, grabbing at looped handles above my head. I chucked my bag under the seat and slid open a small window. I sat back, spread my arms wide, and let the fresh air fill my lungs.

My first-ever hangover.

Friends hopped on at the next stop. Chin high, shoulders back and a gleam in my eye, I told them about my first foray into the world of heavy boozing.

*

Mum and Dad had gone out for the day. Granny was babysitting. By now, the badly signed three-pound cheques were long gone and she hardly remembered who I was.

'Hello Vanessa,' she said, with false teeth sliding out of her mouth. 'Are you still working at the Margarine Factory?'

Granny was at a stage in life where she was forgetful and confused. She'd recently confided to my mum she needed to use 'some of those modern sanitary pads'. Mum handed her a packet of Always maxi pads, and told her to just stick one on and change it every few hours.

On her next visit, Gran complained, 'Golly, those pads don't half hurt when you peel them off! '

Mum had to explain politely that she should have stuck it to her knickers, not her nonny.

On her next visit, Granny appeared in the lounge room, smiling, a yellow substance smeared all over her thin lips. 'This cheesecake is delicious, Vicky. Is it Iceland?'

'Yes, Gran.'

I didn't have the heart to tell her that she'd just eaten a pound of butter left uncovered on a saucer in the fridge.

But her newfound puzzlement meant she was the perfect babysitter. My granny was blissfully unaware that her perfect, well-mannered granddaughter was, in fact, a conniving little shit. Under her un-watchful gaze, I could get away with anything. She didn't know if I was up in my room doing homework or igniting the rabbit hutch with a flamethrower. On this particular day, when I snuck past the lounge room, she was sitting in our big brown chair, feet up on the pouf, squinting at a copy of *Radio Times*. A pair of narrow spectacles balanced precariously on the tip of her nose.

I had Emma, a friend from school, over. She was a popular girl who I wanted to impress. Our playdate started innocently as we sat in the garden, making daisy chains, flicking rabbit turds at one another, and gossiping about boys we fancied. After a legendary game of Swingball, where I got struck by the meteoric yellow ball enough times to warrant hospitalisation, we decided to head back indoors to get a biscuit. I untwisted the Swingball metal pole from the ground, carried the kit into the garage and threw it in the old rubbish bin where we stored it, with some old sun umbrellas and a rake with a missing prong.

The bin was next to the section of our garage devoted entirely to one thing: heavy drinking. Cartons of beer sat one on top of another. Dusty racks clipped to the wall held shiny bottles in rows. Cans, kegs and crates covered the floor. The massive pile of alcohol glistened in front of me like baubles on a Christmas tree. I took in the mountain of festivity at my feet. I'd waited for this moment for years.

'We're not having biscuits today. I'm nicking some booze, Emma. Don't worry, I've got a plan.'

I put my hand down the webby gap next to the freezer, found the backpack I'd hidden the previous day and got down on my knees.

Wine? Beer? Is vodka too noticeable?

A clanging from the kitchen hit my ears, as Granny apparently looked for more cheesecake. My arm shot out from my body, and I grabbed a bottle from the rack in front of me. It was cool in my hand. Without looking, I shoved it into my backpack and did up the zip.

Emma stood near some toolboxes in the corner, shuffling her feet. I gave her the nod, slipped my arms through the straps of the backpack, then squeezed past the wing mirror of the old car filling the rest of the garage. I reached over Emma's shoulder to press the button on the wall behind her. The door clunked as it rose. I held steady as light filled the garage. When the gap was big enough for Emma to crawl through, I pressed the button again. I ducked, then rolled under the descending door like Indiana Jones, and scrambled out onto the drive.

'Let's go.'

We legged it down the road as fast as we could. The bottle was heavy on my back. I was out of breath when we arrived at the recreation ground.

'We did it, Emma!' I said.

The child who had always wanted to grow up was about to take her first step into the world above the knee. A rush of delight spread through my body, and I hadn't even opened the bottle.

The park was deserted but I knew some pesky dog walkers would be by any minute, and guzzling booze in clear view risked a nosey neighbour dobbing us in. My sister Sarah had told me about a hidey place in the bushes where boys looked at magazines with saucy pictures of naked ladies.

'That's where Tommy Fitzgibbons goes to play with his winkie,' she'd said. 'It's a secret camp just to the right of the seesaw.'

We got down on all fours and lifted the undergrowth, then crawled along the worn path. The earth was damp and cold on my knees. Raindrops dripped from the tips of leaves as we fumbled through the scrub. Then light crept through the trees onto an empty patch of soil. We crawled in – it smelled of stale piss. I pulled some thin branches aside to make room. We sat cross-legged, and I unzipped the bag. I took out the heavy bottle. Red wine. I flipped up the arms of the human-shaped bottle opener and, with the sharp tip of the screw, scraped around the top of the bottle to break its seal. For years, I'd watched my parents open bottles of wine.

Like a connoisseur, I burrowed the metal point into the cork and turned the head of the corkscrew, pushing hard, twisting as I pressed down. When it went as deep as I could get it, Emma held the base of the bottle with both hands as I pulled in the opposite direction. There were a few moments of anguish when it didn't budge, then *pop*! As the cork was freed, I fell backwards onto the dirt.

'Victory!'

With no cups and no time to waste, I tipped the bottle upside down, and took a giant swig. I shivered. 'It's like vinegar. Here, try.'

Emma took the bottle and did the same. Her face was deadpan.

What a hard nut, I thought.

We took turns quaffing the ruby nectar, my face scrunching with every foul mouthful. The flavour was rank, but that was irrelevant. I was after accolades, a story and a few high fives. Drinking made me part of something. Accepted. I gritted my teeth, shook my head, and got on with it.

After three glugs, I felt funny. Blobby. The emptier the bottle, the redder my cheeks turned. As I swallowed, the fluid moved through my body, rolling me out like warm dough.

'There's still a bit left. Here, finish it off,' I said, thrusting the bottle at Emma.

She took another quick sip, then handed me the bottle. I held out my tongue and let the last drips dribble onto it. They tasted nasty. I spat the woody sediment onto the ground.

'Blerrughhh,' I said as a shiver ran up my spine. I held the green bottle up to a bar of light that seeped in through the trees. Empty.

I hid it under some leaves and torn-off pages from porno mags. I lay back on the dank soil, letting the alcohol envelop me. My legs were heavy on the ground. I tried to stand up but only got halfway before falling headfirst into the bushes. My arms and legs flapped open and closed to make a dirt angel in the mud. Rolling onto my side, mud on my nose, I giggled and said, 'I feel weird. I think I like it.' I got to my feet with the help of an overhanging tree and, after some staggering around on the spot, made my way back through the gap and out into the park. Emma followed.

On the swings in the sunshine, I swung back and forth, scuffing my shoes along the ground. I was there in body, but my brain leaked from my ears. Stretching out my legs and straightening my arms, I hung my head backwards until my hair brushed along the tarmac. I rocked back and forth as the afternoon breeze flowed over my body.

I was relaxed. Nothing mattered. I seemed to be in the present moment for the first time. I didn't care about before or beyond. I felt far away. Away from school, away from parents, away from expectations. I wanted to stay on that swing with the sun drenching my body, forever.

After a while, my swing slowed to a stop. I pulled my body up, gripping hard on the seat's thick metal chains. When I tried to stand, I melted from the swing, and dropped onto my hands and knees. On all fours, I cackled to myself as blood pooled on the cement. I touched my bleeding knee.

Emma, on the rocking horse, was only about five paces away. I reached out for non-existent objects to hold me up. I bumbled around, stepping sideways rather than forward, swaying from side to side as if waves heaved beneath me. Like I was on the cross-channel ferry heading to Calais, staggering from one side of the boat to the other. I held my breath as my mind drifted to memories of a long drive down a winding road towards a campground surrounded by huge pine trees, my feet dangling out of the window and dust rising in the rear-view mirror. With a huge breath and one giant step, I managed to grab hold of the old wooden rocking horse where Emma sat.

'Your knees are bleeding, Vicky. Are you all right?'

'Yeshhh … you?'

Emma then sheepishly revealed she'd not drunk any of the wine. She'd merely held the bottle to her lips. It meant I'd necked the entire thing in about two minutes.

'I think we'd better get you home,' Emma muttered.

I pulled a twig out of my hair and handed it to her. 'Sorry, Ems, I think I'm a bit pisshhhed.'

Arms linked, we zigzagged back up the road. When we reached the back gate, my buzz was interrupted by waves of nausea. Emma held me up, but my body wanted to droop to the ground. With her hands under my armpits, lifting me like a carer with a wheelchair-bound patient, she yanked my limp body up the stairs. We got past my buttery granny, the only sounds that filtered from the lounge room were her loud snore and some high whistles coming from the box.

'*One Man and His Dog*'shhh on. Thashh my favourite shhhow, Emshy,' I slurred. 'I love shleep dogsshhh. All happy and waggy ...' I could hear shepherds calling their collies in soft Yorkshire accents. Puke hit the back of my throat. I shrugged Emma off and clambered up the last few stairs on my own.

'I'm jjjjuuusst going to pop to the lavvvarrrtorryyy. Shee you shooon ... I'll beee fiiine.'

In the bathroom, I took one step forward, seized each side of the toilet and, with vigour, regurgitated everything but my small intestine into the bowl.

'Yewwwwwwwwww!'

It kept coming until I burped nothing but air. My chest ached. A bit of cheese and Marmite sandwich clung to the edge and purple froth floated on the water. I sat on the side of the bath, took a deep breath. I leaned over, flushed the sick away and wiped my mouth with a bit of bog roll.

Emma went home, and Mum and Dad came back. Rosy cheeks and a sour smell in the bathroom the only evidence of my drunkenness.

I greeted my parents without looking them in the eye. 'I'm just going up to my room to finish off my homework.'

'Did you have fun with Emma?' asked Mum.

Pretty Scandinavians

I had plans for being a warrior, fighting off pain with positive thoughts, determination and breathing techniques. But after 50 hours of labour, I looked at John and whispered, 'I can't do this anymore.'

The baby wasn't budging. I was wheeled off to surgery for an emergency C-section.

I was tired and scared by the time I was on the trolley. Lights whizzed past as I was pushed from room to room. Needles dug into my skin, and the IV drip wobbled next to me as the squashy bag was changed. My back ached from four failed epidural attempts. I shivered with cold, plastic tubes coming out of various holes in my body. I felt useless, like I'd lost control of the situation.

Uniformed strangers, orderlies, doctors, nurses, appeared and faded away. I was nauseated and distressed, with the main event still to come. Everything felt surreal, as if I watched on from above. A numbness enveloped my body. Susan was right. The epidural had gone wrong and I was paralysed. Demonic Clive doll apparitions popped into my mind, Clive's one eye penetrating my soul.

In the delivery room, with huge lights glaring down on me, I heard the clattering sound of metal instruments and the beep of machines. I was certain I was going to die and not meet my baby. My husband would be left to go to the park on his own, where he'd probably fall in love with a young Swedish nanny called Annika and then move to Stockholm, where he'd live in a tiny wooden house near a glacier and forget I ever existed. Panic crashed over me as I pictured the pretty Scandinavian throwing my giggling offspring into the sky.

A voice broke off my irrational train of thought: 'You'll be fine. The baby's heart rate is normal.'

Someone squeezed my hand and I inhaled deeply.

I was asked my name, age, allergies. Ice was rubbed on my skin.

'Can you feel this, Victoria?'

I didn't know if I could or not. If I felt it, would I feel the knife slice open my stomach? What if the anaesthetic didn't work?

Before I could answer, the voices around me became unclear. The loudest sound was my teeth chattering inside my head. A reassuring hand was placed on my shoulder, belonging to a bearded man who told me I was doing well. John's eyes were wide. Sweat ran down his temple.

I mouthed to him, 'I'm scared.'

He kissed my forehead. 'You're going to be okay.'

Neither one of us was sure of that.

The anaesthetist's calm tone, as he explained what was happening to me, put me at ease for a moment. He distracted me with inane chit-chat about old *Rocky* movies. Even in a state of distress, I managed a small Stallone-styled 'Adriiiiiaaann' to break the tension and make everyone laugh.

A white screen, erected below my neck, allowed glimpses. Doctors in masks. Blood on rolled-up sleeves, strained red faces. A crowd surrounded my torso. Their hands swilled inside my abdomen, as if they were scrubbing plates in a washing-up bowl. The discomfort reached a new level.

'Right, are you all ready?' a doctor asked.

There were nods and feet shuffled. Then a pulling sensation.

The doctors moaned like they were in a tug of war as they tried to pull my stuck baby from inside me.

'Right, let's try again after three! One, two, three!'

More heaving and pulling. Then silence, followed by inaudible mumbling. Forceps were handed over my head as a huge weight bore down on my body.

A tear dripped down the side of my face and into my ear.

'One, two, three.'

A shape slid past.

The focus moved from the area around the bed to the other side of the operating theatre.

John's eyes followed the commotion.

'Is everything okay?' I stammered through my chattering teeth.

Then I heard a baby cry.

'If I Do This Well, I Will Always Have Friends'

Age 12

'Come on, get something, Vic.'

My cousins peered at me from behind the door. I snatched two bottles, shoved them up the front of my festive jumper and scurried back towards the entrance of the lounge room.

It was Christmas Day, the one day of the year when everyone in my household (apart from me) was allowed to start drinking from the crack of dawn. Flutes of orange juice mixed with sparkling wine were poured, as thick slices of ham and eggs crackled in the pan on the stove top.

Awake since 4 am, I ran into my parents' room when it was still dark, with the piece of cottonwool I'd found on the landing. Jumping on their bed, I told them, 'Wake up! I've found Father Christmas's beard and heard sleigh bells.'

I'd seen Dad outside my window in the darkness – freezing, creeping around, tapping gently on a tambourine. I wanted to wave and tell him to come inside, but that meant I knew. I wanted to keep my false belief in Santa. Not believing was way too depressing.

'He's been,' I said.

Sarah and I dragged pillowcases full of presents onto their bed, ripped open every gift until we reached the tangerine rolling around at the bottom of each case. Then I went downstairs to see if Rudolph had nibbled his carrot as Dad popped the first bottle of bubbly.

*

Yuletide holidays were spent with cousins and grandparents. Until I turned 12, Christmas was about watching *Top of the Pops*, playing 'Guess the Party Blower tune' (always 'Jingle Bells'), and reading aloud the jokes from the crackers. We either had posh crackers, with toenail clippers and mini calculators, or cheap ones that, for some reason, always contained small ceramic otters.

This year was different.

Since the red wine escapade at the park, I'd been nicking booze from the garage every weekend. I was good at it. Stealing booze became my hobby, my way of making friends, and was guaranteed fun. I was on track to be in the *Guinness Book of Records* (right next to the smallest guy in the world in the tractor wheel). Vicky – the most fall-y over-y, pissed child this side of the M25. All hail!

After breakfast, I opened the rest of my presents under the tree. I tore through paper and threw stick-on bows into black bin bags until there was nothing left.

'Look, Vicky, there's one more,' Mum said, pointing at the tree.

I scrambled underneath, and got poked by pine needles as I grabbed hold of the last gift and tore it open with both hands. My entire family giggled at the sight of my sad face peering into an empty box.

My parents enjoyed playing tricks on us kids (whoopee cushions, glasses of water balanced on doors, cheese sauce milkshakes, black shoe polish on binoculars). I always tried to see the funny side. Being in my family meant laughing along with ridicule and enjoying whatever 'classic' prank they'd sprung on me.

'Good one,' I said, offering a fake smile. I planned my revenge for Boxing Day (cling film over the toilet seat).

At noon, extended family arrived. I watched as Aunty Pat, in her big fur coat and high heels, tottered up the driveway. She carried loads of bags, overflowing with boxes wrapped in bright red paper. Her daughter, Tracey, stood behind her smiling, listening to a new CD Walkman. Pat lifted her arm without setting the bags down and, with one of her red-painted fingernails, pressed the doorbell long enough to be heard.

'Merry Christmas!'

A bottle of white wine slid into the fridge, bottles of whisky were placed on the mantelpiece, and a sixpack of lager was added to the others floating in a big blue cool box.

Alcohol was everywhere, but there was one booze storage facility I'd never been brave enough to break open ... the drinks cabinet.

'I'll try and grab the vodka and gin,' I told my cousin, Lee, as I hatched my plan.

Uncle Michael, who was wearing glowing reindeer antlers, was doing a pretty good version of 'Don't Stop Me Now' with the karaoke machine when I snatched the key from the bowl on the telephone table in the hallway, and slipped it into my pocket.

That key gave me power. With it, I became the gatekeeper – cast-iron fun at my fingertips. It wasn't so much the consumption of alcohol that gave me a buzz. It was the sneaking around, the not getting caught and the praise from my thirsty teenage cousins. Drinking had become the only thing I was interested in. Kids games like tag and hide-and-seek just weren't cutting it anymore. (I'd had to give up hiding-based games, due to always needing the toilet when I crouched behind furniture.) I was rubbish at Cluedo too. I didn't care who murdered whom, or with what. I'd lost my marbles in the Kerplunk set. Operation had a sticky orange sweet stuck in the tongs, and the buzzer made a constant sizzle sound. I'd grown out of toys and board games. Drinking was my game, and with that key, I was team captain.

With it safely tucked in my pocket, I headed back to the lounge room. I plugged the remote into the VCR, plonked down on a sofa bed and kicked back to watch a pirated copy of *Twins*. My three cousins, Daniel, Lee and Oliver, and I, all pretended to be engrossed in the movie to satisfy our mums, who came in at intervals to check on us and give cheek kisses, glasses of juice and Wagon Wheels. Once satisfied, off they popped to get shit-faced.

Twenty minutes into the film, we ditched Arnie and crawled over to the lounge room door. Our heads in a line, we squashed our ears to the wood and listened. Voices had changed; conversations sounded slovenly. I could always tell when Mum was gone on booze – she told the same old story about the time Dad tinkled in a pot plant outside a posh restaurant in Florida, and how he passed out in the hotel room. She had then locked herself out and had to get the lift down to reception, naked, covering her bits with an ice bucket. That story, combined with Aunty Margaret's witch cackle, meant the coast was clear and my covert operation could get underway.

I sneaked out of our kid-friendly lair, past the parents who now sat around the dining table. Squatting behind the couch next to the drinks cabinet, I fumbled in my pocket for the key. With one turn, the heavily varnished doors opened, and I grabbed whatever I could carry and dashed back to the lounge room.

'Well done, Vic! Bagsie having first swigs.'

My cousin Daniel was brimming with excitement. He looked so pleased with me. Making him happy gave me a rush of adrenaline. 'I will be the one testing these fine flagons of liquor, kind sir,' I said in a silly voice and lifted my jumper to display my riches.

I placed them in front of us on the cold tiles. Our eyes fixed on the two long glass bottles. My hasty selections looked like cough mixture and window cleaner.

I spun open the lids and took a swig from each bottle. The first tasted spicy, of aniseed; the second tasted sweet and orangey. I winced and swallowed it. A cavernous row of dark holes appeared before me: my cousins' open mouths waiting to be filled. Like a devious pirate handing out booty to my fellow sea dogs, I poured these revolting liquors down their throats. Each decant was followed by a hard swallow, a squinty face, and, as the alcohol trailed down their insides, a vigorous headshake.

'Yuck, that's disgusting! What's next?' asked Daniel.

A warmness spread from my head to my toes as the liquid oozed into every part of my body. The swigs got longer, as offensive tastes became more palatable with every gulp. I clenched my teeth hard to keep the liquid down, until it reached a point of no return. Getting the alcohol to stay inside my body was my ultimate goal. It seemed a waste to puke it up. After a huge mouthful of the one called Blue Curaçao, though, vomit burst from the sides of my puffed-out cheeks onto the glazed tiled floor. My hand, like a brush into a dustpan, scooped the sick into my palm, and I ran upstairs and threw it in the toilet.

When I returned, everyone gawked at me in awe. I acted very 'Been there, done that'. With all eyes on me, I grabbed the long neck of one of the bottles and tipped the liquor into my mouth. I didn't like the taste, but alcohol offered something I wanted more than anything: acceptance. My drinking philosophy was simple: *If I do this well, I will always have friends.*

I poured a glass of water into each of the half-empty bottles, screwed the lids back on tight, and scooted on my knees across the tiled floor, back to the trove of wonderment. I put the bottles back where I'd found them and the key back in the bowl.

In my bedroom, we lurched around laughing and dancing to 'I Think We're Alone Now'. Then we took turns dragging on stolen Silk Cut cigarettes, blowing the smoke out my window.

From that Christmas Day, the drinks cabinet was my nightclub. I hung out there every weekend, downing strong liqueurs with anyone who would join me.

I became a Drinks Cabinet Binge Drinker.

DCBD.

On my knees, slurping as fast as possible from long-necked, colourful bottles, with no appreciation of taste, quality or vintage. Any chance I had, I drank, pushing my limits. As soon as my parents were distracted by raucous friends, topping up drinks and serving party pies, I was knocking back intoxicating fluids until I saw double.

It seemed to me the more sideways I got ... the more people liked me. Funny stories poured from me, and I spoke with confidence and ease. Drinking made me who I wanted to be. Wild, interesting and humorous. Alcohol made me happy and, in turn, I made my mates and cousins happy. A win/win, just by doing what everyone around me was: drinking until I fell over.

I didn't know it at the time, but my binge drinking and need to be accepted by my peers were going to lead me down a dark path, and it would take a long time to remember who I once was. My youth, drenched in alcohol, drowned out the quirky little girl with the big brown eyes in a sea of chaos. I left her behind in my early teens, alone outside a nightclub in the wrong trainers.

But I was a laugh, right?

A never-ending drinks cabinet of joy ...

Until the doors fell off.

Delirious with Happiness and Painkillers

As they cleared the gunk out of the baby's mouth, a slight hubbub filled the operating theatre. I turned my head to the side, to see the nurse wipe a chubby body with a small blue towel. Covered in a white pasty substance, my baby's skin looked prepped for swimming the English Channel. Bald, like a naked mole-rat. Seeing as John was so hairy he had apparently skipped human evolution, I hadn't expected this.

'Congratulations, it's a boy!'

We were both astonished. Nothing could have prepared us for that moment – from non-parent to parent, from no responsibilities to one *massive* responsibility.

Not even nine months of feeling a human growing inside me.

They handed him to me. He wriggled on my chest with his eyes closed tight, his skin wet. His cheeks were chubby and his head was squashed into the shape of a butternut pumpkin.

'Is his head all right?' I asked the nurse.

'Yes, he got a bit stuck. Don't worry, he'll be fine.'

A camera clicked as I held him to my cheek. I sniffed him and pressed his nose with my finger.

'Hello, little George,' I said. I couldn't quite believe I was holding my own healthy baby boy.

'He's a big boy, 4.3 kilos,' John said as he took the baby and kissed him on the head.

'Thank fuck that's over,' I said.

Delirious with happiness and painkillers, I was trundled off into recovery. I watched John disappear behind a curtain, cradling our screaming bundle of love.

I lay in bed, staring at a fly tiptoeing on the blade of the motionless fan. As I waited for the drugs and the shakes to wear off, I had time to think.

I was worried that I hadn't felt overwhelming love for him when he was handed to me. Everybody had told me you feel a new kind of love when your baby is passed to you, but I was too tired and spaced out to feel anything at all.

What if I don't love him? I thought.

Our new son had lots of smiling visitors that day, excited faces saying, 'Cheese!' It was great being the victorious Mother Earth and creator of life. I'd done okay for once. My parents were proud, I saw it in the way they looked at the new baby. Their attitude towards me changed that day.

*

The afternoon after the birth, after nine months of no booze, someone handed me a glass of champagne. I hesitated for one second, then poured it down my throat.

It felt good to be back in the game. My body was still numb from the epidural, but my hand stretched out for a refill before the bubbles even hit my insides.

'Cheers.'

After my visitors left, the maternity wing was quiet, except for the murmurs of sleeping newborns and the soft bleeps of machines. I held my warm baby and wiped some sleep from the corner of his eye. This first tranquil moment with my darling son was interrupted when a nurse flung open the flimsy plastic curtains.

She didn't introduce herself or ask how I was doing. All she said was, 'Name?'

'Me or the baby?'

'You, of course.'

'Victoria.'

Her beady eyes flicked to the clipboard hanging on the transparent cot next to my bed.

'C-section?'

'Er, yes.'

She pulled my wristband towards her and shoved a blood pressure band around the top of my arm. Her assault almost felt like a warm cuddle compared with the birth. As I was on a morphine drip, her aggressive manner melted off me and into the eyes of the magical rainbow unicorn dancing across the techno cloud inside my mind.

I sat propped up in bed as busy nurses sped around the ward, from one bed to the next, taking the babies out, flipping them over and upside down, giving them a rough once-over. The other women in the ward, also C-section victims, were as off their chops as I was. We sat back, buttressed by soft pillows, observing the mayhem, pumping ourselves with opiates.

When the drugs wore off, the parts of me that had been manhandled started to hurt. I felt my scar beneath the bandages pulling taut. I tried to find a comfortable position, but my body was still numb. At some point, one of my legs went rogue and fell out of the bed. I couldn't lift it. It hung there until the nurse came back.

'What's this doing here?' she shouted.

'That's my leg,' I said.

'Well, don't let it do that again.' And off she went.

Most people would hate being in a hospital bed, but I was well trained at doing nothing, happy to watch the world go by, eating butter and jam off floppy, untoasted white bread. I thoroughly enjoyed having a catheter: I weed without knowing, and I didn't even have to stand. The urine bag filled up as I read the cards tucked in my flowers.

'Look!' I said to John. 'The bag's filling up again. I'm weeing. Brilliant, isn't it?'

He wasn't impressed.

George slept quietly next to me in his plastic bed on wheels. I was drained, but every time I began to drift off, old Grumpy Nuts came back.

'Right, sit up. It's time to breastfeed.'

'Oh, yes, okay.'

What an enchanted moment this will be, feeding my offspring my natural earth nectar, I thought as the nurse undid my gown.

So, I looked forward to feeling all earthy and tribal. But before I could say 'Mung bean', the nurse grabbed my tender nipple. She yanked it towards her like she was trying to get a stubborn tissue from a box.

'I'm not fucking Elastic Man!' I mouthed so she couldn't hear. When a hostile nurse has your sensitive nipple between her thumb and forefinger, you tend to keep quiet.

She tugged back and forth until a thick yellow pus, like paste, oozed out from my assaulted mammary.

'There you go. Now, pop him on.'

Pop him on. Sounds easy.

I lifted him up. It hurt – my caesarean scar twinged. I managed to get him in a rugby-ball hold, with his tiny feet facing the wall behind me. I lifted his head and his little wet lips slipped around my boob, never quite latching on. First fail. I tried again. I couldn't get it in his mouth, he was like a moving target. Fail. His gaping mouth became desperate-looking, opening and closing. He reminded me of those clown heads at the fairground, head slowly moving from one side to the other. Instead of a rubber ball, I was trying to lob my nipple in my newborn's face hole and the aim was off. I wouldn't have won the fluffy dice, that's for sure.

But I kept trying.

The entire east coast of Australia knew when he latched on. 'Farrrkkk!' I yelled.

A baby clamping down on a nipple hurts. A lot. I pulled him off and patted a warm towel over my damaged skin.

Right, deep breath, calm down and try again.

The nurse shook her head in disapproval.

The yellow goo ('colostrum' in nursey lingo) was the extra-special superhero milk babies needed to survive. Life or death. All I wanted was to go back to sleep, and wake up when I could make him a cheese sandwich and take him go-carting.

After an hour of swearing and nipple gripping, I gave up. I had to get the nurse to milk me … manually. Me propped up like a heifer, she collected my tiny drops of thick, yellowish milk in a plastic syringe and squirted them straight into the baby's mouth.

Things didn't get any easier or less awkward during the rest of my stay. To my utter embarrassment, a handsome male nurse walked in and told me to hit the showers.

I wheeled my drip across the room, with my arse hanging out the back of my loose-fitting gown. When I was stripped bare, the male nurse brought into the bathroom what looked like a shammy for polishing cars.

'Right, turn around. Hands against the wall and bend over,' he ordered. His tone combined with my tiredness meant I succumbed. He scrubbed blood from my leaky vagina with gusto, for much longer than it took to clean a grimy oven but with the same vigour. I stood there, legs apart, trying to ease my humiliation by repeating in my head, *He does this every day.*

There were many other unbecoming post-birth moments. The public meetings about my bowel movements; the wearing of giant nappies, like I was an overgrown baby; and peeing myself when laughing, crying, eating, sneezing, coughing or jumping. There were so many 'first's. After a while, I just didn't care anymore. My body became a free-for-all. Poke it. Prod it. Milk it. Scrub it. Squeeze it.

Help your bloody self.

*

Napping was difficult in between bouts of happy visitors, the woman to my right snoring like a dying yak, and the woman to my left having a stream of noisy family members and a phone-yapping husband talking fishing trips.

Once visiting time was over, curtains closed, lights turned down, the ward became quiet. And I attempted to feed George one more time. I reached into the cot and gently lifted him to my boob. His mouth opened wide, and I quickly shoved my whole nipple in.

I fed my baby boy for the first time.

His tiny Adam's apple moved as he swallowed. He squirmed in my arms as I held him tight. Right then, George popped off my boob and opened his eyes, staring straight at me.

'Oh, hello,' I whispered to him in the dark.

He looked so cute in his little hat, wrapped up like a pea in a pod.

A rush of love engulfed my heart.

'I'm your mummy and I love you lots. I promise to be the best mummy ever.'

Cigarettes and Alcohol
Age 13

'Please don't make me go, Mum. I hate it there,' I said as I put on my straw boater. 'Everybody is so posh.'

'Then be posh too. All you have to say is "Toodle-pip" instead of "Goodbye". Just pretend you go on skiing holidays to Switzerland and tell your friends I drive a Range Rover wearing wellington boots, like the Queen.'

My parents had made the peculiar decision to stick Sarah and me in a posh private school. The school was in a Georgian house, surrounded by hockey fields and weeping willows. In 'decorum' lessons, we carried books on our heads and practised falling over in a lady-like manner, without flashing our (regulation brown) knickers. A moustachioed female gym teacher used to measure the distance between the top of my (brown) socks and the bottom of my (brown) skirt. It had to be ten centimetres exactly. My tie had to be in a perfect knot at the top of my (brown) shirt. If it wasn't, I was sent to the office of the most frightening woman on the face of this earth.

The headmistress, like Margaret Thatcher, was stony faced with a domineering presence. Mostly, I avoided being called to see her, but on occasion I got the jab in the ribs that meant it was my turn to take the flak for smoking behind the assembly hall. I sat outside the room on an old church pew, with a feeling of total dread.

'Curtsy!' she shouted at me as I entered. My knees trembled as I obeyed.

She stood up behind her desk and just stared at me.

Finally, she spoke: 'Now, sit!'

She pulled an ashtray closer to her and balanced a long cigar on the lip. A lecture on comportment and her plan for a 'reasonable' punishment followed.

'You will be a wife one day. You must learn how to behave. Smoking is not tolerated here, Victoria!' she screamed as the smoke from her own cigar gathered above us.

I sat there daydreaming as she prattled on. I imagined her digging her nails under her chin and ripping off her human face to expose an evil fembot with gnarly, zapping wires poking out, and an eyeball *boinging* from its socket.

'Are you listening to me, child?'

'Yes, miss. Sorry, miss.'

I left her foul-smelling office with a week of detentions, hoping Daleks would burst through the school gates and terminate the battleaxe.

It wasn't just her, the whole school was stuck in 1955. All the teachers had terrible post-war bouffant hairdos, wore tight tweed suits with A-line skirts, and beige tights that bagged around the ankles above clompy court shoes. Every morning, as I entered the long, leafy driveway, I was transported back in time and into an Enid Blyton book. All I needed was a dog called Timmy and I could have joined the Famous Five.

We did all the things you'd imagine posh people do in school. We baked scones, and said 'Bother' when we pricked our fingers in sewing lessons. We played tennis, and talked about ponies, and Saskia's holiday to Africa, where Daddy had staff and a shooting lodge.

'Guns! How delightful!'

It was all bygone bullshit, and I detested every minute of it.

'I'm fed up. I don't like it there. Please, can I go to a normal school?' I pleaded with Mum.

She knew I was unhappy and told me I could change schools. Also, the fees were bleeding them dry, and she couldn't bear another coffee morning talking about 'how well Arabella is doing in Latin'.

The day before I left, my double-barrelled friends wrote farewell messages on my brown shirt, and the bus driver, at my request, ran over my straw boater. As I stared out the back window of the bus, I shouted at my flattened hat, 'Fuck you, poshos!' while doing a punky V sign. It was total anarchy in the home counties.

I was ecstatic to be out of that musty school, with the dusty books and prehistoric teachers. I needed to be somewhere less brown, with people who didn't have a title, an Aga or a collection of 'family silver'. The following week, I was plopped on a bus to a comprehensive school 45 minutes from home. I had no idea what to expect, but guessed it was going to be the complete opposite of my previous school.

My new school was built in the shadow of a massive power station. A few ugly 1970s-style buildings were joined by cement pathways. I dawdled towards my new classroom, head down, looking at fading hopscotch squares painted on the ground. Mum let go of my hand and kneeled to remove an empty crisp packet that had blown against my ankle.

She then took me by the shoulders and looked me in the eye. 'Good luck, you'll be fine.'

But my overwhelming feeling was I wouldn't fit in.

The girls in my class seemed harder, tougher, than me. I was intimidated. On my first day, one girl said, 'Fuck off, miss,' to the teacher. I was horrified. This was unknown territory, a land where 'Daddy's job in the city' and 'Mummy's antique shop' had no place. I kept quiet, and hid my Waitrose smoked salmon blinis in the bottom of my bag.

*

A name dropped off the register in the first few weeks. One girl was taking time away to have a baby. I saw her, nine months later, strutting down the high street with a pram in front of her and a ciggie hanging out of her gob. I was so innocent in comparison. I didn't even know how to make babies, let alone give birth to one.

The girls at my new school discussed getting felt up by boys, lovebites and fingerings (which I thought was something to do with violin lessons). I was at a stage where I found boys smelly and rude, and all this chat of fumblings in the nether regions was disgusting. But I couldn't help but lean in to the conversations at break time.

'Tanya Turner let Mark Bryant lick her fanny.'

Lick her fanny? I thought. *The world's gone mad. Why would he do that?*

'Kelly McCarthy wanked a boy off in the cinema.'

I made a mental note to ask my sister, Louise, why boys licked girls' front bottoms and what a wank was. Did it mean she had run off with his popcorn?

My new school made me ache for a bit of croquet and a cucumber sandwich. I was invisible for the first few months and simply observed what was going on, until I was able to pick out the good eggs who were potential friends. It wasn't easy. There were all sorts of weird and frightening girls at the school. I believed the huge cooling towers that loomed over us were to blame. They leaked green gunge into the water system, making everyone mean, ugly and a bit fighty. This diverse range of humans included one called Tara, who could do the running man. Older girls made her do it every break time, because her massive bosoms whacked her in the face. She panted like an over-heating Labrador, yet kept on dancing until they told her to quit. It was a mix of humour and bullying. I think she enjoyed it. I certainly did, and cheered her on until her tits nearly fell off.

I avoided a tall, unfriendly girl called Mad Meg. Her mouth wrinkled up like a cat's arse. Her fists were permanently clenched in a threatening manner. I sidestepped her but could often feel her beady eyes following me around the classroom, like she was Action Man.

Mad Meg instigated most altercations in the school. When there was a fight, someone would run across the field, yelling, 'Fiiiggghhhttt!' Everyone flocked to the back of the tennis courts to watch. There was no time to pledge allegiance to a preferred pugilist. No matter what had taken place to lead to the fight, no matter the circumstances or the justification, both fighters got the same treatment ...

We spat on them.

The whole school stood in a circle and coughed up as much phlegm as possible, then launched it onto the scufflers. When the punch-up was over, both participants would have gob hanging off their uniforms and dribble dripping from their hair. Meg never learned, and looked outraged as slobber hit her screwed-up face. Her eyes followed the trajectory of the spit and, like a domino effect, she leaped from one fight to the next, with the viciousness of an angry pit bull.

They weren't all mad and aggressive. There was the swotty crowd, the bitchy crew, the sporty ones, an in-betweeny mob and the girl who could fanny fart on demand. All I could do was turn my eyelids inside out and burp the alphabet, which was nowhere near as impressive, so it took a long time to fit in anywhere. I tried to elbow my way into each group by recalling my plethora of alcohol-related misdemeanours. They all admired my early dallying, but also clearly thought I was a snooty upper-class idiot.

My accent was a bit posh after attending the brown-clad private school. I adjusted it before I got punched and spat on. Pretending to be more 'street' was how I avoided unwanted confrontation. So I cursed all the time – all 'knobs', 'twats' and 'tits' for the first year I was there. I acted like an irritated skinhead in order to get approval, and pretty soon I was another 'cunt', shooting the shit with all the other teenage 'fuckfaces'.

I did okay academically at the school, but my ears had a habit of switching off if a topic was too boring. If trigonometry or Shakespeare dared to be mentioned, I became overwhelmed with tiredness and my head ended up buried in my folded arms. I often had to be awakened by a nudge from a grumpy teacher, as dribble leaked from my mouth onto my furry pencil case.

I had a bad habit of stealing yummy snacks from other students' bags. Mum made me disgusting school lunches: stinking Boursin cheese spread sandwiches or out-of-date stale packets of crisps, accompanied by a bruised apple.

I got jealous. Over the shoulders of chatty friends, I saw the chomping of delicious-smelling cakes, Wotsits and Chelsea buns. I begged for swapsies and got disgusted looks as I held out my mother's rancid coil of a sarnie accompanied by said apple or a brown banana.

If I had pocket money, I spent it on sweets – Flying Saucers and gummy teeth – gobbled out of white paper bags. I was overweight throughout my youth. 'Barrel Body', as my dad liked to call me. I often gorged, alone. I loved pushing Yorkie Bars into my face hole when no one was looking, and stealing Bounty Bars from the snack drawer at home and nibbling all the chocolate from the edges.

After a few months and gaining a few kilos, I found some good eggs to be friends with and fulfilled my destiny of being the class joker. I was mouthy and had a gag on hand for every opportunity. My playfulness often got mistaken for arrogance, so teachers either loved me or had me sit in the corner facing the wall. Annoyingly for them, and despite my tendency to doze off, I glided through assignments and classwork. I got the work in class done quickly so I could spend the remainder of each lesson flicking rubber bands, carving my name into my desk, and playing Russian roulette with my ruler, by smacking at hands before they moved. *Wallop.* I once broke a girl's finger during English.

Still, the only way I knew how to impress my schoolmates was with the amount I could drink ... and smoke. Smoking made me feel cool and sophisticated. While other kids my age did tricks on their BMX bikes or practised new jumps with Double Dutch skipping ropes, I clawed around the local recreation ground, searching for fag butts to smoke. I smoked anything. I inhaled the thin line of smoke from incense sticks, and rolled up dried herbs, like oregano and basil, in A4 paper and sucked the soggy end, then blew out plumes of smoke that smelled like pizza. The paper would be set alight and drop to the ground, making a small bonfire at my feet.

I loved to try anything that made me feel older. I was acting like an 18-year-old when I was 13. After the first year, the girls at my school knew where to come for cigarettes, booze and giggles. I somehow managed to filter out the weirdos and find two amazing friends on my rebellious wavelength. We spent the next few years together, smoking, passing out in parks due to cider comas, getting felt up by boys and doing just about enough schoolwork not to get detention.

At last, I fitted in, and until I was nearly 15, I loved school.

'Sorry About My Tit'

After I'd spent five nights in hospital, we took George home. There'd never been a little person in our car before. I liked it. Leaning around the front seat, I tickled his feet. He looked like a gnome, wearing a green knitted hat and booties. As John pulled out of the parking spot, he gave me a big, excited grin. 'We're taking our son home!'

'Bloody hell, I know. How mental is that? Us, in charge of a baby. I'm surprised we didn't have to fill in more forms, get a baby licence or do any "How to be a successful parent" tests.'

'I think the test starts when we get home,' he said with raised eyebrows.

I turned on the radio and 'Boys Don't Cry' was playing. A good omen.

I wasn't worried, humans had been caring for babies for ages. If a cavewoman had done it (with no Bugaboo or *Save Our Sleep* in sight), then I could too. This was it, my time to prove to everyone what a brilliant mum I was going to be.

As we pulled into the driveway of our flats, I cracked a satisfied smile. With a gleam in my eye, I opened the door, undid his seatbelt, lifted him out and, *doof,* banged his precious, tiny head on the side of the door.

He didn't stop crying for 23 hours and 16 minutes (I was timing it). I spent a whole day and night wandering around the house with no idea what to do.

On my second day home, after no sleep, I opened the front door to the postman, with one breast flopped out of my top. I was so tired, all I said was, 'Sorry about my tit.' And closed the door in his face.

I didn't care. In the hospital, my dignity had been removed, along with my placenta and half of my brain, so nothing fazed me.

*

Then the inevitable happened. John went back to work, and I was left at home, alone, in charge of a life. I knew he had to be fed, but when? And if he slept too long, should I wake him?

I'm not cut out for this, I thought one morning, as mustard-coloured poo squirted up my arm. *I can't do it.*

But, of course, I had no choice. This wasn't like having chosen the wrong salad – I couldn't send him back. I had to suck it up, wipe it down and carry on.

I became so worried about his survival, I decided the best thing to do was to stay awake forever. Just lie in bed with my eyes closed, pretending to rest but with my mind fully alert, ready to jump into action as soon as I heard that newborn cry.

'You all right?' John asked when he came home one night and saw me rocking the baby, black bags under my eyes and wearing nothing but a feeding bra.

'Yes, I'm just going to stay with him for a bit. Make sure he's breathing okay.'

'Stop worrying.'

'I can't.'

It wasn't just the general baby care that made me stressed, it was the immeasurable number of inane tasks that had to be completed: like sterilising bottles, washing vomity burp cloths and hoovering. This whole conglomerate of boringness made my personality evaporate. My cheeky demeanour got suffocated by a haze of cleaning products and I didn't know who I was anymore. I became such a 'mum' that any part of me from before got forgotten about, stored away in the cupboard with the dustpan and brush.

But, to the outside world, I acted like it was a doddle.

'Yes, he's sleeping through,' I lied to my mum on the phone.

'Well, that's great. Oh, by the way, darling, you might want to turn off that video monitor set up in the baby room. I saw John's penis when I logged in last night.'

Woops! I'd set up a little camera that connected to my phone to see George as he slept and given my parents the login. They had retired and were living it up in France, and the time difference meant they checked in just as John, in the buff, was rocking the baby to sleep.

'Sorry about that! I hope it didn't scare you! Anyway, we're all doing great. Don't worry about me – I love being a mum.'

I guessed all mums felt how I did. I didn't want to moan. I didn't want to look like I was failing or being dramatic about my new role, so I kept quiet and hoped the worst was almost over.

When John got home each night, I handed him the baby before he'd even put down his car keys. 'Here, have a baby,' I said, and then collapsed onto the couch. 'And don't take your underpants off.'

The lack of sleep caused me to feel irritable and everything John did made me burn with hatred. I didn't like the way he held the baby, dressed the baby or bounced the baby on his knee.

'Don't wrap him up so tight, he's too hot,' I'd moan as I undid the swaddle. 'Stop fucking bobbing him around, he doesn't like it.'

John had to step carefully to avoid getting a huff, an eyeroll or an exaggerated tut.

*

Days turned into weeks as I warmed bottles, filled the washing machine, and rocked the baby to sleep. I became like a zombie, a nightwalker, awake with the stars. As the sun came up, I tried to sleep, and as it dipped behind the horizon, I was eating breakfast. When my eyes did eventually close, George's cry would ring out and the whole feed-play-sleep routine would start again. My tit-less husband did what he could, but the baby wanted me.

I shuffled from the toilet to the couch, from the changing table to the kettle and back, with my eyes half shut. I padded around the flat with a feeding pillow attached to my waist, and my massive maternity knickers sticking out from the top of my stained tracksuit bottoms. I was capable of yanking a breast out of my bra faster than Quick Draw McGraw with a gun. I became an expert at not wasting precious breast milk, sucking out any drops with a little syringe, like I was picking up diamonds with tweezers. (I'd been able to carry wine into a mosh pit and come out with a full glass, so at least my old drinking skills were useful.)

I was home so much, it made me feel isolated. My old life had fucked off to the afterparty without me. I was left at home with nothing but sore nipples, and an itchy midriff where my stitches rubbed on my folded gut.

As the days passed, my independence faded like a turd in the rain. My entire personality was smothered by a growing mound of dirty nappies and wet wipes. This new life stank. I could not keep up with the motherly responsibilities, the accompanying schedule, and everything life threw at me in between. Since my lovely boy had made his painful grand entrance, I'd started acting like a repressed 1950s housewife who wore a frilly apron, and worried about meatloaf and dusting. That said, the best way to dodge the boring chores was to avoid them completely. If I couldn't see the Everest-sized mountain of washing, it wasn't there. Genius.

I needed some sun on my face and some wind up my gusset.

'Right, it's time!' I said to John as he shaved. 'I'm going to go for a walk!'

I was going to face the outside world. My first junket was a leisurely stroll down the seafront. In preparation, I showered, and spent two hours packing the pram. I had milk, food for me, wipes, nappies, spare nappies, a changing mat, water, a sunshade, cotton wraps, spare cotton wraps, spare trainers, sunscreen, hairbands, an umbrella, a change of clothes for me, two changes of clothes for the baby, my phone, my charger, a nappy holder, a nappy bag, a coffee holder and a squeaky toy.

As soon as I stepped onto the pavement, a car zoomed past me, and I jumped. I moved on with caution. It all seemed riskier than before. I hadn't noticed this pavement being so eroded, and how was I supposed to get down the stairs to the beach? I felt like the green frog in the 1980s computer game *Frogger*. Everything on my route was a potential hazard. Cars, strangers, weather, dogs and potholes were out to get me and hurt the baby. I avoided walking under trees, scared the branches would fall on us. I swerved past bushes, in case a snake leaped out and bit the baby on the nose. I took different roads on flatter paths, clenching the handle of the pram until my knuckles turned white. I avoided hills and inclines, in case the pram hurtled downhill onto a busy road. I took extra precautions in the sun and lathered the baby in organic factor 50. I covered the pram with cotton wraps, like George was a boil-in-the-bag dinner, nearly suffocating the poor thing. I was being irrational but couldn't seem to control my feelings.

Then there was the café venture. Cafés had become smaller. There's no space in those places, no gaps for a pram to fit. When I moved chairs, I was eyeballed as if I was trundling in a wheelbarrow full of steaming cow pats. The busy hipster people hated me. I got their topknots in a twist. I huffed and puffed as I wrangled the pram past the tables and, instead of helping me, everyone looked aggravated. At the counter, I ordered a cup of tea (extra hot, no sugar, with milk on the side) and parked the pram in a corner. I grabbed a cushion off a small tree-trunk stool and shoved it behind my back, then got out my phone, hoping to scroll through funny dog reels on Instagram and wind down for a couple of minutes.

George started to cry. It was louder than standing next to a jet engine on the tarmac. I reached out and rested my hand on his tummy to soothe him, but he then completely lost it. The waitress came over and gave me an understanding 'I-know-what-you're-going-through' face, then passed a teapot full of boiling water over his head. I gasped, then mumbled, 'For fuck's sake.' I pulled the pram closer in a huffy manner, ordered some food (Deconstructed Omelette, with a side order of Losing the Will to Live), and sat pushing the pram wheel back and forth with my foot.

He did snooze, for approximately four minutes, and in that time I wolfed down the eggs I'd ordered way too quickly, which resulted in reflux and some rather unfortunate belching. As I gulped down my cucumber-infused water, the waitress (who I now nicknamed 'Health Hazard') came back over. As she cleared the dirty dishes from the table, sharp knives slid around the plates. As she manoeuvred the deadly stack of cutlery over the top of the pram, I wanted to jump up, grab the knife and plunge it into her stomach. But I did something worse ... an unruly British rebellion.

I didn't say thank you when I left.

I walked at a faster pace back up the hill and gave passers-by a wide birth. Every person was a probable paedophile or the child snatcher from *Chitty Chitty Bang Bang*. I think if anyone had dared to utter a friendly 'Good morning', I would have lurched at them with my front door key and rammed it into an eyeball.

I got home, shut the front door and locked myself in. I decided going outside wouldn't be necessary for a while. I'd wait until autumn. The autumn that was in 15 months' time.

Being home felt safe but there was no off button for this motherhood thingy. Eat. Feed. Sleep. I had moments of respite in the strangest places, like sitting on the toilet for a few minutes longer than required. Squeezing avocados in Aldi until security moved me along. I often hid out by the washing line. There was a little step where I sat and caught a bit of sunshine on my face. All I wanted was a moment of peace, a moment of me.

Then back to the grind. I was spinning a hundred plates on long, wobbling sticks all day long and, at times, my patience smashed into a million pieces on the ground. As soon as one thing worked, something else went wrong. If he was happy, my back hurt. If my mastitis cleared up, he had runny poos. There was no window into the world I used to know.

Some days, I sat on the couch crying, ignoring the baby, wondering how I was going to get through the day without breaking in two.

'I should have got a dog,' I whispered to myself as I picked a scab off my nipple. 'I wonder if sea monkeys would be dead by now?'

My paranoia and tiredness didn't abate and soon … all I could think about was drinking.

I needed an escape. I'd been at home for four weeks. I deserved a reward for all my hard work. Surely a few drinks wouldn't hurt. I knew I shouldn't drink and breastfeed but, honestly, by that point, I didn't give a flying pig's arse.

Drinking was what I knew, it was my way out of this. Drinking was how I took part in life. The idea of feeding diluted gin to my precious angel did not worry me one bit. I never even paused to consider the impact a hangover would have on me taking care of a newborn. All I could think of was to drink, to be myself again. *Drink. Forget about this shit. Drink. You deserve this. Drink.*

I'd been good at being good. I'd kept the baby alive and now needed a bit of the old me again.

*

One afternoon, I packed the baby into a carrier and headed out to town in time for happy hour. I found a pub with a view of Manly Wharf and ordered a beer. The barman gave me a disappointed stare as he realised the massive stein of German lager was for me.

Yes, I'm carrying a newborn and ordering a beer the size of an elephant. Deal with it, I thought. I stared at the amber liquid flowing from the tap into a cold, misty glass. He handed it over and I felt a piece of me return.

The baby weighed about the same as the beer, so, after finding a seat, I lifted him out of his carrier and balanced the two weights, each arm taken up, in a satisfying baby/beer equilibrium. Then I took a huge gulp that left a white moustache under my nose.

'Ahhh.'

The liquid flooded my body. I felt an instant release. The woes of motherhood drifted away.

It would have been a perfect moment … if I hadn't sneezed and pissed myself.

'Bless you,' the barman said.

I looked up and smiled, then crossed my legs, hoping to soak up the damp patch.

Little Knotted Bracelets
Age 14

'Wait, wait, I can't keep up!' I shouted.

I'm running as fast as I can, but can't catch up with them. Then I'm on my knees on the school playing field. Tears run down my cheeks, my skirt is covered in mud, and there are two small wrapped-up boxes next to me.

Why is this happening?

*

I'd been away with my family to France for Easter, and my two best friends, my good eggs, had gone elsewhere, together. I didn't think anything of it. I couldn't wait to catch up on all the gossip and laugh about the stuff we'd been up to. It was a gloomy, drizzly morning. The rain dribbled down the window of the science lab where I was unpacking books from my satchel.

I had presents in there too. Little knotted bracelets I'd spent ages choosing at a cosy seaside gift shop. With a few minutes to spare before the bell went, I ventured out into the playground to see if I could find them.

They sat on a concrete step, kicking at something on the ground and talking. I called out to them, waved with enthusiasm, and hurried across the playground.

Those two girls were my world. We spent weekends at each other's houses, dancing round in our pyjamas to David Bowie's 'Changes', rolling around on the floor, snorting at each other's daggy dance moves. We got tipsy together on stolen bottles of Malibu, smoked badly skinned-up spliffs together, and talked about boys. I truly loved them and thought we'd be friends until we were three mad old ladies in a nursing home.

I was wearing a red denim jacket. I visualised the bright sleeves extended before me, holding the little pile of gifts as I approached, smiling.

They raised their heads and looked at me. I knew right then there was something wrong.

I didn't have time to say hello.

They whispered something, giggled, got up and ran away in the opposite direction.

I laughed and followed them, the gifts toppling out of my grasp.

'Hey, guys, where are we going?'

I couldn't keep up and tripped over. They just kept on running.

I didn't understand the joke. *What are they doing?*

Stopping to catch my breath, I watched as they ran up the track beside the playing field.

I stared at them getting smaller and smaller, until they were out of sight.

Not knowing what was going on, I slumped down onto the damp grass, feeling confused, my tears mixing with the droplets of rain that ran in lines down my face.

I don't know how long I sat there, it felt like a lifetime.
My two best friends didn't speak to me again.
I had no idea why.

Snot and Free Cake

I would not let 'Health Hazard' win. I had to go out again. It was that or buy a lemon and a bottle of gin. I packed the pram full of enough baby-related shit to survive an apocalypse (and a pandemic), then headed out the door. I strolled down to the little shopping village to buy some milk and found myself filling in a form outside a church. I decided it was time to attend some torturous daytime activities with George. Playgroup, to be exact. I was about to come face-to-face with two things I'd always managed to avoid: God and other people's children.

Friendly faces welcomed me as I tipped the pram back to manoeuvre it through the narrow doorway. An older lady, who sat at a grey fold-up table, asked for my name.

'Victoria,' I said, wanting to sound a little bit posh.

She raised an eyebrow and with her sharpie wrote *VIC* on a big white sticky label. She slapped it onto my cardigan much harder than a church-going lady should.

'It's song time. You can join in … Vic.'

I looked over at a circle of women bouncing babies on their knees. I sat cross-legged on the 1970s-style orange and brown carpet. My baby was fast asleep in the pram parked next to me. I didn't know what to do, so I joined in … solo. I felt like a knob clapping along to 'Dingle Dangle

Scarecrow' without a child. I elbowed the pram to wake him but, for the first time ever, he was totally zonked.

I thought about leaving, but the girl next to me yanked my arm.

'Come on. This is a good one,' she said pulling me up.

I found myself following her, walking single file, doing chugging-train arm gestures to 'The Wheels on the Bus'. Fuck me, that's a long song. There are so many verses. I didn't know the driver had so many jobs. Checking tickets, beeping the horn and moving passengers back. I felt like I was in a horrific drug-induced psychosis. Around and around the room we chugged.

I looked like a weirdo on day release. I did all the singing and actions by myself. Each time I circulated past the pram, I booted the wheel with my foot, but he didn't stir. Unsupportive brat. Eventually, the song ended, and I collapsed onto the floor completely out of breath.

The pretty girl in charge asked us to put the babies on our shins and jiggle them as we sang 'Row, Row, Row Your Boat'. I held out my hands as if I was holding an imaginary baby and sang along. I smiled as my invisible infant jigged happily on my knees. One woman pulled her real, non-invisible child away from me. I didn't blame her.

I thought, *What the hell am I doing?* But I was too far in to stop.

After ten painful minutes and three more awkward songs, the nuttiness was over. I lay back on the floor and stared at the fan whirring above my head, as I heard the other women around me leave. I stayed on the orange and brown carpet in my comfy cardigan with a tissue stuffed up the sleeve, wondering how I could share tea and cake with these women.

Then, of course, George woke up. I glared at him as cute dimples appeared on his round cheeks. I shook a finger in my baby's face and said, 'Be awake next time. You made me look like a twat!'

As I turned to go outside, the lady from the entrance stood right behind me, squinting.

'Only joking. Hahaha,' I gibbered as I pushed the pram into the garden, her unholy stare burning a hole in the back of my head.

There were plastic toys scattered across the grass, tables set up with paints next to mini easels that contained what looked like Jackson Pollock paintings, and rosy-cheeked new mums sitting on colourful rugs.

Smiling at some familiar faces as I headed towards the free cake, I decided that if I was busy eating, nobody would bother me. I grabbed three slices of sponge cake and a caramel slice, balanced them on the pram handle and wheeled myself over to the swing set in the shade.

I'm not great with chit-chat. The 'getting to know you' bit of friend making is tiresome for me. I don't care where people come from or what their husbands do for a job. I want to know how many people they've slept with and what their relationship with their mother-in-law is like. I want to get to the good stuff. So I avoided starting any inane conflab and sat in the corner, stuffing my face with sugar and carbs, absorbing this strange new world.

The sun-drenched garden was a minefield of dirty nappies and snotty tissues. There were children running in different directions, crashing into each other at full speed and banging heads. It was like Toddler WrestleMania. One mega baby, yogurt around its mouth, leaped off the top of a climbing frame and landed on identically dressed twins (*The Shining* came to mind). The unsuspecting evil angels responded by throwing punches in every direction. Their mothers tried to prise them apart. Hair got pulled, fists flew, knees got grazed and bloody; I even saw tiny teeth latch on to a finger. Then, as if by magic, bandaids appeared from leather handbags.

'Sorry. Archie is expressing his feelings through biting at the moment.'

Some mums did their best to undo sticky situations, while others sat back and watched the battles unfold. It was like a gladiators' arena in there. Fight till the death, or until one of the contenders' owners put down her coffee and intervened.

'Tilly! Darling! Let Wolfie have Thomas. It's his turn!'

Arms got pulled as troublemakers got hauled to the naughty step, screaming in denial, 'I had him firrrsssttt! *MY* Thomas!' The clashes either ended in a soggy tear-filled cuddle or women with angry faces dragging screaming red-cheeked children through the wooden gate towards naptime.

If the children weren't fighting, they were having their noses blown. The only way to avoid catching a terrible disease in this place was to wear a full hazmat suit. Every little cherub in there was slobbering, leaking or wiping mucus on the furniture. It was Día de los Muertos, the Mexican Day of the Dead parade. Zombified gob-dribbling mutants pacing towards me, their tiny germ-ridden mitts reaching out to join hands and sing a song about the bubonic plague, 'Ring a Ring a rosies, a pocket full of posies …'. It was the stuff of nightmares.

I folded my last piece of cake into a paper napkin, slipped it into my bag and backed out of the garden, then headed into the church. I imagined waving a burning stake as I fended off the snot-saturated undead. Pulling the pram backwards out of the fire exit without touching anything but a lamington, I ran for my life.

*

The next morning, after bathing in bleach and hosing down the pram, I tried music class. It was just as painful. An eccentric middle-aged lady wearing child-like bunches sang everything she said. The class then had to repeat it back to her, matching the tune.

Her: 'Good dayyy tooo youuu.'
Me: 'Good day tooo you.'
Her: 'The toilets are inside on the left.'
Me: 'The toilets are inside on the left.'

I must admit, George loved it. He clapped with joy and shook maracas like he was Bez from the Happy Mondays.

After the class, I sang everything I did.

'I'm wiping your bum and have shit on my elllbooowww.'

'Now, please go to sleeeeeep, so mummyyyy can mourn her social liffeeee … fa la.la.la.la.'

I loved George with all my heart, but this botty- and booby-based existence left me gagging … to get totally hammered.

Jim Morrison is Angry with Me

Age 15

I was on a bridge, buying acid.

'Yes, of course I've done it before,' I lied to the dealer. 'Do I get a discount for two?'

'Do you, fuck!'

I was with my new friend, Tina. I had met her outside the Spar convenience store on the village high street a few weeks before. She was leaning up against a brick wall smoking a rollie. She wore Wallabee trainers with purple flares and looked like a member of Candy Flip. I thought she was cool and, well, I needed a mate.

'Here you go.'

As I handed over two screwed-up five-pound notes it started to pour. Big raindrops made dark spots on my bomber jacket. I noticed the guy we bought the acid off was fidgety. He had scabby hands, ratty features and a weird smell emanated when he spoke, like off milk. He wore a long brown trench coat with scuffed Nikes that looked two sizes too big. He dug around in his deep pockets and pulled out some Rizla papers and a Bic lighter, then a little clear bag.

I saw small squares of paper, like tiny stamps, sitting along the bottom edge. He squeezed the bag open and fiddled around trying to grab two of the small squares between his thumb and index finger. He then placed the tabs on my open palm.

'Right, see ya!'

The grubby boy turned and sauntered off in the other direction. I slid the squares into a little plastic compartment in my foldout wallet, then Tina and I pulled our coats over our heads and legged it to the train station.

After buying a ticket, we sat huddled together on a cold metal bench. Water filled a gutter above us and emptied noisily over the train tracks. Our plan was to take half each, wait for the 18.39 to Reading, go to the pub and have a pretty normal time. We hoped for a slight buzz and, if we were lucky, some fucked-up trippy visuals.

I ripped one of the tiny tabs in two and stuck it on my tongue. Tina did the same. Then we waited ...

For 45 minutes. Nothing. Not one laughing rainbow pixie in sight.

I went into the pissy public toilets and looked in the smudged metal mirror to see if my pupils had changed.

'They look normal,' I said to Tina on my return.

'Must be duds. We may as well take the other half.'

I opened my wallet, and took the other tab out and split it in two. We each took a sip of Fanta, swallowed hard and waited for a reaction. As the rain lashed down around us, we sat together, making flowers from the foil insert of our cigarette packets.

We waited to get high.

And then the train arrived.

We hopped on, feeling a bit dispirited, annoyed with ourselves for spending ten quid on what was probably an offcut from a fuzzy felt board.

We arrived in Reading and headed to our usual haunt. We flashed our fake IDs at the burly bouncer, and at the bar ordered two pints of lager. The place was dead. There was no DJ, no atmosphere at all, just a few red-nosed codgers propped up at the bar, clasping metal tankards.

Just as I was about to say, 'Screw this ... let's go home and watch *The Krypton Factor*,' a lovely warmth spread throughout my body. Battered by an overwhelming psychological mind blizzard, the only thing I could do was raise my arms above my head and let out an animalistic moan.

Tina looked at me.

I slowly brought my hands down and grabbed my drink, then headed over to a small table near the jukebox. I could feel eyes following me across the room. I sat down and looked at my friend. 'Holy shit, Teen. This is mental.'

She was very still, her eyes wide and her jaw clenching.

'You all right?'

'Not really.'

'Me neither.'

'I guess we just have to go with it.'

'Okay.'

We sat in the corner, side by side, holding hands, and allowed the trip to take us away.

I was propelled into a world beyond reality, where words and time had no meaning. Where I was but was not. My brain cracked open like a coconut, and colour spilled over my forehead and into my eyeballs. Then my eyeballs melted out of their sockets and dripped onto the floor.

I held my hands out, turning them, wriggling my fingers. A trail followed my hand as I waved it in front of me. I could see through my skin, as my veins pumped blood along my arteries. It was amazing and frightening all at once. I felt detached from my body. Disconnected from who I was. 'Dub Be Good To Me' played on repeat over the crackly speakers behind me. Tina stood, then turned her bomber jacket inside out, so she looked like a giant orange. As I stared at her, I contemplated my existence.

Scabsy, the guy we'd bought the LSD from, had told us it would be a fun ride. But this wasn't fun. It was intense, with a big dollop of weird. As we spiralled into this psychedelic soft-edged vortex, I started to regret my hasty 'Hey! Let's do acid' proposal.

After a while, the music went quiet. All I heard was voices chattering, murmuring things I couldn't understand. I cupped my hands over my ears, only to hear the even louder sound of my beating heart. People walked past the table, back and forth to the bar, but their figures were unfocused, the lines of their bodies distorted like a yeti in a faded photograph.

'Let's get out of here.'

Somehow, we stumbled from the pub to the train station. Around that time, there would usually be a few Goths comparing winkle pickers near WH Smith, and groups of strung-out city boys with loosened ties falling down escalators but, on that night, I was surprised to find wild beasts roaming the platforms. The voice over the speaker was no longer a kind one, announcing train arrival times and delays. Instead, it shouted in a booming voice like the Wizard of Oz.

'What a naughty girl you are, Victoria. You're going to be in big trouble.'

My heart raced with fear and excitement. 'This is fucked,' I said to my jittery friend, who sucked her elbow, looking perplexed.

We got on the train, and I leaned back in my seat. It felt like hands were touching me from inside the backrest. *Go with it*, I said to myself as I let the illusory hands massage my back. For a moment, I relaxed a little. There was nothing to do except let the drug run its course. We had to ride it out and hope that our trip down the yellow brick road didn't end with us both being sectioned.

Our trippy voyage became more intense as the heavy minutes ticked loudly by. Just when we thought a cloud had lifted, chaos descended upon our brains. Our thoughts went from surreal to terrifying. We got off the train and, with wobbly legs, headed in the direction of home. Walking through a spooky forest didn't help. The trees were alive, branches reaching out to touch us, but luckily we bumped into a happy goblin, playing a flute, who led us home. We ran upstairs to hide in my bedroom. Awake and afraid for what seemed like a lifetime, I was confused and rambling. A poster of the Doors Blu-Tacked to my bedroom wall was transformed, the faces changing from serene indifference to anger.

'Jim Morrison is angry with me, Tina.'

'Think happy things. Just think happy things,' she said. As she spoke, her head split in two and melted over her body, like one of Salvador Dali's clocks.

I squished my eyes closed and wished away the horrible images, only to be met by a growling wolf lurking behind my eyelids. I tried to sleep, but the trip was long and unforgiving.

After 12 hours of intense brain melt, including having drawn on our knees weird monkey heads, which talked to us, we rocked backwards and forwards in the corner of my bedroom, while the torture subsided. As birds began to tweet outside the window, Tina and I fell asleep.

I managed to hide my little escapade from my parents. We said we had gone to a mate's house to watch *Grange Hill* and make mix tapes. I did feel a bit guilty that I'd been in my room falling down a multicoloured wormhole filled with monsters, wolves and general peculiarity, when they were watching the national lottery draw in the lounge room. But I was doing what teenagers do, acting how anyone would act after losing two best friends. I was consciously getting unconscious. Blocking out my pain with whatever stopped me hurting.

'Well, that's acid done, Tina,' I said the following morning. 'What do you fancy trying next?'

Mum Shorts

I tried to set aside my need to go out and get wankered by being 'Yer normal, everyday mum'. I bought some unflattering mum shorts, I hummed as I hung out the washing and I spent endless hours folding little onesies. I even considered getting a trendy 'Mom Bob' haircut, but I would have looked like the volleyball out of *Cast Away* in a wig, so I refrained. For the first time ever, I had a routine. It was boring but necessary.

I woke when the baby woke, I showered and got ready for the day before John went to work, and spent blissful days striding down the seafront, proudly pushing George in his off-road pram. At intervals, I sat on park benches, where I dug around in my shirt for the heavier boob and sat feeding as I watched surfers catch perfect curling waves. My nipple scabs (sorry, guys) had softened a bit by then, so the feeds got longer and easier.

I enjoyed the connection I had with my baby. Sometimes he popped off my boob and turned his head to look around, then latched back on with ease. I felt proud I was able to feed him. I was proving to myself and everyone else that I was a great mum, that I was doing everything the small leaflet at the antenatal clinic told me to do (apart from using it as a coaster for my cup of tea).

Then, one afternoon, my perfect baby vomited blood. It spattered over the white cotton wrap I used to shelter him from the sun. I was beside myself. I called John at work, 'I'm worried, can you come home?'

The midwife was due to visit that day, so I went home, stood in the kitchen and did the only thing I knew to do: bobbed him up and down over my shoulder, and sang him an insane, creepy lullaby. When the midwife, a gentle lady with soft hands, arrived, she placed him on a little scale on the dining room table and, as digital numbers ticked up, shook her head.

'This is not good.'

'What, the sponge?' (I'd prepared a nice lemon drizzle cake for her arrival.)

'No, the baby! He's lost too much weight. It looks like you're not producing enough milk. The blood is from you, from your cracked nipples.'

This was 100 per cent my fault. *Oh God.*

'Is he going to be all right?'

'Yes, but you need to get a pump, express six times a day, top up with formula, get a steriliser, note down every feed, use a syringe to excrete extra colostrum, and take him to the clinic every day to be checked and weighed.'

I nearly passed out. As if I wasn't tired enough?

The feeling I had as she told me all this was like nothing I'd felt before. A fierce force rumbled up from within me. I felt solely responsible for whether my baby lived or died. If I couldn't manage this one job, I was letting everyone down, and we'd potentially have to go back into hospital or worse.

After an hour of giving instructions, the midwife left. John, the baby and I all cried. We were scared – the situation felt out of control.

What if I can't get enough milk? What if he doesn't take it? What if he drinks too much and pukes it all up again?

I was overwhelmed, to say the least, but the process, as most do, started anyway. I swallowed, put my worries aside and got on with it. There were no other options. I had to get some goodness into that baby and make him better.

*

Thus began one of the most gruelling periods of my life. A never-ending stream of duties on repeat. On occasion, I peered into the fridge at a crisp bottle of pinot grigio. It looked so cold, so delicious. I imagined the fluid slipping down my throat, easing my concerns …

But I didn't do it.

I buckled down, strapped my tits into the pumpy pumps and farmed as much milk as possible. Days turned into nights. There was a dark hollow in the couch, in the shape of my body. For weeks, I fed, pumped, slept when I could, and watched episodes of *The Office* on the iPad as George slept in my arms.

At a clinic visit, a stern lady told me if I didn't breastfeed, I was a bad mother and that formula feeding was destroying humankind. As she waffled on, I sat looking down at my hands, just like in the headmistress's office when I was at school.

After making it through many sleepless nights, twenty boxes of tissues, every episode of *One Born Every Minute* and a few consultations with a less critical paediatric nurse, we got there. My brilliant husband became a dab hand at washing up and sterilising plastic bottles, and my boobies started doing what boobies are supposed to do. The baby got back on track.

At last, I popped out the other side of this milky nightmare, but I was ruined. A mess who had aged ten years. My back gave in from not moving around, and the amount of muffins I'd eaten created a tractor tyre around my midriff. I felt like utter shit – fat and unhappy. I thought about drinking through my anguish, but I was honestly too tired to open the fridge door. Even at my lowest points, when I wanted to drown out the stress, when I couldn't bear the thought of changing another mustard-coloured nappy, I still didn't drink. My baby was too important.

I was surprised by this. Surprised I had gone so long without my reliable crutch and surprised I was still half-human without it. It had been natural for me, since I was a teenager, to drink. I was astonished I felt so much love that I was willing to do anything to make sure George was okay. And I noticed some changes from not drinking. I started writing, something I'd always loved. I could think more clearly, and putting pen to paper seemed to relieve any stress I was feeling. The waking up without a hangover was a delight.

I had a little window into what sober me might be ... it was like peeking from behind a curtain into a new world filled with happy techno and rivers of fizzy water. Any self-doubt I had before I became a mother disappeared. I became more in touch with myself. This unclouded world was both an interesting place to visit and also very ... ordinary.

I felt utterly normal without alcohol.

Normal and a bit boring.

Being at home with George meant I had no stories, no quips or adventures. Yes, some bits of it were enjoyable, but a lot was mundane. And, as time passed, I could feel the perfect-mummy persona fading. My daggy shorts were falling, and the space between me and my binge-drinking habit was getting smaller. Any fanciful ideas of not drinking again were disappearing down the plughole – that big stein of beer had tasted so good. A night out was getting closer. I was ready to push over stability and kick ordinary in the ball bag.

One day, I sat at my laptop and searched *Will my breasts explode if I don't feed my baby for one night?*

It was a good result.

One drink can be detected in breast milk for about 2–3 hours, alcohol from two drinks can be detected for about 4–5 hours, and alcohol from three drinks can be detected for about 6–8 hours, and so on.

Not a problem, I thought. *I'll only stay out for a bit. I'll have two glasses of wine and toddle off home before 9 pm. Easy.*

Now all I had to do was find some equally bored mum friends to join me.

Big Fish, Little Fish, Cardboard Box

Age 16

'I'm going to the disco at the village hall, Mum. Then sleeping over at Nicola's. See you later. Happy New Year!'

'Yes, see you later, darling. Have fun.'

I sneaked a folded twenty-pound note out of Dad's wallet and did a victorious backwards moonwalk out the back door, and into the cold, dark night.

I saw the exhaust fumes from my sister Sarah's car, which was waiting up ahead. I jumped in and hid in the footwell until our house was out of sight. We picked up some of her college mates and, together, headed off to embrace oblivion.

*

My sister was 18 when she started going to raves. She'd slip on a catsuit and a bum bag, some Fila trainers and a beanie, then head off in her Fiat Panda to a petrol station outside Reading. Cars queued down the road, filled with people waiting for the venue to be confirmed. A payphone rang, an address was scribbled down on the back of a fag packet. Giant maps were unfolded as spotty kids pinpointed the whereabouts of the next illegal rave. A thumbs up and off they went. A convoy of old bangers blaring techno would hit the M4 motorway, destined for a farmer's field, barn or abandoned warehouse.

Each Sunday, my sister bounced through the front door midmorning, chewing on gum, rattling on to me about the magical sights she'd seen. Her jaw quivered and her teeth chattered as remnants of her night out swam in her bloodstream.

I envied her. She had a boyfriend with record decks set up in his bedroom, and spent weekends bumbling around the countryside in friends' pokey cars, nodding along to crappy recordings of previous dance parties played on shitty stereos. Electronic beats with heavy basslines, euphoric piano and ethereal female vocals floated from her bedroom.

The rave scene charmed me, not in a cosy Miss Marple way, more in a creepy werewolf from the 'Thriller' video way. I knew I was too young to go to raves, but I wanted in. I kept on at my sister: 'Please take me with you. Please, I'll do your chores forever!'

After cleaning her bedroom and doing the dishwasher for a few months, I persuaded her.

*

The thump of music echoed in the night as I took a huge pull on a spliff. It crackled as a seed popped inside. I kept the smoke in my lungs for as long as I could before blowing it out like I was a fire-breathing dragon. I passed it to the driver and sat, jigging my legs to the beat.

We parked in a damp, muddy field outside the venue. It was freezing. Hundreds of eager ravers were getting out of cars, their cold breath visible in the black sky. Through the fog, I saw people huddled together in the darkness. Dots of red from lit cigarettes glowed. Hands moved quickly, passing drugs, powders and broken-up pills, followed by bottles of water as tablets were washed down.

I stood rubbing my palms together to keep warm, blowing hot breath into the space between my hands. I had my chewing gum in one pocket and my Marlboro Lights in the other. I was ready to get wired.

I looked over to where a line of people stood. Mist escaped from the main entrance, where the big, red-faced bouncers patted down pockets, searching for baggies of drugs. I put my finger into my bra and felt the two little pills tucked inside a secret pocket. They didn't even make a lump. Before I reached the entrance, I took half a pill, with a sharp swig from a can of warm Coke, and stuffed the other half back under my clothes. I smiled at the bouncers as I stepped into a huge hall.

Sweaty, wide-eyed people, with glow sticks dangling from their necks, swarmed the space. Strobe lights beamed across the room, towards a podium full of performers in cages. Huge speakers bookended the stage, decks were set up in the middle and backdrops hung from overhead. People dressed as massive robots manoeuvred on stilts among the crowd. Cutting through the darkness, lasers sliced up the venue and kaleidoscopic visuals were projected onto huge screens.

The DJ leaned his head to one side and, with his shoulder, clenched a headphone to one ear. He mixed and scratched records on the decks, controlling the ravers' high with banging choons and peaky crescendos. He nodded and sucked hard on his cigarette as he slipped one beat smoothly into the next.

Alongside the DJ booth, an MC freestyled, hyping up the crowd, shouting down a mike demanding we 'MAKE SOME NOISE' or 'MOVE YOUR SOUL! LET'S GET MOTHER FUCKIN' OUTTA CONTROL!' He swung his dreadlocks from side to side as he held the mike at an angle close to his mouth, spitting out rhymes, then held it high over his head when the music paused, reaching to the sky like an evangelist preacher. The room lit up. Whistles and klaxons resonated around us until the beat rose and sneaked back in.

I nodded to the music and made my way through the mad stomping crowd. I found a good spot near a big speaker, necked the other half a pill, then, for the next ten hours, danced like I was fighting my way out of a spider's web.

A boy wearing a brain-surgeon-style face mask with *E* written in felt-tip pen on the front marched on the spot next to me. A girl chewed on the inside of her cheek while massaging strangers' shoulders, and a shaggy-haired boy did 'big fish, little fish, cardboard box', dancing with his feet wide and knees bent. His eyes were like saucers, and he had sweat dripping down his temples. Dealers with dirty baseball caps weaved their way amid the throng, offering Es, whizz and Charlie under their breath.

As I peaked on my pill, the ambience kicked up a notch. I felt the music, rather than heard it. My mouth turned down into an ugly gurn. My teeth chattered as if I was stuck in a freezer. I hung out in scabby toilets for longer than I should have, begging for more chewing gum and asking wasted strangers, 'Have you come up yet?' I made friends and promises while perched next to a hand dryer: 'Yeah, man, we'll be mates forever.'

I kissed a boy with spit in the corners of his mouth. The gentle touch of his hands on my back made me so high, I vomited on the floor. Someone else rubbed my back. Everyone in the venue was as twisted as me, so my 'lost it' behaviour was appropriate, and accepted. My huge eyes, dripping brow and blotchy face made me one of the crew.

When the noise of the klaxons got too intense or my rush wore off, I went back to my sister's car for chill time. I stuck on the Stone Roses, skinned up a giant doobie, and dozed to 'Fools Gold' until I took my next pill. My jaw ached from chewing and my legs throbbed from hours of stompy dancing, but I never felt unwell. I was happy to be part of something. Every bone in my body felt alive, and I didn't want it to end.

*

When I got home, I sat on the end of my bed and closed my eyes as the beats buzzed around me. I loved being part of this crazy whistle posse. I could get totally wasted and no one cared.

I skinned up in carparks and made holes in my jeans as little boulders of hash fell into my lap. I waited for friends, wearing beanies, going on mushroom hunts in the freezing weather; and had long comedowns in strange places, including bus stops. I collected colourful flyers to stick on my bedroom walls with Blu Tack. They had names like Fantazia, Mythology, Dreamscape, and I think one was called Amnesia. They featured optical illusions of never-ending staircases or huge eyes with laser beams streaming out of the pupils. The flyers were emblazoned with DJ's names in big black letters in order of popularity: Carl Cox, then Jeremy Healy and Paul Oakenfold.

The rave scene was a place where my overindulgence was invisible, where my addictions were tucked away into a nice leather bum bag, along with a torn-up Rizla packet.
This is it, I thought. *I've found where I belong.*

Fluffy Jumpers and Tupperware

Via the hospital antenatal classes, I was connected to a group of girls who'd popped out brats at the same time I had. Every Monday morning, we met at a park that overlooked the ocean. It was nice getting to know women who were balancing in the same unsteady boat as me. I was intrigued to hear how others coped, and if they felt like shoving their heads in the oven the way I did. There were tears during our first meeting. We took turns having breakdowns, all of us so tired and overwhelmed. But after each get-together, I felt lighter, knowing others were struggling through the same hardships as I was.

My new mummy friends were organised, with magical foldout boxes of Paleo snacks and pre-prepared squishy tubes of organic purée. They were all in their mid to late 30s, with successful careers, shiny diamond rings on their fingers and huge mortgages. These women were grown up compared with the friends I had before: they had PAs instead of new piercings, and perfectly plucked eyebrows instead of tattoos. Happy running a market stall selling jewellery, I had never had a city job and had travelled for the previous ten years, so I felt immature by contrast. I was a dodgy wheeler-dealer compared with these smart career women, but I didn't feel judged, I felt accepted. I liked this strong-minded, powerful group. They were kind and generous. I could tell we were destined to get very sozzled together.

I knew that beyond the frivolous baby chit-chat, fluffy jumpers and Tupperware containers, we were all anticipating the chance to show our true, deviant selves. The hedonistic booze hounds who guzzled shots, pulled our skirts over our heads, and ripped our shirts open when the guitar solo at the beginning of 'Livin' on a Prayer' was played. I was gagging for the opportunity to see these modest mums let their hair down. So, when the topic arose, I leaped at it. At last, a chance to go out and be my old self. *My God, I deserve it, I haven't been out in ages. One night won't hurt.* I was determined to be the life and soul of the party again, and wasn't going to let a baby stand (or crawl) in my way.

'Let's have a night out,' I declared, as we packed snacks into our many-faceted nappy bags. Those five simple words represented my return to binge drinking.

*

It took a little planning. I found the list I had been secretly squirrelling away, jotting down all the jobs I needed to do before leaving home to get pissed. I carefully ticked off each task, then expressed milk into small plastic pouches. I put two in the fridge and one in the freezer. I set up a CCTV spy contraption in the nursery so I could observe the baby from my iPhone (and changed the password in case Granny and Grandad were on willy watch). I sat John down and discussed feed times, rocking techniques (sway, don't jiggle), optimum burping positions (on knee or over shoulder boulder holder) and stuck emergency phone numbers on the fridge.

'If the baby is choking, should I grab him by the ankles and swing him around the room?' John asked.

'Er, no. Please don't do that,' I said, hoping he was joking.

I formulated a top three list of my most sleep-evoking songs:

1. *'Daisy Bell' (Please change the word Daisy to Georgie.)*
2. *'You Are My Sunshine' (Please change the word sunshine to Georgie.)*
3. *'What I Am' – Sesame Street Remix*

And added a forth:

4. *Only to be used in extreme circumstances: 'Mama' by the Spice Girls.*

'Right, there's a curry in the slow cooker. Don't forget to stroke his forehead as he falls asleep, he likes that. I'm off to get ready.'

I padded my bra, in case of leakage, stepped into some massive knickers that held in my gut, and stuck on a sanitary pad for security purposes. A hard laugh or a low twerk would be too risky otherwise. I topped up my mascara, hung my head upside down and gave my hair a makeshift backcomb with my fingertips (I was going for a tumbleweed/just let out of the asylum look). I did all this pre-party preparation while sipping on a huge gin and tonic. It was only my second drink in over 11 months, and I wanted to drain every drop. The ice made a clinking noise as I tipped up the glass. A cold slice of lemon landed on my nose as I forced the last trickle towards my gaping mouth. The liquid warmed every part of me.

I kissed my family goodbye and headed off into the night.

I remember telling myself a little lie as I walked up the hill: *You're going to have a few drinks, dance and then come home.*

I meant well, I really did.

'G'day, how are you? Return to Manly, please. Are you having a nice evening?' I asked the bus driver.

I have an annoying habit of being overfriendly with people I don't know. I pour myself over strangers like warm custard. I don't care if it's a member of the royal family or a bus driver; I would have chatted up a curtain rail if I thought it would buy me a drink. He handed me my ticket and gave me a strange look.

The bus dropped me near my local haunt: a grubby hotel with cheap drinks and dirty tunes. I waved like a maniac at my friends when I saw them. All kisses and compliments: 'Look at you', 'You look amazing', 'Love your dress.'

The first few drinks were perfect (as they always were). I was within my preordained limit, interacting, nodding and making jokes at the right points. The girls were all drinking wine. Their glasses were fuller for longer. I was knocking them back quickly, I was so excited to be out, and not thinking about the baby at all. I didn't even consider looking at my phone to check on him as he went to bed.

With each trip to the bar, I headed further into my predictable descent. I had mentally given myself the green light to get tanked. I was gulping beers, slamming shots and necking wines. My minimal good intentions were quickly annihilated, my self-care sucked into a black hole. Faces and places began to seem distant; my happy, coherent demeanour disappeared.

'Are you okay?' someone asked.

Someone else was holding me up.

'Yesh, where's the toilet?'

I was hoping a tactical vomit might increase my chances of staying out. I managed to bang closed the door of the little cubicle and lurch towards the toilet. Five minutes later, I flushed my night away, along with a shot of tequila and some bitter-tasting puke. The pressure from heaving, combined with the fact I'd just given birth, made me pee myself a bit. The pad did its job but before I sat down at the table, I tucked my sequinned dress up between my legs in case of any seepages. Then, instead of going home, I took a deep breath and carried on.

Back at the bar, I bought two drinks. I couldn't see the money in my wallet and just slapped down some coins and a note, hoping it was enough. My drinks sploshed over the sides of the glasses as I bumped into tables. I looked over to my friends. They were all sitting with their backs straight, sipping full glasses of wine. None of them looked that tiddly – more like they were at a tea party, chatting about the weather and what accountant they used.

I couldn't remember much from that moment on. I flashed in and out of consciousness: an awkward crotch grind, an angry bouncer with puffy hair chucking me out into the rain, a stumble to find food, and the sound of my moans inside a toilet.

Who are these people?

Where am I?

Then a cab.

My body flayed around the back seat. I closed my eyes and spun like I was on a Waltzer. Vomit rose. I reached out for anything to be sick into. My hands made their way down my handbag strap, then to the zip. I opened my bag and projectile vomited into the small silk-lined space. My aim wasn't great and the pure volume of sick worked against me.

I shouldn't have had that kebab, I thought as I prepared for round two. I tried to make my regurgitation quiet (drunk quiet) and ducked out of the driver's view. *If I can't see him, he can't see me*, I thought as vomit spilled over the sides of my bag and all over the seat.

'Are you okay, love? Do you need me to pull over?'

'Yesh please, I've had too much to drink.'

I leaned out of the car before it came to a full stop and emptied my stomach into the gutter. My homemade pavement pizza slid towards a drain, and I mumbled 'Shorry' to the nice cabbie.

He handed me a tissue and drove me home.

*

I found my door key in the bottom of my rancid, soupy bag, then tried to open the door. The key scratched over the copper-coloured lock. It wouldn't slide into its designated hole and my arm got tired from trying. I collapsed in a heap and my key fell to the floor.

'Open the door, it's me,' I said, with my head lolling around on top of my useless body.

Then I passed out on the doormat.

John heard my wails and opened the door. My body was flopped backwards on the carpet, and my legs stuck through the front door like I was the Wicked Witch of the West. A stream of sick seeped from my handbag.

He carried me to the bathroom, where he hosed me down, like a zookeeper washing a muddy elephant. I sat in the bath in my sequinned dress with warm water flowing over me.

My sweet husband didn't tell me off, or ask me where I'd been or why I was wearing a bow tie. He just wrapped a fluffy white towel around my body and told me to sit on the couch while he got a glass of water.

When he returned, I was slumped on the floor, moaning like an injured polar bear. Fast asleep.

Dry Humping Care Bears
Age 17

'Is that nice?'

'Yes, it's rather lovely, thanks.'

I sounded like I was complimenting a cheery café owner on a particularly yummy chocolate brownie, but I wasn't. I was lying on a sofa, and a willy pointed up at me from an undone pair of jeans. I was stewed on Lambrini, a sour pear cider, and had smoked enough skunk to kill a grizzly bear. I actually didn't like this boy that much, but he seemed to like me. So, I closed my eyes and pretended not to feel sick as he kissed my neck and encouraged my hand down to his groin.

Sex was never something I'd been into. Disgusting stories from my older sisters, and tales of the fanny lickers and boys with sharp fingernails scratching around inside the undies of tarty girls at school, had put me right off.

I had no interest in dry humping Care Bears under my quilt, like some girls boasted about. The thought of letting anyone near my lady garden made me feel queasy. While I had no urges to speak of, certain fiddlings in the lower parts were expected of me as I grew older, so I had to feign a level of interest in all things clammy and squishy. I didn't want to come across as a prude. In fact, I didn't want to come across as anything at all.

DIY sex was my first port of call. I listened in on a conversation about female masturbation one lunch break. The girls shared a packet of Minstrels, and the sound of the bag being squashed made bits of the dialogue cut out like I was hearing a badly tuned radio. What I got from it was that Stacey Gibson had made herself feel funny after rubbing her undercarriage vigorously in her cubbyhouse. She said you had to twiddle with your bits until your body went stiff.

It didn't sound very enjoyable, but I tried that night. I wriggled and buffed and pulled and tweaked. Nothing. No joy, no funny feelings at all; the only feeling was of a scouring pad having been rubbed between my legs. I lay back on the floor, crossed my legs at the thigh and squeezed the pain away. It was a disappointing result, which made me wonder what I'd done wrong. Was there a particular flap or nub that I should concentrate on? Had I been going in the wrong direction?

I limped over to my friends the following day, with some questions: 'Just asking for a friend.'

It turned out the girls had failed to mention you were supposed to think sexy thoughts when partaking in the downstairs guitar solo: 'Tell your friend she needs to think about sex.'

I waited a week, then tried again.

Before I went to bed, I stared at the poster on my wall of Gordon the Gopher. A hand puppet wasn't the sexiest character to lust over, Basil Brush might have been more arousing, but he was all I had.

Then, I got under the covers and squeezed my eyes shut. *Think sexy thoughts. Think sexy thoughts.*

But I was too young to envision anything arousing. I lay there wondering how I could get my hands on a pair of rollerblades and why my sandwiches didn't have the crusts cut off that morning.

I ended up with a sore fanny and a fading curiosity about anything sexual. I wasn't ready to take any more awkward steps up the sexy ladder. Willies would have to wait, flopped over the bottom rung until the chaffing had healed.

*

As the years passed, the tight parting between my legs started to crack open, not because I wanted it open, but because everyone else's were open and I had to follow suit. Boys no longer needed a crowbar to prise my knick-knacks off. All they needed was three pints of strong lager and a packet of prawn cocktail crisps.

Once I discovered alcohol, lewd interactions became easier. Beer was my sex aid. It softened me and made my underwear accessible to those who showed an interest. I was shy without booze, scared of fingers, tongues and erections until I was at least a few drinks in, then the more, the merrier. Boyfriends expected me to 'do things' and because I was apprehensive, I drank.

I drank to the point of not caring.

I drank to feel accepted.

Loved.

My sexy side became available during pub opening hours. I should have hung a mini chalkboard on my pants, displaying opening times and other helpful information.

Closed Mondays. Slippery when wet. Look, but don't touch. Men at work.

I was doing what my mates were: using my body to get good stories and fit in. Having tales of wanking off a boy in the bandstand at Forbury Park, or getting my tits vigorously rubbed by an electrician in a graveyard, pimped my personality. Boys wanting to fiddle with me was confirmation I was a worthwhile person. So, I got cockeyed on pints of Scrumpy Jack cider, then got off with, nibbled, spooned and canoodled with as many boys as I could, as often as possible. There were tussles with bra straps, and angry-looking lovebites that I proudly hid under poloneck jumpers at school in the middle of summer. I never stopped to think if I liked these boys or if they were good enough for me. I never considered my own pleasure, my own self-worth.

I had many short-term boyfriends, hot and heavy two-week romances that ended at train stations after unsatisfying cinema snogs. I visited all the bases, the tits, the fannies and the jobs, but, at 17, I'd still never done the deed. I didn't want to get pregnant. I was concerned a quick game of hide the sausage would put an end to my youth. I didn't want to end up like the girl in my year who had suddenly disappeared halfway through term. I stayed with boys for short periods, then dumped them before the question of rumpy-pumpy came up.

*

Towards the end of high school, I got a serious boyfriend. He was sweet and loving. We passed the time sneaking around parks, smoking hash and heavy petting. A typical first-love teenage romance. We called each other cute names and bunked off college to suck each other's face off in the back seat of my car. It took a year of dating before I finally gave in. I starting taking the pill a month before and bought condoms; I acted responsibly. I loved him and thought waiting meant he would respect me and not think I was a slag (yay).

My parents went away, and he and I got tiddly on cheap, vinegary wine. I switched off the lights in my bedroom before we got down to business. I thought sex would hurt or something would get punctured. I was scared of bleeding or farting, or, worse, him not liking me afterwards.

I took a big gulp from the wine bottle on the bedside table and lay back on the bed. I tried to relax, but my body was rigid. All corners, awkward and angled. He wriggled around a bit and got into position on top of me. I took a deep breath and clenched my teeth, then felt a sharp pain, followed by some humping and very uncomfortable eye contact. This kerfuffle went on for a couple of minutes until he made a noise that resembled an over-zealous tennis player, and it was game, set and match.

It hurt, but not in a needing-to-scream-loudly sort of way. More of an internal scream. I swallowed, and winced. Probably not the best sexy face ever.

'That was, er, nice,' I said.

'Let's do it again in a minute.' My boyfriend smiled proudly.

I couldn't stomach a second serve. I got up, went to the bathroom, and sat on the toilet, holding a piece of bog roll, feeling empty. I reached down to my vagina. It was sore and swollen, like a warm jacket potato between my legs. I sat cupping the spud, staring at the screwed-up toilet paper in my hand, feeling like I wanted to cry, but not knowing why.

It wasn't his fault; he was lovely and had done everything right. I just wasn't ready.

I thought I should have necked more booze and blacked out the clumsiness of it all. There was too much rummaging, too much panting. The foreplay and the sex reminded me of a school trip to a farm near Oxford, where we had all lined up to milk a cow. There was a lot of pulling, changing of hand positions and grip pressure until the milk pumped out. My boyfriend might as well have mooed when he climaxed. But he seemed to want it and I felt it was only right to oblige. Supply and demand, like a milk round.

*

Over the following years, my sexual escapades didn't really improve. I showed men I cared about them by gratifying their desires, and pretended to be part of the sexually charged teen culture, part of the dry-humping marathon. But I was just going along with things I thought I was supposed to do. I did what was expected of me, rather than experimenting because I wanted to. Sex, even kissing, never felt natural to me.

Instead, I watched TV out of the corner of my eye as overenthusiastic boyfriends lashed their tongues inside my ear. I read care instructions on the labels of boys' t-shirts as they gnawed on my tits. They thought I was in a state of orgasmic euphoria when, really, I was wondering why cold-water washing was required.

I sometimes tried new things in the hope I might find one I enjoyed. The 69 position was the most unsatisfying. I couldn't imagine anyone ever doing it twice, to get to 70. Suffocating on a penis just wasn't pleasurable. I was a breathe-in-through-the-mouth-out-through-the-mouth sort of girl. So, when partaking in French kissing, blow jobs or the upside-down double guzzle (I made that up – thank you), I'd have to come up for breath, like a humpback whale.

Throughout my late teens, I had sex very rarely, and when I did, I was juiced up to my eyeballs on grog. I temporarily cured my insecurities with wine or beer, which made sex feel much easier. I drank to block out my sordid misadventures with spotty, Lynx deodorant-smothered, horny teenage boys. I knew they happened, but the memories were vague. All I knew was a lot of toilet roll was involved and condom packets were hidden in neighbours' wheelie bins.

This type of awkward, unsexy scenario carried on throughout my 20s and early 30s. Without booze, I found sex too personal, too serious and too real. I felt I was better off doing it in a blackout, to avoid dealing with the intimacy.

I'd rather have just visited a dairy farm in Oxford.

Hungover

The following morning, my two worlds collided.
   'You'll have to get up, Vicky. George needs feeding.'
   'What?'
   'The baby's hungry!'
   Oh, yeah.
   Shit …
   … the baby.

Free Beer Here

Age 18

'Here you go. Hang this on your door.' Mum handed me a sign that read: *Free beer here!* 'Have fun,' my parents said in unison before they turned and left.

I had two crates of cheap beer, a TV and a bag of clothes. I sat on my bed, had a moment of missing Mum and Dad, then found a bottle opener. I stuck the sign on my door and waited for my new intellectual university buddies to arrive. Of course, signs like that don't attract the studious sort, so all my newfound friends were binge-drinking, pot-smoking losers like me.

The few months before uni had been messy. A pick 'n' mix of drugs and alcohol, doof parties in farmers' fields, and comedowns in Ford Cortinas. My long-term boyfriend dumped me. So, I fit the teen cliché by becoming an inconsolable brat. I slouched around, ate alphabet hoops from the tin and had sporadic bursts of crying while playing Tetris. My parents were concerned, but quickly became less so. That summer, I ground down their patience into a speck. I despised them ... and the feeling was mutual. I was moody and 'emotionally challenged' from all the speed I was taking in break-up binges. My need to escape their authority meant I was hunting down lines, dabs and drags on a nightly basis.

One night, after telling Mum and Dad, 'You can't tell me what to do!' for the hundredth time that day, I went to a house party with a local drug dealer called 'Disco Dave', who carried a Tesco bag full of class-A drugs. I snorted chalky lines until I didn't know my own name. I fainted, and someone found me on a kitchen floor, as pale as a ghost, hardly breathing. I was okay, though a bit unnerved.

The next morning, Mum brought me a hot chocolate. As she placed the mug on top of a pile of books next to my bed, I felt a deluge of guilt. She sat down and her eyes filled with tears. She reached out and held my foot through the blanket.

'You know we love you, don't you, Victoria?'

I nodded, unable to speak. I knew my parents loved me, but I couldn't reciprocate. I was too far gone, busy falling into a chasm so deep, no one could reach in and pull me out.

When she left, I crossed my heart and promised to slow down a bit.

Heading off to university is going to be a fresh start, I said to myself.

No drugs, Vic. (Unless they're free or particularly good.)

*

I was accepted into a marketing degree at Luton University, through clearing, which was how unis and colleges filled course vacancies. This process was made available to teens who were lazy, passed exams by writing answers on their forearm in blue biro, and argued endlessly with their parents.

I arrived full of anticipation, but Luton was an uninspiring place, foggy and wet. On my first day, I dawdled around the town centre, where chimneys met the sky, and two-up two-down Victorian townhouses with ornate masonry shared party walls. Their ground floors had been converted into crude mobile phone shops and discount stores. Big stickers on windows announced bargains, but the deals can't have been that tantalising – the locals looked miserable. They mooched between shops, weighed down by bags of shopping, while mumbling about bus times. Employees with underarm sweat patches, and lanyards dangling from their necks, stood in doorways, smoking, staring at the ground; a few teenagers hung about near a cashpoint, taking turns to spit in the direction of a pigeon with one leg. Even the market stallholders, who, I would discover, were normally cheeky and chatty, looked forlorn.

During orientation week, the police gave us a talk about safety. The bad news? A high chance I would get mugged. The worse news? It would probably be at knifepoint.

Free beer and a battering. Welcome to Bedfordshire!

Over time, I got to know and like Luton. The booze was cheap, I wasn't the drunkest person in town and, actually, spitting at one-legged pigeons was pretty fun. I labelled myself the party girl from day one, while still vowing not to take drugs. I made it my responsibility to brighten up this dreary metropolis. I was witty, pretty, and, as far as anyone knew, keeping it together. What had happened at school with my two best mates meant I was desperate not only to make new friends but to keep them. And the only way I knew how to make people happy, and like me, was to be three sheets to the wind, whiffled, fried, off my bloody tree, blind drunk.

I never went to one lecture the whole time I was at university. The only thing I learned was how to drink a pint of snakebite and black (beer, cider and blackcurrant) in under three seconds – a Luton record. And how to collect my student loan payment without being in attendance as a student.

Unfortunately, my plan not to take drugs and to get everyone to like me backfired. The local dealer lived below me and all my hall of residence flatmates hated me. I fried onion rings at 3 am. I ate the carefully labelled food in the cupboards. I slurped milk straight from the carton, and never did any washing up. I stomped around; played house music loudly; banged on doors and windows, having lost my keys. I was a staggering, dribbling mess, a nightmare of a flatmate.

There was one guy who found my antics amusing. His name was John. He ambled around the campus in a thick Aran jumper, carrying a bottle of Johnnie Walker on his way to social events. He had a gap in his teeth, which I found endearing. He never complained about me stealing his cornflakes.

As far as I was concerned, everyone apart from me was dull. Students studying! *What boring fucks*, I thought. University was about having a good time. If I managed to get a laugh, get pissed, have a few snogs, that was all that mattered. I spent my days doing nothing, and my evenings lurching between basement bars and 50p-a-pint Irish pubs.

I'd never been a big liar. I had told my parents a few in the past, denying I threw the rice pudding down the toilet or ate the Smarties off my sister's birthday cake, but nothing major. Now, though, I told a uni buddy I couldn't meet her because a friend had been hurt in a car accident and I had to go to the hospital. Of course, I was just hungover, lounging in my pit with a can of Lucozade and some Marmite on toast. This showed a new side of me: a person who told big lies to cover up a problem. My heavy drinking had caused me to be devious in this way and, once the hangover faded, I felt awful.

And when I felt awful, I did the only thing I knew to do. I drank more, hiding my shame under a Vodka Red Bull and copious pints of lager.

My next few months at university were a blur of big nights out, pub crawls and pill popping. My inhibitions were squashed under a few pints of Stella. I stayed awake for days on end, smoking huge spliffs as I watched sunrises over the misty Luton skyline. I was still hurting, I guess, with no tools to deal with my pain.

*

One night, just after snorting a line of dirty speed off a DJ's turntable, I was introduced to a girl. I was still holding a finger to one of my nostrils, making sure no crumbly remnants dropped out. As I reached out my hand to shake hers, I inhaled deeply through my nose, hoovering any rogue granules stuck in my nasal passage.

'Hi, I'm Vicky.' I sniffed.

'Oh hi,' she said, as if she knew me. 'I've heard about you. You're the one who's always drunk and off your trolley on drugs, right?'

Any colour still in my cheeks drained and I snapped out of my buzz.

It was the first time in my life somebody had implied that my behaviour was not okay.

I'd never realised people thought of me as anything but cool and fun. Yet, here was this stranger telling me I had a 'reputation'. I was humiliated. I turned and walked towards the nightclub's fire exit. I went back to my halls of residence, crept past my flatmates, hid in my room and cried. Was this stranger right?

A lolloping mess, I lay in bed, watching *Countdown* and smoking roll-ups. I was going nowhere fast. (Even in my Morris Minor.) This should have been a pivotal moment. Being known in Luton as a befuddled, bleary-eyed idiot should have been enough for me to go on the straight and narrow, and become a barrister or something. Instead, I packed my bags and left university the next day, my bad habits travelling westbound on the M25 along with me.

Mum and Dad were not impressed with my decision to leave uni, and it was clear that living at home again wasn't going to suit me. They still didn't like my 'attitude' and I thought they were twats. But what could I do? I was so disoriented and uninspired. Normal jobs didn't appeal to me, and I had no idea what I was good at. The school careers adviser had told me I should be a vet. (Who the hell were the school careers advisers in the mid-nineties?) Seven years of study, just to get kicked in the fanny by a horse.

My parents had wanted me to study topics I had no interest in, like French, English and marketing. I should have done an art course or a degree in design; there lay my passions. The creative side of me was desperate to be unleashed, but my parents didn't believe 'artsy fartsy' types ever made any money in the real world. I was stuck between what they expected and what I wanted. The arguments now reached a point where there was no going back. After a particularly nasty exchange, I grabbed my car keys and did a wheel spin out of the driveway.

I then did what a lot of lost souls do when life doesn't go their way.

I went to Brighton.

Sour Milk

I felt so hungover I could hardly move my head. John handed me my son. I looked at him wiggling in my arms. His tiny fingers wrapped around mine. I couldn't feed him. My milk would taste like Kahlúa.

'You're going to have to make him a bottle. My milk is spoiled.'

I felt a lump in my throat. A ball of shame and self-loathing that felt so big it might choke me.

My husband sat down on the bed next to me. I leaned into him. He put his arm around me and gave me a squeeze. I sensed he felt sorry for me, that he wanted me to be okay, but there was another feeling that lingered between us.

An unnamed melancholy.

He didn't say anything. We sat there for a few minutes in silence because what needed to be said was too confronting. My heart sank because I knew I had failed.

When John's grip loosened, I hid my face. I avoided eye contact, worried my sadness would confirm his concern for me. He slid his hands under the baby and lifted him onto his shoulder, and I was left empty handed.

As John exited the bedroom, I looked at my baby, George, his cheeks all podgy, his chin resting on his tiny hands. I knew I was not capable of taking care of him.

I put my hand inside my top and felt my boob. It was hard, engorged and painful to the touch. I got up and looked in the long mirror, inspecting the area that hurt. There was a red rash that stung when I touched it: mastitis, an infection from the milk build-up.

I grabbed a red bucket that still had sick swilling around the bottom, and sat on the edge of the bed, squeezing milk from my sore boobs.

'You Are Under Arrest'
Age 19

'Bollocks!' I cursed as I glanced into my wing mirror. Blue lights flashed behind me, so I stopped the car and wound down my window. As the police officer marched over, I thought about what I was going to say. She leaned down with the breathalyser and asked me to blow hard into the small plastic pipe.

I was too scared to speak and, as I blew, thought, *Well, you've really gone and fucked yourself this time, Vicky.*

*

Until that point, I'd been enjoying Brighton. I'd moved in with a mate from home, Tom, and he agreed if I made him and all the boys he lived with cups of tea on demand and did the washing up, I could sleep on their couch for free. I had no money, so it was a good deal. (I also cooked roast dinners in the electric kettle by re-boiling potatoes until they were soft, and accompanied them with a tin of cold Spam.) Tom and I talked in pirate voices most of the time. I have no idea why.

I got a job in a pub and, each day, made my way down the cobbled lanes to the seafront. The seagulls squawked above me, and waves crashed over the pebbled beach. I'd never lived by the sea before, and the fresh air cleared my constantly foggy, hungover head.

I met a group of amazing girls at the pub and, together, we were a force of nature – a pack of wildcats who stole pints, slept around, and flirted with doormen until they gave us wraps of coke. It was the era of the ladettes: girls who could drink men under the table and swear like sailors. A culture that represented my friends and me perfectly.

We all had nicknames – Bogfish, Pants, Spanner, Lozza, Spen, Big Vic and Smelly Kelly. I was the youngest and affectionately known as 'The Baby'. Collectively, we were called 'The Flies' because if someone had drugs, we were all over them like flies on shit. We thought the name was brilliant and flapped our hands like little wings when we greeted each other.

I was happy in Brighton; I had strong friendships at last. These girls proved themselves to be loyal and dependable, and we soaked up everything Brighton had to offer. We had dance-offs at the Big Beat Boutique, necked strong Es at Massive Attack gigs and music festivals, and cried laughing as we recounted stories from our nights out. We rolled from bar, to club, to house party, arm in arm, with not a care in the world. It was a wonderful, crazy time.

Alcohol was our drug of choice, followed swiftly by ecstasy, speed, cocaine and weed. We did whatever we could get our hands on. All eager to push ourselves to the limit. As for me, when I reached that limit, I still wanted more.

*

On the night of my arrest, I'd had a few pints during my shift at the pub. That led to a couple of shots before last orders. After work, the staff headed to The Escape, a nightclub near the pier, and my car was parked in a short-term space, so I had to move it, rather than get a ticket I couldn't afford to pay.

I was bladdered, driving the wrong way up a one-way street, when I saw the lights.

The police officer looked at the result on the breathalyser and arrested me. I'd well and truly crossed the line. I sobbed, and begged the officers to change their minds.

'Please, I won't do it again. Maybe you can just drop me off at my nan's and we can forget this ever happened?'

'You've been arrested for drink driving. You'll be spending the night at the station.'

She wasn't being mean, she was doing her job.

My door clicked open, and the officer took my arm and led me to the police car. I slumped into the back seat. The smell was a combination of sweet fir tree and vomit. A black metal screen separated me from the front of the car. Trapped. I could not believe where I was. My own stupid choices meant I was on my way to jail for the night.

With each passing second, the alcohol wore off and the reality of the situation sank in deeper. I managed to lift my head a little during the drive to the station. I watched people laughing in queues outside pubs, a couple holding hands as they ran across the road. All the blurry, colourful lights of the city whizzed past the window.

My drinking was going to have consequences for once.

I spent the night in a cold cell, with a toilet in the ground and blood splattered on the walls. The howls and whistles of other inmates floated along the corridors, and I was scared.

There was also screaming and crying. The screaming came from the lady next door, but the crying came from me. Big tears dripped down my cheeks. I blubbed for hours, wiping lines of snot along my bare arm as I succumbed to the reality of what I'd done.

I wasn't in touch with my parents. We hadn't been speaking since the fight, so I didn't call anyone. I sat on the bed in the freezing cell until the sun came up. I heard footsteps and a rattle of keys, then the police officer told me I was free to go. She breathalysed me again and gave me a letter with my court date. With a shaky hand, I signed some papers, and walked out into the street.

*

A few weeks later, I sat with a solicitor in the waiting room at the courthouse. The people awaiting their day in court all looked troubled and damaged in a way that I wasn't. I wondered if this was how my life was going to be: court dates, fines and subpoenas.

An angry-looking man with a combover and deeply furrowed face sat opposite. He had on a stained white vest that was too small and his hairy gut was on display. He spoke in a gravelly voice about his case to a solicitor. She wore a sharp suit and leaned back to avoid getting spat on. I watched the angry man pause, mid-sentence, adjust his weight onto one butt cheek and let off a succession of huge farts, like three bursts from a ship's foghorn.

Paaarrrp. Parrrpp. Parrrp!

The poor solicitor didn't flinch. She probably dealt with offences like that every day. For some stupid reason, I was mortified, so I blushed. The culprit carried on his chat as the overpowering pong hung between us. In that moment, as the whiff settled, I promised myself I would never commit a crime again.

Then my name was called. I was the next number in line on that rainy Tuesday afternoon.

I felt very uncomfortable as I stood in the dock in my smart shirt and admitted my guilt. 'I'm so sorry,' I said to the magistrate. 'It was a stupid thing to do.'

It wasn't dramatic, there were no wigs and gavels. No rattling of chains or being dragged out of the dock. It was clerical. Paper was stamped, names were signed.

I got a fine and a year's ban from driving.

As I left the courtroom, I walked past the other offenders awaiting their fates. I didn't look or feel part of this farty felonious world, but I was.

I was a criminal.

I paid the fine and arranged to get my car towed. As I watched it get loaded onto the back of the truck and disappear down the road, I felt my life disappearing too. But the major problem was that the only way I knew how to deal with strong emotions was to drink my way through them.

What else was there?

A Conga Line of Broken Promises

It was after 10 am by the time I went into the nursery. I stood in my dressing-gown, feeling ill, staring at my sleeping baby.

'I'm late for football. I've got to go,' John said from the hallway.

'Sorry,' I said, a second after the door closed.

I put my hand on George's chest and felt his ribs as he breathed in. His body was as warm as a hot-water bottle. Stroking his soft cheek, I pulled over his small body the blanket he'd kicked to the bottom of the cot.

I stood watching him for a while. Going out last night with the mums, the wine followed by the shots, and the ill-fated taxi ride, all meant I'd lost precious time with my baby.

I felt a tingle in my boob as the milk let down. I took a deep breath, trying to repress the shame. 'I'm sorry I broke my promise to you,' I whispered.

He couldn't hear me. He was asleep and would be for a few hours. I plodded back into the bedroom, climbed into bed, shoved a pillow behind my back, and sat there staring at the photo hanging wonkily above my chest of drawers.

I was pregnant, posing on a beach in a blue-and-white-spotted swimming costume, looking over my shoulder at the camera; happy, excited. The day the photo was taken, John and I had set up a little picnic and spent the afternoon lazing by the ocean, chatting about what type of parents we would be.

I remember saying, 'I've enjoyed being pregnant and not drinking has been easy. I thought I needed to drink to have fun, but maybe I don't? I'm going to try and stop.'

In that moment, I'd really meant it.

Now, in bed, hungover, I was unable to care for my child. A barrage of feeling hopeless attacked my hungover head. Self-hate tore through me. Suddenly, I couldn't catch my breath. My lips and hands started to tingle, and a massive tidal wave of panic rolled over my body. I held a finger to my neck – my pulse was beating fast, as if I'd run up ten flights of stairs.

I'm having a panic attack, I thought. *I'm going to die.*

I suddenly felt like I was standing on the edge of a skyscraper, with my toes hanging over the world below, and the floor beneath me was going to crumble away. At this moment, the party girl and the mum were flung against one another, we crashed and it hurt. Unease saturated my body as a thought flashed in my mind: *Drinking alcohol is causing you to be a shit parent right now.*

Before George, I'd never had anyone who relied upon me. This baby, sleeping in the adjacent room, needed me. As the reality of the situation descended, another wave of panic ripped through me. My body trembled.

I heard him cry.

I felt so unwell, so full of despair, that I lay there, ignoring him. Bending a pillow around my ears, I waited until his sobbing slowed down.

Oh God. What am I doing?
You're a mum now, Vic. Go to him. Go to your baby.

I got up, rushed into the room and scooped him up. His face was as bright as a tomato. His body, warm against mine, took away some of my anxiety.

'It's okay, sweetie. Mummy's here.'

After a long cuddle, I pulled myself together. I showered, brushed my teeth, got dressed. Even though I was full of regret and self-loathing, I got on with mothering.

The panic subsided but I felt it lurking all day, just out of sight, like a sneaky stalker. John got home from the footie and, before he could even lean in for a kiss, I said, 'I've been feeling awful. I think my panic attacks are coming back.'

'Coming back?' he replied. 'Have you had anxiety before?'

'Yes,' I said with a bowed head. 'Yes I have.'

It was true. I *had* felt like this before, many years ago, and it was a place I never, ever wanted to visit again.

Overdosing with Big Bird
Age 20

I hopped on the bus to a run-down area of Brighton, and knocked on the door of an unknown geezer's flat. A strong smell of hash wafted out as he opened the flap of the letterbox.

'Yeah?'

'Oh, hello.' I pushed a small wad of cash through the gap and said in my ridiculous posh accent, 'Fifteen ecstasy pills, please.' (I didn't add 'old chap'.)

'Wait there,' he grunted.

I twiddled my thumbs. A grubby hand pushed forward a small zip lock plastic bag stuffed with the white chalky tablets. Then he warned me, 'Careful. They're pretty strong.'

I didn't flinch. That was good news – the stronger, the better. I bent down and said, 'Thanks, it was nice meeting you.'

I almost shoved my hand through the flap for a firm handshake. I sounded as if I was trying to impress a bank manager, not buying drugs from a greedy dealer. My very British polite side blurted out of me if I was stressed. A fight-or-flight reaction. Go posh or go home.

I had 15 Es in my back pocket. Excited, I rushed back to my flat to show my mate Kell. I slid open the bag and handed her two pills. She slapped her hand to her mouth and swallowed hard. I did the same.

And so our eventful evening began.

Eyes rolling, we chatted with friends and danced to cranking tunes on grubby dancefloors, then headed to the loos and took another two Es. I spent most of the evening in a toilet gibbering at strangers and jigging like a mad banshee. I was wasted, with a pocket full of drugs. I never considered saving them or giving some away. I took another two. And another two. Kell and I were in a club, then in a flat. Sitting on a bench in a seafront gazebo sheltered from the cold wind. We were both completely off our tits, wandering around Brighton until the sun came up.

By 11 am, I was home, curled up with a blanket over me, trying to come down. I was worn out and hoped to drift off to sleep as *Sesame Street* babbled on the TV.

Then, out of nowhere, an immense fear rushed through my body. I went from feeling high and blissed out to feeling like I was going to die. I couldn't catch a breath.

A distorted Elmo and Big Bird danced on the screen as numbers were flashing up: '1, 2, 3, 4, 5, 6, 7, 8, 9, 10, 11, 12.'

Marbles rolled around, colours jumped out of the TV.

Then children sang along to the theme tune, as my entire body started to shiver.

Kell looked at me. 'Are you all right?'

'I'm dying, I can't breathe,' I said. 'I'm going to swallow my tongue and choke to death.'

She got me some water, but I couldn't hold the glass to my lips. Water spilled onto the floor.

'Let's go outside and get some fresh air.'

'Okay.'

My juddering legs hindered me walking downstairs and out onto Brighton Beach. I was going in and out of consciousness, my body not doing what I wanted it to. My head was lolling around. I couldn't walk straight, I could see my limbs in front of me but felt disconnected from them. I began to heave. Nothing came out. Then I collapsed onto the cold pebbles.

'I love you, Kell. Say goodbye to everyone for me and tell my family I love them.' I lay back and accepted my fate. I was going to die, right there, right then, and it was my own stupid fault.

Before I closed my eyes, I said to her, 'Call an ambulance.'

Then I passed out.

*

The next morning, I came to expecting to be in a hospital bed, but Kell hadn't called an ambulance. She was paranoid we'd get into trouble for buying drugs. Instead, she'd called some friends, who'd taken me home, carried me upstairs and put me to bed, hoping I'd sleep it off.

I rubbed my eyes and got up. The ground felt uneven. I had to grab the door frame to keep upright. My mouth was parched, and my vision blurry. Worst of all, the fear was still there.

It hadn't faded at all.

It was worse.

My body felt so tense, my toes were curled, gripping onto the carpet. I tried to call out but couldn't speak, my words wouldn't join together.

Am I going mad? Have I gone mad?

I am. I have.

I made it into the bathroom and looked in the mirror. A sad, scared person stared back at me. The colour was gone from my cheeks. My eyes were dark, with big bags underneath. I looked older, troubled.

'What's happened to you, Vicky?' I asked my reflection. 'Where have you gone?'

The drugs seemed to have taken part of me. Emptied me out.

I turned on the taps, collected some water in my cupped hands and splashed it onto my face, hoping to snap out of it. I watched the water drip off my face. I imagined my skin melting off too, until nothing was left apart from blood and exposed bone. My own mind took me to the most frightening possible scenario.

My flatmate knocked on the door. I turned off the taps and walked past her, feeling too scared to look her in the eye. I was too nervous to even speak. She reached out to touch my shoulder and I lurched out of the way, as if touching me might feel like touching sadness. I didn't want her to feel it too. I didn't want anyone to ever experience my pain. Instead, I went back to my room and closed the door.

Sprawled out on the floor, I looked at the cracks in the ceiling paint. My body was screaming for help, but only I could hear it. Friends couldn't see the panic simmering within me, nobody could get close to it. The silent cry filled my existence from that day forward.

I was embarrassed I couldn't be the person I had been. My friends wanted me back and I wasn't there anymore. Fear had taken me by the hand and its grip was firm. Each day, I was pulled further into this petrifying dream-like state. I'd abandoned myself, set the real me adrift, and all that was left was this stranger in the mirror.

I was a visitor in my own body, and this unwelcome guest wanted to push me in front of a train or shove me backwards into my grave. I couldn't see a way out. My mental health was deteriorating by the hour, and I had no idea how to cope.

I stayed in my little room, hiding away from the world, ignoring the phone and not answering the door. I sat on the bed, trying to push out the dread from my body. But it was impossible, the fear had found its host and would not budge.

Normal tasks became unbearable. My heart pumped hard in my chest, as if I was running away from a knife-wielding murderer, when I was just making toast. Sweat appeared on my brow as I spread the jam.

I heard whispers, words floating inside my head: 'Kill yourself. You may as well die.'

But I didn't want to die. I wanted to feel normal again.

But I wasn't sure I was capable of living like this. This felt worse than death. At least death offered peace.

My day to day consisted of different levels of panic, flashbacks, and the constant fear of my own death. It was an endless cycle of negative scenarios swirling around my brain. I held my fingers to my throat, checking my pulse rate, then rubbed my forehead with my thumb and forefinger, rocking back and forth. It was a nervous habit I had, like a patient in *One Flew Over the Cuckoo's Nest*. Lying on the bed, I muttered to myself, 'You're not dying, it's just a panic attack. You're not dying, you'll be fine. Get a grip. YOU'RE NOT DYING!'

Nobody knew what to do. I lost my connection with friends, family and with the world. The panic wasn't detectable to an outsider. I didn't have blood pumping out of a cut or snot running from my nose. I wasn't hopping all over the place with a jippy knee. You couldn't see my illness. It was a noiseless monster buried inside my brain. This made it hard to explain to anyone, and when I tried, I sounded self-indulgent, paranoid, like a severe hypochondriac. Basically, everyone thought I seemed bonkers.

People offered advice: 'Try meditation.' 'Think more positively.' 'Breathe into a paper bag.' 'Snap out of it and go for a long walk.'

They might as well have asked the ocean to stop making waves. The darkness inside my brain was a power much stronger than me. The wall of dread would take more than a paper bag to demolish. Panic had set in, like a heavy rainstorm.

I vanished. I moved into a flat on my own, and descended into a private hole of fear and discontent.

*

I went to see my doctor. 'I've gone mental, I need help.'

He referred me to the local psych ward, so I took the bus to the other side of Brighton. A big red-brick building loomed over me. The smell of bleach filled my nostrils as I entered the grey waiting room. I sat there, hoping I might be mad enough to be sectioned.

The psychiatrist was ancient, and his office smelled of biscuits. 'Sit down,' he demanded in a rather stern voice.

I sat down.

There were holes in the plastic seat cover. Nervous patients must have picked at the foam as they were being seen. I was picking at it too. My chair was positioned in the far corner of the room, quite a distance from the man in the white coat sat hunched over his desk. The lino floor stretched out in front of me.

I told him my name and said I thought I was having a breakdown.

'Did you wet the bed as a child?' he asked, without turning in his chair.

I was baffled. 'I'm not sure,' I said.

'Can you name all of the Queen's children?'

'Erm, no.'

He shook his head. Mumbled something into the desk, then scratched his head with a fountain pen.

My hands gripped the foam seat. I felt angry. I was being spoken to as if being evaluated for a Victorian asylum. I'm sure I did wet the bed sometimes, and I couldn't name the Queen's children – not because I was mad, but because I didn't give a flying ceremonial shit about the royal family.

I'd reached out for help, and this was making me feel worse. I got up and stormed out.

At home, I picked up the phone and called my mum. 'I've taken too many Es and I've gone a bit mad. Can I come home, please?'

My parents drove down to Brighton and picked me up. 'I'm okay,' I lied as Dad loaded my belongings into the boot. By the end of the journey home, I'd revealed the true extent of my panic.

'I think we need to get you to the doctor, Vicky.'

'Okay,' I said.

They put me to bed when we got home and called the family GP.

'Can I get you anything, Vicky?' Mum asked, stroking my forehead.

'I'm fine, don't worry.'

I was trying to sound positive, faking normal, but as Mum talked, I peered over her shoulder, wondering if the packet of paracetamol on the shelf behind her would be enough for me to do myself in.

Doctor Morrison came, said I should rest, and that was it. Rest. But sleep was impossible. I became an insomniac, pacing the hallways at night, begging silently for my brain to calm down. I became agoraphobic. The front door was my nemesis. I knew it led to my freedom, but there were a billion psychological locks to undo before I could even consider crossing the threshold. Easier to stay on this side, easier to stay in bed.

Mum tried to get me out some days. If I did make it past the front door, everything made me panic. Trains. Packed carriages full of cold stares and tepid cups of tea, crumpling newspapers, and the sudden, frightening sound of other trains shooting past the window. My mind jumped to morbid thoughts of my head being lobbed off as I leaned out the window to grab a breath of fresh air, images of my severed, bloody bonce rolling around on the tracks.

People. Being with friends or strangers made me feel odd. I saw pulses pumping in necks, every line in every forehead and every pore, intensified observations of faces I knew well: fear gave me an evil superpower. I was able to see inside someone's body, see their organs jumping out at me. I watched human interactions and bodily reactions with a newfound concentration. A simple touch felt like an electrocution, zaps on my skin making me lurch away from comforting embraces or meaningful hand holds. I wanted to see inside people to find out why their bodies were functioning so well while mine was breaking. I hardly ever engaged in conversations. My mouth was dry, and I didn't know what to say anymore.

Food. I was aware of it every single time I swallowed, and thought it was going to get lodged in my throat. When I ate, I envisaged my death. My hands clasped my neck, and my face went blue. My fear of choking took hold every dinnertime. I felt my Adam's apple rise and fall with each forkful of food. I chewed for much longer than usual and took incessant sips of water, trying to wash the food down. Everything that passed down my oesophagus felt as big as an orange. My parents watched on as I struggled through each meal.

Weather. The sun was too bright, and the rain made me cold. I feared being struck by lightning or killed in a flood. I sweated profusely in the winter, with huge beads trickling down my forehead. Birds tweeted on tree branches outside my bedroom window on warm spring mornings. Their song made me desperate to feel better, to be able to enjoy the weather. On hot summer days, I sat inside under warm blankets. Knowing I couldn't get out of bed or act like a normal human being made me withdraw even more.

Myself. I was scared of me because I didn't know myself anymore. I was boring, reclusive. I couldn't see how I was ever going to get well. Every morning, when I looked up at my reflection after brushing my teeth, I wondered who I was. *Who is this girl? Who are you now, Vicky?*

I couldn't believe my flippant drug use had caused this, had caused me to lose myself.

Every morning, thoughts of suicide sneaked into my consciousness. *Today? No. Maybe tomorrow.*

I typed 'Panic attacks' into Yahoo. There were a few articles on fight-or-flight responses and meditation, but mostly it was old-school tactics meant for actors who were stressed before a big role or audition. My anxiety felt more hardcore than puking behind the stage curtain before the matinee. My big breakout role was the simple act of getting out of bed in the morning. At least actors got applause.

The fear turned me into a hypochondriac and the internet turned me into a bogus doctor. Self-diagnosing gave more symptoms. I spent days trawling through online essays on panic disorder and anything related to mental illness. I read so much information I could have stolen a kidney and sold it on the black market, but I was desperate to find a snippet I could relate to. I found nothing. Nowhere could I track down data on panic resulting from having overdosed on ecstasy. Maybe it hadn't happened before? I concluded I was the only person on the planet who felt the way I did. Of course, that increased my feelings of isolation and impending doom.

My mum was very worried. At my lowest point I asked her and Dad to hold me down because I was going to jump out of a window. Not because I wanted to die (they lived in a bungalow), more because I'd lost control of my actions. I felt as if I couldn't stop myself from doing something stupid. It must have been terrible for them to witness their child so fragmented. I could see the pain in their eyes. They had no idea how to handle this. We were all lost and confused. Time wasn't healing me, and my depression deepened as I struggled to stay mentally afloat.

One morning, Mum sat me down on the sofa after coaxing me out of bed with the promise of a chocolate Penguin. (Previously, she'd tried a bottle of rescue remedy.) She placed her hand on mine and asked, 'Is this because of something I did wrong? Were we bad parents? Is that why you were taking drugs?'

I burst into tears and said, 'No, this is my fault. I thought I was invincible. You're the best parents ever. All you did was teach me to be invincible, Mum.'

It was true, nothing they had done had caused this. It was me trying to fit in, trying to be cool, rebellious, and attempting to fill the void left by my school friends. We had a cuddle and a cry. I ate my chocolate Penguin, feeling remorseful I'd made her question her parenting ability. I wished I could be better, do better. I hated how my illness was making everyone feel bad.

I had lost my mental Status Quo.

Down.

Down.

Deeper and …

Down.

I spiralled, trudging around the house in my manky bathrobe, looking sad, watching *This Morning* with Richard and Judy, eating badly, sleeping too long, body aching, mind reeling.

I was a total and utter fucking mess.

Home by 10 pm

A few weeks after the big mummy night out, my hand hovered over a 'Going' icon on my Facebook page. It was the first time I'd hesitated over an invite. It read: 'Carly's Birthday Bash – Next Saturday at The Wharf Bar. Bring your dancing shoes.' I wondered if Birkenstocks counted as dancing shoes. The photo had a circle of arms reaching in to form a big 'Cheers!', with frothy pints and bubbly flutes of champagne meeting in the middle. It looked enticing.

I can do this.

I'll go and prove that I can drink in moderation.

The terrible anxiety-filled hangover had faded into my past like a bad dream. My body had chosen to compartmentalise the anguish, box it off in a place where my drinking habit and my conscience couldn't see it.

Admittedly, that hangover had been challenging. Anxiety had buzzed around me like an annoying March fly for a week. I'd missed playgroup, ignored phone calls, and eaten junk food for three days, but I wasn't going to let that one night of overdoing it destroy my reputation for being the top party animal. I was ready to take off my mummy hat and climb back into my comfy drinking pants.

After clicking 'Going', I slotted the stems of two large wine glasses between my fingers, and grabbed the cold bottle of chardonnay that had been looking sad and lonely in the fridge.

'I'm going to Carly's birthday bash next weekend and I'm going to moderate my drinking,' I said to John as I spun the lid off the bottle. 'I'm going to be home by ten pm.'

'Okay,' he said.

I poured our wines and left it at that.

I'd like to say here that I had just one glass of wine and went to bed, but there was a bottle of red burning a hole in the cupboard under the kitchen sink, and, well, it had been a long week. I deserved a little reward for all my excellent parenting. Anyway, George was asleep, and I needed some adult time, to wind down. A bit of Mummy Wine Time.

Sounds innocent. It wasn't.

'I'm going choo do it,' I slurred as I tried to pack the dishwasher two hours later. 'I'm going to go to the party and stop after two. I will be the best moderate drinker the world hash ever sheen.' Then I staggered into the bedroom, collapsed on the bed, and dribbled red wine on the pillowcase.

*

In the week leading up to the big shindig, I was as determined to succeed at moderation as I was to start the diet on Monday, and take back my library book, a year overdue. I made promises to George and me and played out a drinking fantasy in my head. It was the same one I had before every party. It was how I kidded myself into believing I could be a normal human. Someone who could stop at one. Having a delusional fantasy about how I 'might' behave allowed me to get excited about going to the party.

The fantasy went like this.

I'd arrive at the Wharf Bar a little late, looking windswept yet glamorous. I'd be cheerful, bright eyed and everyone would be happy to see me. I'd sit on the edge of a high bar stool, with my legs crossed, sipping slowly at my one glass of wine. My pinky finger would stick out like I was a character from *The Great Gatsby*. I'd reel off yarns about my 'crazy' day and my friends would lean in to hear what happened next. Occasionally, I'd throw my head back in laughter, showing a row of perfect white teeth. I'd be hoping everyone thought I was funny, and my anecdotes cheered them up. I imagined, as the night progressed and people in the room got droopy and out of control, myself perched on my bar stool, feeling superior. I'd smile politely at wonky partygoers, and when my one glass was empty, I'd leave. Easy. I'd made people happy without ralphing on their shoes and I was going to go home feeling smug.

Outside, I'd try to hail a cab in the rain and a handsome man would offer me an umbrella. I'd thank him and our eyes would meet. I'd get in the taxi and he'd be left astonished, alone on the pavement as I disappeared into the night. I'd be home in time for *Ninja Warrior* and be 100 per cent capable of caring for my child the following day.

It was fucking ridiculous, I knew.

I'd been hunting down this drinking fantasy ever since I was a child flicking through the thick glossy magazines that sat under the telephone table in our hallway. I imagined I was the woman in red lipstick, holding an elegant bottle of liqueur, and I envied the glamazons at my parents' parties, swanning around in kaftans, sucking Blue Curaçao through stripy straws. I wanted to drink like the sophisticated women on TV who sat on the front of yachts in huge floppy hats and giant sunglasses, holding a wide-rimmed martini glass. After each binge, I kept my chin up, believing I could achieve the impossible next time. I had to.

Even as I pulled my jeans on, sipping on a cheap chardonnay before I left the house, I was still saying, 'You've got this,' knowing in my heart, *You haven't got this at all.*

I entered the Wharf Bar with my moderation fantasy at the forefront of my mind.

I had one glass.

Then I ordered a bottle.

Then shots.

There was no perching on stools, or handsome strangers in the rain.

I ended up at a karaoke bar, downing shots and hogging the mike as my baby slept soundly at home. The last thing I remembered was a man coming to the bar and telling me I had a giant cushion attached to my bottom. I reached around and discovered a huge pillow, not scatter size, European, stuck on my bum with chewing gum. I grabbed my full glass of red and downed it in one go, hoping the wine rush would hide my utter embarrassment.

Blackout.

I woke up in the middle of the night, with my heart beating hard and a dry mouth. I stumbled to the bathroom, filled the toothbrush pot with cold water and drank it down. When I caught a glimpse of myself in the mirror, I saw I had mascara smeared under my eyes, and my skin looked red and blotchy in the bright light.

What are you doing?

My night had gone off course so quickly. It was the first glass that did the damage. As the wine hit my bloodstream, my good intentions evaporated, I left my body, and I liked it. Being away from daytime me for a moment felt good.

Drinking meant the mum disappeared for a few hours and the party girl took over. I enjoyed shutting the door on mundane.

Drinking meant I got to remember who I used to be.

I stayed in bed the next day, mentally punishing myself, and listened on as my life happened without me. I heard George cry. I smelled pumpkin roasting in the oven. I heard plates being slid from cupboards, pans clattering and the mixer whizzing. I heard John get the pram from the garage and the zip of George's little dinosaur anorak.

The front door closed and off they went to the park without me.

My phone buzzed.

> Hey, Vic, did you get home all right? You were hilarious! Do you remember stealing the tablecloth and climbing the horse statue?

I turned off my phone and closed my eyes.

Later, sometime in the afternoon, I heard them come back.

I got up, crept into the hallway, and stared at my family. They were watching *Peppa Pig*, George's head resting on John's hairy chest. It must have felt soft, like a carpet. They had a blanket over them. I wanted to join them, pick up the end of the blanket and snuggle in. I didn't. I just stared, longing for the comfort they were feeling.

I have failed. Again.

I've become a spectator, a bystander in my own life.

I really am a piece of shit.

Good Old-Fashioned Brainwashing!

Age 21

Help reconnect with people, the leaflet said. *Find others who are suffering*. That was enough. After my drug-induced fizzle-out, I needed to reconnect with the world.

Still filled with anxiety, I drove up to York, in the north of England, where I anticipated finding some answers to my permanent negative state of mind. The leaflet had been brief, but it represented something. Hope.

A sticky name label was patted onto my chest and a large group of people began to congregate around me in the hotel lobby. A voice over a loudspeaker told us to head to the big double doors and find our seat numbers. I was met by a suited, smiling usher. He asked me to take off my watch and place it on the tray he was holding. I complied. He directed me into a huge conference room buzzing with people.

I found a chair. There was some dramatic music, and a charismatic American dude took to the stage. On a flip chart, he drew a diagram using circles and arrows. It represented how we all lived within our comfort zones and how life was better experienced outside of these parameters.

Blah, blah, blah.

We all clapped, some cheered. Women gazed, infatuated with this somewhat unattractive fat, bald man. He had a presence, though, a charm that was intoxicating, and by the end of the weekend, I was gazing too.

He blathered on for hours about finding our true meaning and letting go of insecurities. I soaked up every gooey phrase like a lentil soaking up water and, soon, my mind was a mashed-up dahl of inspirational quotes and authoritarian procedures. I succumbed to it all with pleasure and gusto. It was just what I needed, and I dived headfirst into every task and workshop.

The other attendees were smiley and welcoming. Some had been to the sessions before and were there to aid us newbies. The alumni wore similar clothing: women in long dresses and men in sharp suits. They seemed savvy, worthy of respect, but as the weekend progressed, it became apparent they were all a teeny-weeny bit mental. They didn't blink much, and as we revealed our stories to each other, I realised they were all vulnerable, damaged individuals looking for help, just like me. The crowd of fuckups felt like home. These people understood me because they were suffering like I was. A room full of desperate souls seeking restoration.

Through various processes, problems were agitated out of each of us, because each task churned up insecurities. Before I knew what I was doing, I found myself crying with a small group of strangers and holding hands with people in a circle. I even told a random person next to me I loved them. I fell backwards into the arms of my dependable new friends. I hugged and nodded a lot. I sat cross-legged and listened like an obedient dog waiting for a command. I did 'love bombing', holding the shoulders of a person in the group, looking them directly in the eye and saying 'I love you' over and over again, until we both fell to the floor in a heap.

'I let go of all my power,' I said, throwing my hands up to the sky.

'Say it louder.'

'I LET GO OF ALL MY POWER!' I shouted. It felt awkward, but I did it anyway.

I had no idea what any of it meant, but I felt happy for the first time in ages. For a few blissful days, my panic subsided.

After I'd let go of my insecurities (and my $500 tuition fee), I was set up with a 'buddy': a skinhead girl with a bright smile. She introduced herself as Mel, and told me she was going to take care of me and support me in the outside world. I admired her; she was an assistant, a person who had 'done the work'. She had lots of insightful knowledge. Chin resting on my open palms, elbows digging into the hard cement floor of the conference room. I took in all her wisdom. As I stared, I noticed empty holes in her ears and nose. She'd removed all her piercings. I briefly wondered why.

Her voice and story were intoxicating. I trusted her because she'd been through stuff. She ached and had fears like mine, so it felt natural for me to open up to her. Together, we shared our problems and hopes, our dreams and failures. She was my new best friend, and we spent the whole weekend squeezing each other's shoulder blades in a supportive, yet slightly painful, manner.

After rather a lot of 'releasing' and 'connecting', we all regathered in the hall to hear the final presentation. The same guy waltzed onto the stage, and we all cheered and screamed like a group of Tom Jones groupies, our fists pumping the sky, doing loud wolf-whistles. I didn't throw my knickers up on stage but I did shout out 'YEAH!' in a weird accent.

The tubby, bald American demanded we take the tools we had been taught about over the past 48 hours and start spreading the message while following the instructions set out in our workbooks. (Things like introducing yourself to a stranger every day, getting up at the same time each morning, making your bed and saying positive mantras in the mirror. Simple, yet controlling-by-nature, tasks.) We nodded in unison as he spoke, making mental promises to take our newfound knowledge into our normal lives and into the lives of the mere mortals beyond the four walls of the grand hall. I felt like a missionary being sent away to spread the good word.

For the big finale, we had to get up on the stage, one by one, grab the mike and tell a room packed with over 500 people our three deepest secrets.

I didn't hesitate. *How wonderful that I can be in such a trusting environment.*

It was an enlightening few hours. I managed to contain my laughter by pinching my nose throughout the public shaming. One guy got up, and told us that when his wife was out, he took the broom from a corner of the kitchen, put a condom on it and stuck it up his arse. I nearly spat out my water.

I didn't understand why he needed a condom. And wouldn't the thought of rectal splinters have quashed his irresistible urge? Surely the handle of a washing-up brush or a plastic whisk would have been more appropriate? And how did telling this story free him? I'd have thought informing a room full of strangers you liked shoving brooms up your back passage would only make you feel more vulnerable.

Maybe he hoped that, by being so honest, he could sweep the whole debacle under the carpet?

After his awkward admission, a wild-haired lady divulged she did wees in the shower (*Doesn't everyone?*) and had shagged her best mate's husband. Then a young boy said he feared wooden spoons and watched too much porn. We all clapped as each person blurted out their secrets.

They didn't applaud so hard for me when I revealed I had once stolen five packets of Hubba Bubba chewing gum from my local shop, lied to my parents about drink driving, and was madly in love with the charismatic baldy American leader. I blushed at him as he stood at the edge of the stage, his face frozen in a knowing gawk. He also rubbed his hands together in a greedy way, as if to say, *'Another helpless groupie for me to take advantage of. Excellent, mawahhhahaha.'*

He had a room full of them, clawing for his attention. I'm pretty sure he used his power to sow more than seeds of wisdom. Something inside me sank as I stepped off the stage, but I buried the emotion under a layer of delusion.

*

When I got home after my enlightening weekend, I felt a little better in me noggin and was eager to go to the next event, in London the following weekend. It was $1500. I didn't have any money, and wondered if I could weasel in by offering to help in some way: peel potatoes or polish the charismatic American's plums.

I tried to get some friends to come along and jabbered at them in a snooty fashion. I droned on about my so-called 'Group Awareness Training', about how amazing it had been and how I was part of an incredible network of like-minded people.

'I've done this course and learned about the tools to live a better life. You must come.'

My best mate Kate thought I'd completely lost it when I told her she needed to 'Work on herself'. I failed to recruit anyone for the expensive 'self-actualisation' weekend. I didn't care; I had a new gang, with morals, wisdom and hypnotic stares.

I called my 'buddy' Mel most evenings, to check in. We chatted for hours on the phone. She was kind and understanding, but was going through a severe bout of depression. I felt useful; she needed me, and I was able to make her feel more positive. Another susceptible soul in need of a guiding hand, she listened and understood what I'd been through. We were both hurting and wanted to help one another.

Perfect contenders for a bit of good old-fashioned brainwashing!

I'm not totally stupid. The signs of this group being a cult were clear. I'd say I was 50 per cent indoctrinated. My brain was being rinsed and lightly blow-dried, rather than washed. After about the first 24 hours of being there, I had an inkling the faction was seedier than I first thought. The rubbing of the hands and the breaking of my soul alluded to a darker undercurrent. It felt uncomfortable, like when my jeans were too tight after gorging on naan bread. I had a greasy, windy feeling in my tummy as I started to join the dots.

Some of what I'd seen that weekend had been overbearing behaviour by those in charge, and perhaps traumatic for those on the end of it. Teenagers attended with their parents, taking part in the 'group confessionals'. The process cracked people open, and it was painful to see these young, fragile minds get covertly manipulated, kids being humiliated in front of their parents. I understood that confronting emotional stuff could be beneficial in the right environment, but this wasn't. It seemed soul destroying for them.

Still, the pyramid of power was obvious and I felt the compulsion to step up the ladder. I wanted to be an assistant – someone in charge of meeting and greeting new disciples, and controlling the environment through stringent routine tasks. These serious-looking henchpeople meticulously lined up the chairs, stood rigid at the end of the rows of seats, like linesmen at a tennis match, and made sure everything was in its exact place. I guessed these nuances were designed to train the brain not to question instructions, a sneaky way of teaching us who was in charge. This was why Mel had removed all her jewellery. Control.

Wanting to give them money, money I didn't have, to move up the ranks within the hierarchy, felt wrong. Then I asked myself, *Why can my friends live life from day to day without this group? Why do I feel like I need it?*

Needing this group started to feel creepy.

One morning, I was reading a newspaper on the train and saw a little ad on the back page that said *CULT HOTLINE – call this number to find out about cults or to save a family member.*

I dialled the number and asked them about the group. I thought they'd say, *Don't worry, it's just a self-help group. It's fine.*

I was surprised when the lady on the other end replied with, 'Yes, we know a lot of families who have lost children to that cult.'

I didn't go again.

*

Sadly, panic re-emerged over the following weeks, which led me down some other alternative routes to try to get better. I had acupuncture, it hurt. Reiki didn't hurt enough. I booked in to see a clairvoyant, who cancelled due to unforeseen circumstances, and I ended up being hypnotised by a lady in a purple sorceress's dress, sitting side-saddle on my parents' bed, like she was riding a broomstick. Too witchy.

'Imagine a beeeach with waves lapping at your feeet,' she said, like a sad ghost.

'Er, okay.'

'Now, close your eyyyes and count dooown from a hundred, very slooowwwly.'

I did as the witch ordered: visualised the scene and started counting backwards. When I got to zero, I pretended to be asleep, in case she got angry and hexed me. I lay there, motionless as she described a peaceful scene where panic dissolved into grains of sand falling slooowly through an hourglass, then she clicked her fingers and declared, 'You're back in the rooom, Victoriiaaa.'

Before she mounted her broom (with a condom on it), she scooped up her belongings and prophesised, 'You will never feel anxiety agaaaiinnn.'

She was wrong. What a load of old bollocks, I wasn't hypnotised at all. I was groggy, tired. The fear was still very present.

The spooky purple hypno-witch recommended meeting with a regression expert. She said it might reveal why I was so anxious. I didn't fancy it because I thought it was rubbish. People were always either Cleopatra or King Henry VIII in their past life, never a street urchin or an accountant. I told hypno-lady the reason I had panic attacks was because I had shoved bucketloads of drink and drugs down my throat for the past ten years, not because I was Genghis Khan in a previous existence.

Having flushed a bit of (my parents') money down the toilet trying various remedies, none of which worked, I sought some conventional help that didn't involve human sacrifice or handing myself over to a sect. I hadn't wanted to take antidepressants because I feared putting any more drugs in my body, but I had run out of other avenues, so I gave in to my mum's wishes and saw my local GP again.

I was prescribed antidepressants and referred for cognitive behavioural therapy (CBT). I attended a weekly meeting with a gentle lady called Ruth, who, with care, helped me rewire my brain. Hence, my recovery began. Having someone who understood my problems was a huge relief. Ruth had come across people like me before, as she had cured many drug-addled, panic-stricken souls. I wasn't alone, there were other people like me, and it was strangely reassuring. I knew I was in the right place.

During one session, Ruth asked me to close my eyes and describe what I saw inside my head. I was scared of confronting the darkness in my mind. I squeezed my eyes shut hard and straightaway was greeted by a furious monster. He looked like the creature the Honey Monster from the Sugar Puffs advert, spinning around inside a tornado of rubbish as he hurled objects at me. It was petrifying up there.

Ruth told me to keep my eyes shut and imagine I had a gun. 'Take it out. Kill it. Shoot the monster!'

I was surprised we were resorting to a gun battle, but did what she said. I imagined holding a black machine gun, like

Tony Montana at the end of *Scarface*, and mowing down that Mother-Fucking-Cockroach-Cereal-Killer!

I did it. I shot him. I killed him.

Bang.

His furry body hit the deck in slow motion, yellow fluffy hair falling into a heap.

I opened my eyes.

In that exact moment, I realised I, not the fear, was in control. I had the upper hand, the power to stop the monster. It was within me to cure my problem.

'You've done it, Vicky. You killed him.'

'I know, it was easy. I didn't know I was so strong.'

I could see the ravenous beast twitching behind a little glass window. He wasn't quite dead: just badly injured and knocking to come in, banging on the glass that separated him from my brain. I didn't let him in – it was that simple. *Don't let the panic in.* I was determined to leave my big yellow enemy out in the cold.

I'd always thought it was people, places or things that made me anxious, but it had been me all along.

I realise this process of visualising my problem might sound weird as, but it truly worked. I felt all the turmoil from the entire year lift. 'I feel amazing, Ruth. I feel, erm, a bit better!'

I did. Something had altered within me.

Ruth had given me a pebble when we first met. 'I want it back when you feel better.'

It represented that fateful day when I collapsed on the cold stones of Brighton Beach. I kept it in the back pocket of my jeans. If I was feeling fear, I could reach in and hold it. The pebble reminded me how far I had come and how determined I was to never feel like that again. The pebble was my panic and the time had come to give it back.

After the monster-visualisation epiphany, I handed it to Ruth. 'I don't need this anymore. I think I'll be okay now.'

She took the pebble from me, and our hands cupped. She wished me well and I thanked her. I never saw her again.

I hoped never to see that monster again either, but no such luck.

Invisible

I was in my usual spot on the couch, as George slept with his head resting on my lap. I tried to watch a YouTube video on 'the best way to fold a bed sheet' without waking him. The housework was done and I was having a quiet week. Trying to make up for going out. Trying to be a normal mum.

I'd been to music class once this week. I'd played the *EastEnders* theme tune on a xylophone, and popped into playgroup, where, over crumbling Anzac biscuits, I engaged in conversations about sleep times. This morning, I'd mashed up veggies, cleaned surfaces and wiped George's face with spitty hankies.

I had successfully parented.

I even ironed a few shirts, something I had told John I would never do: 'When we get married, just know – I am not one of those wives who darns socks and irons shirts.' But guilt about drinking, and the sight of the shirts hanging off curtain rails around the house, like the ghosts of suffragettes, meant I unhooked them and ironed out the creases. I hoped to get a few brownie points.

Today had been good but most days …

I didn't recognise myself.

I hated to admit it, but I was finding being a mum … well, dull.

There were only so many times I could fake smiles over poop anecdotes and look excited about pushing a baby on a swing for an hour.

I couldn't tell anyone, though.

That would make me a bad person.

I couldn't say out loud that motherhood was hard and boring, or that I was daydreaming about packing a suitcase and sneaking away in the dead of night, quietly shutting the garden gate behind me.

George moved a little, and I nearly dropped my phone on his head. I stroked the side of his face until he settled and wondered if he deserved better. Did all mums consider running away? Did others reminisce about their lives before children?

The transition from party girl to mother was a bit trickier than I had imagined. I'd gone from having glitter boobs at Glastonbury, being independent and travelling the world, to being stuck in a flat on my own with a crying baby.

And it sucked.

No one had told me I would be so isolated, that a little person would be so dependent on me and so demanding. It was such a huge responsibility.

Before I had George, I imagined keeping the free spirit within me alive when I was a mother. I wanted to cling to the party girl with no roots, still be someone who stuck pins in maps and booked tickets. I thought I'd stuff the baby in a sling and be off galivanting across the globe with my family in tow, getting my camera stolen by baboons, hiking up mountains, watching the sun set over the Ganges – but here I was, in a room with beige wallpaper, paying a high rent for it, watching a video about bed sheets.

I looked down at some smudged brown banana on my white trousers and let out a huge sigh.

I'm boring now. All I'm good for is a healthy packed lunch and a bedtime story.

I'm just a comfy-cardiganed bottom wiper.

Someone who rubs her heels and moans about being on her feet all day.

Just a mum.

Just a boring housewife.

I felt overlooked nowadays. An inconsequential blob. Like my life before parenting never happened. It made me want to run out to the street and shout, 'I've ridden fucking camels through the fucking Sahara Desert, for fuck's sake!'

But I didn't. I sat on the couch, wondering where the Vicky I'd known had gone.

The only thing I was looking forward to was baby bedtime and an astronaut's-helmet-size glass of white wine. I was drinking more during the week, more than ever before. But what else was there to do, how else was I supposed to feel okay about all this?

A pattern emerged, but I couldn't seem to stop it.

I was good.

I got bored.

I thought about being bad.

I was bad.

Then the hangover, accompanied by a visit from Mr Anxiety Monster. He was sitting at the end of my bed, filing his nails, waiting to pounce on my sanity.

Then *paff*! By Wednesday, he was gone and I was back raising a glass to the sky.

A self-inflicted woe on repeat.

Lately, a few things had gone wrong. There were little fractures in my parenting. Signs I was sinking.

George's first time at day care, his teacher called and said, 'Did you forget to pack his lunch, or does he just really like cheese?' I'd grabbed the wrong container from the fridge and sent him in with an entire block of cheddar.

The previous Tuesday, I locked him in the car and had to call the fire brigade to break him out. Two handsome firemen told me to 'Be more careful' and my cheeks flushed as I lifted my crying son out of his seat. I felt terrible.

Also, my dinners had been a bit lazy. My homemade organic mashes had been replaced with shop-bought squeezies: little packets of processed food with twist-off caps.

I know it wasn't as if I locked him in a cupboard under the stairs, like Harry Potter's aunty and uncle, but I thought my perfect-mum persona was slipping.

Recently, I'd been hiding how much I drank. I told John I stayed out because my friends made me, and that I only had a few. I didn't tell him I went to an afterparty and danced on a speaker. I kept secret the fact I woke up slumped in the hallway armchair with a saveloy sausage sticking out of my top pocket.

I didn't think I needed to worry him. *I'm not an alcoholic.* (Even though I'd failed every online 'Are you an alcoholic?' test.)

People with drinking problems didn't look like me. There were no rock bottoms here; I was fine and dandy. I wasn't eating out of a dumpster or injecting heroin behind the 7-Eleven. I wasn't selling my body for a hit of crack or passed out on a park bench with a bottle of Jack Daniel's clenched to my chest. I was a mum who deserved a break, a binge drinker, a partier who got shitty hangovers.

But, secretly, I thought I was fading away, disappearing between the cracks.

I felt trapped in a cycle with no way out. I was stuck in a pinot gris purgatory.

I was sitting in a place where people couldn't see me. Couldn't see my problem.

I tried to tell a few friends how I was feeling. 'I'm having anxiety when I'm hungover,' I blurted out to a mate over a hot chai at a café one morning.

'The hair of the dog will sort that out.'

'But I'm getting really anxious every time I drink.'

'Get a grip, woman. If you start drinking vodka in the morning, then you might need to start worrying. You're fine.'

'I feel like I'm losing it.'

'It's just a hangover. Everybody feels like that.'

'Really? After a night out, the other mums post smiling pictures of themselves. They've been for a ten kilometre run or they're with their kids at the park. They all seem to be having normal, happy days, when I'm lying in bed looking like roadkill – unable to move my head.'

'They're probably running to the toilets to regurgitate kebab between each selfie. Don't worry about it.'

But I *was* worried.

I looked down at George, his eyes were open. He yawned and stretched his arms above his head. His skin had little red marks from sleeping on his teething rattle. When our eyes met, he stared back at me and smiled, then stuck a thumb in his mouth and drifted back to sleep. Just the sight of me was enough to comfort him. I leaned down, and put my nose on his cheek and breathed him in.

Then I had a brilliant idea.

What if I get pregnant?
Maybe if I get pregnant, I could stop drinking.

*

Anything was worth a try.

The Stump

Age 22

I'd put my hellish year of anxiety, cults and antidepressants behind me. I decided never to take drugs again. It had caused so much turmoil, and I truly felt like I wouldn't survive another drag on a joint or not-so-'cheeky' line. That part of my life was over.

My getting-better goal when I was suffering from anxiety back then was to be able to sit in a pub and drink a pint. My objective was to get back to normal life, which, for me, meant getting back to booze. I never once blamed the alcohol for my illness, I blamed drugs. Holding alcohol responsible meant giving up on being me and I wasn't at all ready for that. I was only 22, and I wanted to jump back into life, to start having fun again.

It was time to get drinking.

'A pint of your finest ale, please, sir!' I asked, sounding as if I was a thirsty explorer back from the Kalahari Desert.

The barman handed it over. I tipped nearly the whole pint down my throat in one go, then had two more. All my mates gathered around me and cheered my return to alcohol.

'I can't believe I haven't drunk anything for a year. I think I've got a lot of catching up to do!'

I'd been living with Mum and Dad while I recovered from my mini mental breakdown and, honestly, it was wearing thin. Their house was a B & B back then and they needed my old bedroom for guests, so I was relocated to the garden shed – the Stench Den, as I called it. It smelled like a hamster cage and the walls rattled in the wind. Even though I was out of their living space, our relationship deteriorated by the day. They were annoyed with me for not paying my way and using their home like a hotel. I was annoyed that Mum stopped leaving mints on my pillow and cleared the buffet breakfast before I woke up.

Once I was feeling more mentally stable, and to make the relationship with my parents bearable, I blagged a shit job in a Mexican-style restaurant. I hated it. I had to carry huge trays of potato skins above my head for hours on end, and smile as I listed the options: 'French fries, savoury fries, curly fries, cheesy fries or fries, fries.'

The response was always the same: 'Got any chips?'

I got my revenge on dumb customers by asking, 'How many potato skins would you like? Two skin, three skin or foreskin, sir?'

I never lasted long in jobs I hated, not being one to bow down to authoritarian types. This time, I had to quit after my initiation back into heavy drinking made me look like an idiot.

I got black-out mullered on a night out with work people, and a colleague's mum discovered me on her landing at 3 am, squatting and taking a piss on her thick white carpet. My co-worker promised she wouldn't tell anyone, but on my next shift, the entire staff was smirking at me. I was mortified. I spent my last stint there hiding behind the industrial fridges, crying into my sombrero. When the manager discovered me, instead of telling her what had happened, I threw my apron on the floor and said, 'Shove your chipotle refried beans up your arse.' And that was that.

*

It was time for a new start. The money I'd earned was enough to buy a round-the-world plane ticket. I bid farewell to my disgruntled parents, and handed them back the key to the Stench Den, kissed them on the cheek and promised to give them a good Tripadvisor review.

Now, imagine a map with the route of a plane looping from London to Bangkok.

Touchdown.

I slung my backpack on, jumped into a bright yellow taxi and headed into the depths of this mysterious city.

At Khao San Road, the main backpacker hub, I found a cheap room with a fan. It wasn't much different from the jail cell in Brighton, so I felt very much at home. There were stains on the pillows, cockroaches scurrying under the bed, and the shower was a bucket in a big plastic barrel. The fan made a loud clattering as it spun around. The room was roasting, so I put some cash and my passport in my little money belt, then made my way downstairs to discover Bangkok's nightlife.

I visited bars that pumped out techno and reggae from small speakers. I met an odd woman from Holland, who danced as if she was climbing a ladder. I rambled around the steamy streets, going from pub to club to hotel. I witnessed a lady blow out the candles on a birthday cake using her vagina. I watched a Thai boxing match between two toddlers. I declined some opium, and ate some fried ants and skewered scorpions. When I got back to my hotel, I collapsed onto the yellowing mattress. I was rat-arsed and the room was spinning around. Lurching forward, I made it to the toilet, where I threw up.

What a night, I thought as my head hung deep inside the bowl.

I opened my eyes. Remnants of insects – thorax, legs and antennae – floated in the foamy spew. I wiped my mouth on a forearm, then flopped backwards onto the cool floor tiles. I lay there, laughing aloud about my momentous night out.

When I awoke, I had a bad headache, but no fear. The night had been eventful, and I loved every freaky minute of it. I was me again. But, this time, nobody knew who 'me' was. I was free.

Travelling gave me the ability to morph into whoever I wanted to be. I was a panic-free girl with the world at her feet. There was no expectation to be the funniest person in the room. I became calmer, more introverted, happy to be on my own. I didn't care about other people's opinions, and I felt a sense of independence. My life was simplified by going away, my choices were all my own. No pressure, no one to disappoint. The chaos of the past few years melted away, and a shinier, happy girl stepped out into the big wide world.

Bangkok and I became buddies. The people never stopped smiling and the food was incredible. The sights and smells invigorated me. Everywhere I looked, there were interesting spectacles to absorb. Temples with monks in orange robes, kneeling in prayer; street vendors throwing noodles into pans, making big plumes of smoke; dogs with emaciated bodies and nipples like cow udders, sniffing the ground or growling at tourists. In the evening, bars appeared from nowhere, and overflowed with young travellers who were eager for new experiences and cold beers.

I was finding myself by getting lost in the huge city. Every day, I woke up early, and wandered around with no plans and no maps. I took in the quietness before the traffic and car horns. I walked in parks, and watched old people, with lined faces, practise slow tai chi in silence, and I sketched the skyline in the back of my diary. I traipsed around for hours, meeting locals and trying spicy, undisclosed meats from sizzling hot plates. I chewed dried squid that a toothless man had arranged in lines on a wooden frame. It was just me and the streets.

In the evenings, I sat on the kerb with a beer and watched. People came and went. Weird characters sat next to me and unloaded tales of adventure into my twitching ears. Friendly faces gave me advice on spots to visit, hidden beaches and blue lagoons. Stories floated around me, whisperings of the past. Every step I took along the worn cobbled foreshore of the river felt like walking an ancient path. I couldn't work out what was true and what was legend, and didn't care. Pessimistic expats gave me warnings: accounts of travellers going missing after heading over the Burmese border, having stumbled upon ganglands and weed fields. It was all very exciting, and I drank up the mysterious stories as eagerly as I did the cold beers.

Japanese backpackers were a pleasure to hang out with. Their sweetness touched my heart; their hands covered shy smiles, their faces full of innocence. I played pool with these gentle souls, and the only interruption was the occasional tap of the balls as they slid softly into pockets. I ate dinner with dark-haired, serious Israelis who'd come travelling after completing mandatory military service. The men were handsome, with curly locks and tanned skin; the girls beautiful and abrupt. I shared books and *Lonely Planet* tips with friendly, beer-swilling Germans with orange bum bags, and had breakfast with early-rising Scandinavian girls who had Nordic white-blonde hair and fierce blue eyes.

I met a bloke called Nigel Miller, who had changed his name by deed poll to Don Reno San Tino, which I thought was the best thing ever. I also met a Geordie who said, 'Thank you very much' after every sentence. 'I went to the beach, thank you very much,' or 'I'm going to grab dinner, thank you very much.' I liked him. His accent made me homesick (thank you very much). On a bus ride, I met a tall man who looked like Roald Dahl's BFG – he had a big nose and spindly fingers. As night fell, his hand snaked its way onto my upper thigh, and he leaned in and whispered in my ear, in a long Texan drawl, 'I'm here to meet girls, sweetie pie, and maybe make love?' I had never needed the toilet so suddenly, and got off at the next station, feeling queasy.

I also met a girl who contradicted everything she herself said: 'I nearly hiked up a mountain today, but I didn't. I almost stubbed my toe yesterday, but I didn't.'

I hoped she might fuck off, but guess what?

There were so many weird and wonderful people to pass time with, doing nothing. The best conversations were simple nods and smiles from these strangers. Silence drowned out egos and language barriers cut the crap. These cultural blockades created peaceful interactions that ended in swapped email addresses and well wishes. Sometimes, just passing a beer to an unknown nomad was enough for us to become kindred spirits.

I soon had the garb and the hippie attitude. I started saying 'man' a lot and had a new interest in tie-dye. My new-age image attracted like-minded, no-shoe-wearing, nose-pierced people and I enjoyed being a more chilled human. My trousers got baggier, my hair grew shaggier, and my pace slowed.

On scorching hot days, I sat on a sunbed next to a rooftop pool, under the polluted skies of Bangkok. I read, and daydreamed of being a writer one day. I bought books by philosophers and travellers. I devoured *The Alchemist*, *Jonathan Livingston Seagull*, *On the Road* and *The Beach*. I loved the idea of being a nomad. I felt an affinity with these drifters, these characters in the novels I was reading. They spoke to me from the pages. I had whimsical images floating around my mind of never going home and living out of a bag forever. I got a tattoo of a quote from *The Alchemist* – 'it is written' – inked on my foot in Thai script. It represented the happier me; everything that had transpired, and the panic and depression, was for a reason. It was all meant to be.

Travelling gave me space. I had time to unwind and listen, find a beach bar, grab a drink or ten, and sit waiting to spark up a conversation with a stranger. At breakfast, over sweet poached eggs, I spent hours scribbling my adventures down in bulging diaries, describing my day using poems and funny drawings. I kept every train ticket, menu, business card and map, all taped between the pages of these scruffy journals. I didn't ever want to forget.

*

When the pace of Bangkok got too much, I headed southeast. Koh Samet island was a picture-perfect location to unwind, with white sands and a clear, flat ocean lapping at its shores. It was paradise. Days passed of doing nothing at all. I strolled along the coastline, taking the time to decide which tree to tie my hammock to. I drew shapes in the sand with my toes and sat feeling blissful as the warm breeze passed through the trees above my head. I slept in a ramshackle hut, and ate meals at the local market: fresh fish, and curries laden with lemongrass and basil. I sat on the roadside, taking mouthfuls of food while jotting paragraphs in my diary, and finishing letters or postcards to my friends back in Blighty, as the motorbikes zoomed past, and the sun disappeared below the horizon.

I liked being alone.

I stayed in that hammock for two months, until I met two sweet English boys, Pete and Rich. They told me about full moon parties on an island in the south of the country. It sounded fun. I jumped on a train with them and headed off. A couple of boat rides later, we landed on Haad Rin Beach in Koh Phangan

The island was a tropical Eden, a textbook hippie haven with a clear, glistening ocean. Quirky bars lined the palmy oceanfront, where beautiful girls sat braiding each other's hair and dreadlocked boys practised throwing fire sticks as the waves washed over their feet.

I'd found my ideal spot. I bought some orange fisherman's pants, a low-slung bag for my towel and book, then spent the next month doing nothing but drinking, snorkelling and playing frisbee.

*

On New Year's Eve 1999, the motley crew I'd attached myself to and I made our way to the site of the world-famous full moon party. The bars had signs written on pieces of driftwood: 100 Baht Buckets, Special pri. These small metal buckets contained a bottle of Thai whisky, a can of Coke and a strange energy drink that contained formaldehyde – just in case my brain wasn't pickled enough. I'd had a sip of one before and hated the syrupy sweetness, but it was New Year's Eve and I wanted to avoid passing out before midnight, so I grabbed a straw and joined in.

Now, I was not a slow-paced drinker. I poured it down my throat like I was filling up a car with petrol. I was a guzzler – or 'The Gulper', as I was nicknamed – so this kind of high-volume alcohol was a disaster for me. I could gulp wine and beer, no *problemo*. But this stuff was different; it was rocket fuel, chemically enhanced crazy juice. The first few sips, then having jelly legs … and midnight was a very hazy start to the new millennium.

The bucket was handed around a circle of people. As soon as I passed it on to the person next to me, another one was handed to me. I took it and wrapped my lips around the bundle of straws. It went on and on.

'Happy New Year,' I said as I kissed a man in a cowboy hat on the cheek. Then I remember being handed an ice-cold bottle of red wine.

In and out of consciousness, lying on the beach covered in sand like a chicken schnitzel, dancing on a speaker, friends helping me stand, stumbling together down a dusty road. I looked down at my fumbling hands as my right thumb rolled back the little cog in a cigarette lighter. My other hand then came into view and the flame met the wick of a small round firework.

The explosion was loud. Straightaway, I knew something had gone tits up. I could feel liquid dribbling onto my bare feet. Staggering around in shock, with my ears ringing from the bang, I couldn't make out the extent of the injury. It was too dark.

I called up ahead, 'Hey, guys, er, I think I may have blown one of my fingers off.'

Happy faces turned pale. Someone found a head torch and, through the darkness, we saw bone protruding from where my finger had once existed. The top of it was completely blown off. The skin was burned, blistered, and blood spouted out. Pete wrapped a t-shirt around my hand and Rich hailed a taxi. I was lifted into the back seat. Blood dripped off my elbow and onto the floor.

'I'll never play the piano again!' I quipped, before passing out.

The taxi pulled up at the tiny hospital. I was plonked in a wheelchair and rushed into the emergency unit. The room was brightly lit, with chairs and buckets on ripped lino flooring. A whiff of death and excrement pumped out of a manky air-conditioning unit and insects rained down from the ceiling. I heard zaps as mosquitoes got fried on an electric machine above my head. It was like an episode of *M*A*S*H*. Beds rattled past, people cried out in pain and curtains were pulled closed as victims of motorbike accidents were wheeled in.

I listened to the howls and moans as a nurse gently assessed my wound.

The alcohol was still swimming around in my bloodstream, doing lengths up and down my body, making me feel quite woozy and numb. At that time, my pain was minimal. Bearable. The nurse was kind, speaking softly and doing her best in these terrible conditions.

'*Farang* be more careful. No play fire.'

She leaned over and stretched her hand towards a rusty metal bucket. There was water swishing around inside. She scooped up a needle that was floating on the surface. It looked used. There was no plastic covering. No disinfectant nearby. No surgeons. Just me, the nurse, the scuttling cockroaches and the rusty bucket of death.

I shook my head at her. 'No needle.'

'Sure, lady? Maybe pain?'

'No needle,' I repeated.

I clenched my teeth as the kind nurse sawed off bone with her tiny hacksaw, then cleaned and stitched up what was left of my finger, with no anaesthetic. Needless to say, the excruciating pain sobered me right up and my jaw ached from the trauma.

They did what they could, but I could see I needed surgery. My finger was gone from the middle knuckle up and the bottom part was at a funny angle. The nurse bandaged me up and handed me some painkillers. She held my uninjured hand and whispered, 'Bery strong lady.'

Just as I drifted off into a strong-painkiller-induced coma, I saw the nice nurse get harassed by a six-foot-six Russian tourist who had a tiny piece of coral stuck in his toe. He screamed like a baby as the nurse tweezered it into a napkin.

What a wimp, I thought as I fell asleep.

I called my parents after a few days. I lied and told them an evil drunken stranger had thrown a firework at me. I was too embarrassed to admit I'd lit one when pissed. 'It just missed my eye, so I was lucky. It could have been so much worse.'

They believed me, as always.

I cut my Thailand trip short and flew to Australia to get better medical care. Both my sisters were living in Sydney, so

THE STUMP

I had a choice of sofas to surf once my finger was all better. The kind English boys helped me get back to Bangkok, where I hopped on a plane with my arm strapped to my chest. I had to say farewell to my Thai paradise, and thanked Pete and Rich for being so kind to me. I was extra sad because I was a little bit in love with Rich. I left part of my heart there on that perfect island, along with the top of my finger.

*

Sarah and her partner, Dan, an old mate of mine from Brighton, met me at Sydney airport, and we headed to a local medical centre. On arrival, the doctors asked me for a urine sample. I supplied it with pleasure, and my name was called out. The doctor asked me many personal questions: about my stay in Oz, previous work experience, my qualifications, schooling, etc.

Gosh, they're thorough here, I thought.

Then he asked, 'What nursing experience have you had?'

'What? I'm here for you to look at my finger. I blew it off.'

'Oh.'

He'd been interviewing me for a job. The urine sample was for a drug test.

'Shame, you're the best candidate so far!' he said.

When the knobhead noticed my arm was bandaged up to my elbow, we each expelled an awkward laugh, and he sent me to the nearest emergency room. But he kept my urine.

I was in hospital for a couple of weeks, getting the break sorted and having skin grafts. 'Keeping some length', as the doctor put it. Being an inpatient was boring. I couldn't drink or go out to any Aussie pubs. I didn't know anyone, and my sister was working. The only distraction was the old lady in the opposite bed, who shouted and screamed at night, and kept me awake. I couldn't help but be worried for the old bat. Every time her gurgling sounds came to an abrupt halt, I headed to her bedside, worried she'd died. One time, her eyes snapped open. She sat bolt upright in the bed, grabbed me by my gown, then pulled me towards her until my nose touched hers.

She shouted in my face, 'GET BACK TO LONDON!'

I didn't help her again.

One morning, towards the end of my stay, I awoke to find a note under my pillow from a doctor. It read: *Hey, if you want someone to show you around Sydney give me a call 078865544 – Love Sam.*

This doctor had been injecting pain medication into my left buttock at night … when I was asleep. I'd never seen him or spoken to him. You can't ask someone out having only introduced yourself to their arse, especially if they're unconscious at the time! I declined the kind offer by putting a reply in my underwear and slept with one (brown) eye open from that night onwards.

*

My new year really had gone off with a bang. My finger did heal (disappointingly, it didn't grow back). I stayed in Australia for another year, I worked, selling insurance, waiting tables, picking fruit and renting deck chairs. Whatever I could get. I did lots of drinking and bonking too. The whole time, I never saw the Harbour Bridge, the outback or a kangaroo. I was too busy being wasted or hungover. Travelling gave my drinking the opportunity to develop without repercussions. I drank every day, under the guise of being sociable. My habit got absorbed into the crowd, diluted into another round of shots and a pile of excuses. I surrounded myself with people who were just like me. Party people, with itsy bitsy drinking problems. That is, people who thought it was okay to get drunk seven nights a week.

Travelling was a backpack full of endless justifications. I could always find a reason to drink. I was celebrating, rejoicing in being free from panic. That fact alone was enough for me to be consistently reaching out for a bottle opener. I would drink for no reason or any reason. I had an endless list of excuses – another beautiful sunset to watch, a birthday, a sacking, a pay cheque, a dumping, a rekindling, a missed flight, a new arrival, a long day, a bad day, a good day or a boring day.

Just like that rebellious kid with the key to the drinks cabinet, I had the answer.

The remedy for the world's wins and losses.

Alcohol.

Always alcohol.

Operation Wombfill

I was totally obsessed with doing pregnancy tests. If I had a funny twinge, stubbed my toe, sneezed, or felt a tiny bit nauseated, I was in a bog, peeing on a stick.

It was a secret new addiction.

I told John I was ducking out to get groceries, and sneaked to the chemist to grab a fistful of different tests. Electronic ones that indicated weeks you were pregnant, ones that tested fertility, and cheap ones that I hoped were wrong. I went to great lengths to hide empty packets in bathroom drawers or in the bottom of my underwear box. I constantly added notes to the calendar in my phone, planning the best times to have sex on ovulation days. I had little code letters in the corners of the date boxes. O – ovulating, S – Sex, D – due on. It was an undercover mission executed with military precision. My enemy was my period and my target was those two blue lines: 'Operation Wombfill is go.' I even started wearing camouflage, but no one noticed because, apparently, the army look was 'super hot right now'.

I spent afternoons hovering over public toilets next to busy carparks and waited in line outside café lavatories, my hand firmly clasping a stick inside my shoulder bag. Poor George, in the pram, must have wondered why Mummy kept disappearing behind graffiti-covered doors and coming out looking sad.

But I kept faith, always optimistic that the last test was wrong, and the next one would change my life and save me from myself.

Two lines, come on.

I craved that perfect window of sobriety again. Nine idyllic months with a perfect reason not to drink. It was the opportunity to climb out of this hole I was digging myself into.

But there were never two lines.

Just one pathetic faint line that took far too long to appear. It was torture.

So I drank to make myself feel better.

'Is there anything that will help?' I asked the doctor. 'I feel like I've tried everything and nothing is working.'

It was true. I'd googled *8 weird ways to get pregnant fast*, and wore socks to bed, ate more pineapple, avoided predatory fish (dead and alive ones), had acupuncture, slept in total darkness, and had even started eating yams in the hope of having twins.

'Have you stopped drinking alcohol?' the doctor asked.

'Yes. Of course I have!' I lied.

I was lying more than I ever had before. I had lied to a friend a few days before when she asked if I was hungover.

'You smell like a brewery.'

'No, just had a couple of beers at quiz night.'

When, in fact, I had four pints of pale ale, four shots of vodka and was smoking cigars in a pub doorway at 2 am. I was hungover as fuck. But I was holding a baby, and wasn't exactly going to tell her that.

I lied to my family too when I said I was okay. I wanted them to believe I was fine, so I put on an act and laughed away my misery.

The truth was that my drinking was seeping into every evening, and if I wasn't doing it, I was planning it. I thought about drinking when I should have been thinking about nappies, and what was for dinner.

I hated it but couldn't seem to stop.

I posted photos on Facebook, me with George, making sandcastles or playing in germ-infested ball pits. I beamed at the camera, I looked happy and proud, but the smile was not genuine. It was a show, to keep everyone around me happy. Stop everyone from worrying.

*

At dinner one night, I did have a moment of honesty.

'I don't think I can have any more children, John. My body isn't working.'

'Don't worry about it. We have George. He's enough.'

He was right. George was enough.

But.

Not enough to stop me drinking.

Nothing was.

The thought of not having another child was too painful. I blamed myself, which changed my drinking habit from normal to necessary.

I no longer drank for fun, or to be the life and soul of the party.

I drank because I needed to.

I drank to dim the panic.

Something else was happening too.

My darling husband's face had lost its softness, its look of forgiveness. The expression that had radiated nothing but love had been replaced with one that told me *I'm worried about you*.

He showed his concern for me in subtle ways. A tight hand squeeze, a warm knee touch, bedroom visits with beakers of orange juice, warm embraces and his rough palm stroking my forehead. One morning, he sat for an hour holding a cool flannel to my flushed cheeks as panic ripped through my body like a wildfire. It must have been awful for him to see me like that and I sensed a sadness as he popped painkillers out of their crackly packaging onto my palm.

'Did I come home with you last night?'

'Yes.'

'Did the babysitter see me?'

'Yes.'

'Are you angry with me?'

'No.'

He hid his disappointment. But I knew it was there.

Because I had noticed this change in him, I was trying to avoid going out. I moved between safe places. I went to the shops, to the chemist, to the post office, I had quiet dinners and movie nights. I wanted to show him I was okay, so his old face would come back.

But it was gone.

When he was at work, it was only me and George. I felt happier with just him because I knew I couldn't let him down. It was us against the world. I cherished long walks on cool days. I buttoned up his little hooded jacket and strapped him into the pram, and strode down the seafront with a cold wind blowing in my hair. Together, we sat on a low wall overlooking Manly and shared a blueberry muffin. I popped morsels into his little mouth and held my hand under his chin to catch all the crumbs. We watched as seagulls floated above our heads and surfers glided to the sand on crystal clear waves.

In those moments, I found peace.

As my child grew, he amazed me; his love and cuddles filled me with hope. I managed to keep my nose just above the waterline, above the panic that was biting at my ankles.

From the outside looking in, you'd think everything was perfect. A mother who had it all: a lovely son and a kind-hearted husband, a nice apartment, and lovely friends. But the loss of myself was weighing me down and the single line on the stick was breaking my heart.

So I drank.

I knew what I was doing. In the end, I didn't feel like I had a choice. I created a blurry world around me in which I was so pickled, so entrenched, that I couldn't see a way out.

A Tsunami

Age 27

I was half-cut, leaning on top of a piano while on holiday in Australia with my family. It was Boxing Day and I'd downed a few flutes of buck's fizz for breakfast. The TV was on in the background, but it was drowned out by my very tuneless version of the Carpenters' 'We've Only Just Begun'. Dad walked over and interrupted my rendition.

'There's been an earthquake. I think it's Thailand, Vicky. Come and look at the news.'

Images of Koh Phi Phi filled the TV screen. I couldn't understand what I was seeing.

'There's been a tsunami, Vic. It looks like where you live.'

Everything slowed down. I sat in the hotel lounge, transfixed. It *was* where I lived, it was where my beach bar was, and where my boyfriend was …

Everybody gathered round. We watched in stillness. The death toll on the side of the screen flicked up from the hundreds to the thousands. People came and went, brought me drinks and food on trays. But it sat untouched next to me on the wooden floor.

It took me a while to comprehend the extent of what had happened. A tsunami. A wave. It seemed unreal. I had no idea what to do. Should I go there? Fly into the disaster zone?

I went upstairs and grabbed my little pocket address book and ran my finger down a list of names. I called some numbers. A flat tone hummed in my ear. No connection. Phone lines were down.

I sat on the floor with the phone off its hook next to me, trying to come to terms with the fact that all my friends, and my boyfriend, were probably dead.

'I have to go there,' I said. 'I have to see if I can find him.'

*

I'd moved to Thailand after getting my work visa in Australia, and had met Jai while walking along the beach late one afternoon. I was studying to be an English teacher in the tourist hub of Patong, and was heading home when a smiling face caught my attention.

'Hello, my teacher,' he said.

'Oh, hello,' I said as I walked past.

The next day, he was there again, smiling.

'Hello.'

'Hello again.'

'Beer for you?'

I sat with him on a concrete block.

We didn't say much. We just sat.

'*Chok dee.*'

'Yes, cheers,' I said back.

I couldn't help but fall in love. He was charming, with his dreads that almost dragged along the ground and a smile so big it nearly split his face in two. The little bag slung over his shoulder carried his only belongings: cigarettes, a tatty wallet containing ID, and an extra pair of board shorts.

'I lub you, Wic,' he said after our first kiss. That was it. I had myself a lovely Thai boyfriend.

*

We moved together to an island near the town of Krabi, where we opened a bar on an abandoned squid boat. It was perfect. I spent my days swinging in a hammock, and my nights surrounded by travellers and alcohol. Having my own bar felt like being Tom Thumb plonked in the drinks cabinet of my youth, only now I could help myself with no fear of getting into trouble. The hostess with the mostest, with a smiling hippy man by my side.

I loved island life. I ate freshly caught crab with the sea-gypsy community, read dog-eared books discarded by long-gone travellers, and snorkelled in the clear blue ocean. I fished for my lunch with a hook, a piece of string and a stick. I felt like Huckleberry Finn.

Each morning, with a stonking hangover, I made my way to a communal concrete slab next to the well, where groups of inquisitive Muslim women gathered. They stood in a huddle, expertly scrubbing their bodies with soap and powdering themselves with talc, while managing to hide their bodies under long, colourful sarongs. Holding my bucket of cold water, I stood there awkwardly, not sure how to wash with a sheet wrapped around my body.

I would do a dodgy knot at the top and bend over to collect some water. Without fail, my sarong hit the floor each time I reached up and poured the freezing water over my head. The women giggled with delight, and never got bored with seeing my pasty white body, and the silly face I pulled as I bent and picked up the sarong.

They let out a communal groan when an older lady came over and taught me a special way of tying it on … but, on occasion, I dropped the sarong on purpose, to give the women a laugh. Naked little kids, in hysterics, pointed at my white bottom, so I sidled away like a crab, clutching my shampoo bottle, laughing, with my sodden flip-flops slapping against the concrete.

There were funny people coming and going, and I had a stoned, smiling boyfriend. I could have stayed there forever, but Mother Nature had now got in the way.

*

According to the news, flights had started taking aid to the worst-hit areas. I made the decision to go back to Thailand and try to find Jai. I was scared, but knew I had to go.

I waited until the aftershocks had passed, and called the airline. I explained my situation and they reserved me a seat on the next flight. I think the lady on the other end of the phone could hear the worry in my voice: 'I need to get there. My boyfriend is missing.' Most people were flying out of the disaster, rather than into the thick of it. She took my name and never asked for payment.

I hugged my worried family and headed to the airport. I felt numb, but they and I were very British about the whole thing. 'Chin up, old girl,' I repeated to myself. 'Worse things happen at sea.'

Not the best mantra, under the circumstances.

A TSUNAMI

*

The flight that morning was like nothing I had experienced before. There was total silence on board. For the two hours from Singapore to Thailand, a terrible stillness filled the small space. My fellow passengers had traumatised, haunted expressions frozen on their faces. If eyes met, they instantly filled with tears.

We were all on that plane for the same reason: to find out if loved ones were dead or alive.

It was too blunt to fathom. We were too scared to discuss the possibilities of what lay ahead. Most people sat with heads down, clasping the arm rests. Some prayed and some sat staring at the seat in front. As I put my passport in the holder in the back of the seat, I caught the eye of the lady on the other side of the aisle. I felt sadness heaving up from within as we locked eyes. She reached over and took my hand. Our support for each other dangled in the aisle, as we were joined in a mutual fear of the unknown.

I whispered to her, 'It will be okay.'

She nodded. We both knew it wouldn't be.

We squeezed hands tighter, and didn't let go until the flight attendant came down the aisle and broke us apart with the offer of a cold drink.

Just before the plane landed, the lady took my hand again.

'Good luck,' she said.

'Yes, good luck,' I whispered back.

That afternoon was one of the most surreal and saddest experiences of my life. Every single person on that plane knew they were landing in a nightmare. We helped one another get bags from the overhead lockers with polite thanks and tender smiles, a gracious moment of normality before we entered the disaster zone.

I disembarked and walked through the arrival gate.

There were hundreds of people waiting, but there was no noise. No movement. I watched on as people around me tried to make out who was there to meet them.

I stared as people counted heads.

One, two, three ... eyes flitting from face to face.

Who is here and who hasn't made it?

A simple head count determined how this was going to go.

Numbers. Missing people. Disappeared from families. Some of those there had missing children, others had lost spouses or parents, and many stood alone.

One man kneeled on the floor with his son next to him. They shook their heads in despair. I heard the younger man say, 'They're gone.'

I looked away, embarrassed to be part of this intimate moment – the incomprehensible moment he discovered most of his family were dead.

My eyes darted to where some other people convened. They embraced hard. Others shook hands, having been met by strangers with bad news. Sobs and wails echoed throughout the small airport. I watched, sat on my suitcase and waited for a bus, witnessing lives change before me. I saw hope transform into sorrow with a few words.

'She didn't make it.'

'I held on, but I lost him.'

'I can't find her.'

There was so much hopelessness. As the bus pulled up, the lady who'd held my hand appeared, carrying a toddler in her arms, smiling. She squeezed that child with all her strength, and I knew she was one of the lucky ones.

I acknowledged her with a weak thumbs up and flung my bag onto the bus. I watched from my window as families slowly walked towards the exit, towards the worst day of their lives.

I headed into town to join in the search.

*

I got off near the market where cheerful food vendors usually sold meals off the back of ramshackle motorbikes. But instead, lining the streets, were hundreds and hundreds of coffins.

Men kneeled, tools in hand, nailing planks together, sawing at big panels of wood. Dust sprayed across the road, the sound of hammering and revs of electric power tools ricocheting off buildings. The streets had become like a workshop. Busy, serious men were getting this essential, yet unfamiliar, job done. A factory line of workers passed the empty coffins down the hill to be stacked. I followed the trail until a wall towered over me. Thousands of finished coffins stood like a huge wooden mountain. The pile was taller than the buildings around me. There were so many, all waiting to be filled.

I was handed a face mask by one of the men. I wasn't sure if it was to stop me inhaling all the fumes from the machinery or because of the dust in the air. I put it in my pocket and walked towards the harbour. As I approached, people gathered and huddled in small groups, I presumed to meet friends on boats returning from the islands.

A ferry chugged along the inlet, and a gust of warm wind blew into my face, carrying with it an intense smell. It took me a moment to comprehend what it was …

Death.

It draped over me in the humid air, like a dense fog. The smell was putrid and made me retch. I turned my face away from the breeze, but it got stronger as the boat got nearer. I now realised what my mask was for and put it on, covering my mouth and nose, but there was no way that thin plastic veil was going to block out the stench that encircled me.

I kept my gaze in the opposite direction of the approaching boat. All I saw were the faces of the waiting people, pale and ghostly. As the boat docked, people turned away, quickly. The deathly odour entwined with the smell of the boat's engine. My interest overtook my fear and I turned back to look. The boat sat heavily in the water, its cargo weighing down the huge vessel. I heard someone shouting in Thai, and ropes were thrown and tied. There was a small commotion as some locals approached the men on board. They had a discussion, then called others over to form a line. With the boiling midday sun bearing down on my face, I watched them unload.

At first, I thought it was rubbish bags, tonnes of waste brought in by the wave, but it was piles of dead people, all lumped on top of one another. One by one, the bodies were passed from the boat to waiting open-backed trucks. The men held one arm and one leg each, lifting the corpses through the mob of onlookers. They did so with respect and care.

People clambered to get a glimpse – tourists, locals alike, to see if it was their husband, child or friend, scanning the bodies for any scar or tattoo, anything they could distinguish to confirm identities, but the bodies were bloated from being in the water. They looked inhuman and unrecognisable. People who were there craving answers, turned their heads, covered their noses and mouths with handkerchiefs, and looked distraught, as they held on to supportive partners.

What amazed me was the complete silence. It was the only way we could mutually pay our respects to these lost lives; we all connected without speaking. Eyes were screaming, *Please don't let it be my child*. Words were left unsaid.

I saw relief at times, as officials handed people photographs of survivors awaiting reunions in hospitals but, further up the line as the bodies passed, I knew when someone recognised the little pink shorts or the colour of a shirt as belonging to one of their own. There were quiet sobs and low mumbles.

'No, no, please no,' people said as they walked alongside the bodies, accompanying them to a place of rest.

There must have been a thousand people waiting for the boat. What I knew as a hectic market square teeming with activity had become a makeshift morgue. A never-ending number of dead bodies, big, small, Thai and European, were carried from water to land.

Hands rested on shoulders, and tears wiped from cheeks by strangers. I heard the chants of monks in the nearby temple. It was terrible and peaceful all at once. For an hour, I watched this awful scene unfold. I was numb, I couldn't contemplate that what I saw was real. I walked away when the second and third boat pulled up at the port.

I drifted back up the hill into town and continued the search for my friends. Most of them turned up at local haunts over the following days, with stories of how they had survived. Some friends had held on to trees as water flooded over them. My friend Emma held on with one arm around a palm tree and another gripping her fake Louis Vuitton suitcase. It was all she could think of doing as the wave crashed onto the sand. My friend Thierry managed to scramble up a tree and watch in disbelief as the resort he'd finished building the week before was decimated below him.

Not every story I heard was one of survival. There were endless tales of loss, waiting and not knowing, hoping and then not finding.

I didn't know what to do. Communication lines were all down, boats were busy helping with the clean-up, nothing was running as normal, but I had to get to my little island. I persuaded a fisherman to take me. Thais are superstitious, scared of the spirits of the dead coming to haunt them, so many stayed in the mountains for weeks afterwards, too frightened to travel on the unpredictable ocean where so many lives had ended. I was lucky to find a brave local willing to help me.

Just before I jumped aboard, someone shouted my name. I saw a friend, who said my boyfriend had been spotted. A military boat did an inspection of the island and had seen him walking around.

He was alive.

Feeling utter relief and perched on the front of a long-tail boat, I headed over to the island. As we approached, the engine cut, and as the boat noiselessly glided towards land, I saw the space where our bar once stood.

The FUBAR (Fucked Up Beyond All Recognition) had lived up to its name. There was nothing left. It was as if every page from a copy of *War and Peace* had been torn into a million tiny pieces, then thrown up in the air to spread over a vast area of land. I hopped onto the sand and straightaway spotted my Marks & Spencer bra hanging from a tree. As I plucked it from the branches, there was a tap on my shoulder.

'Hello, Wic.'

It was Jai.

'I'm so glad you're okay. I was worried I'd lost you.'

'Don't worry, Wic. I find big bag marijuana in wave. I stay in the mountains, smoke for one week. No problem.'

I laughed. His big smile and ridiculous story cheered me up. We walked along the beach, holding hands. He told me he'd run inland with the wave at his ankles, after waking the people sleeping in bungalows, shouting, 'Water coming, run!' Some managed to scramble onto the backs of trucks, others legged it as the wave destroyed everything behind them. I felt lucky to have him, especially after seeing so much suffering back at the port. We wandered around in the clutter and debris, picking at things that were left over from our lives before the wave. I found some water-stained photos, broken CDs, and books with water-soaked pages bulging from their covers. A few bottles of spirits, comfortably planted in the sand, were salvageable.

I plucked a bottle of vodka from the ground, cracked the seal, turned the twist-off cap. Sitting on a washed-up log among the rubble, Jai and I took turns swigging the strong liquor until it was finished. The alcohol eased some of the weight off my heart. We stared at the horizon as the sun disappeared over a calm Andaman Sea. As we sat, hundreds of single flip-flops washed up at our feet.

A Life Vest

In a pub toilet, a damp pregnancy test was balanced on my knee. As I waited, I read a wonky flyer, Blu-Tacked to the door, about a ska band playing at the venue in a week's time. People chatted in the bar area, and the Beatles' 'Blackbird' played over the speakers. One of my favourite songs.

The alarm on my phone buzzed. Even though I'd expected it, I got a fright. I jumped, knocked the test off my lap, and it landed upside down near the sanitary bin.

I leaned down to pick it up, expecting to turn it over and see one line turning from a very soft blue into a dark navy.

This time it was different.

I looked up at the ceiling, took a deep breath, then looked again.

Two lines emerged.

The colour deepened.

Two solid dark blue bars.

And I exhaled.

Positive.

I'd been drowning in these bloody pregnancy tests for months. Now a life vest was thrown in my direction, and I clung on to it for dear life.

Hope.

I sat back on the toilet and tried to take in the moment.

All the chaos would be over.

The anxiety monster would piss off back to its cave, and I would be free.

Another baby.

Another chance for me to be the mum I always planned to be. Sure, I was going to bloat up like a dead whale, suffer heartburn, claw hands, piles, and all the other side effects of growing a human being inside my body for nine months, but anything was better than this pesky drinking problem I'd developed. Even cracked nipples and incontinence.

As I sat in the little cubicle, a heaviness lifted from my chest.

I listened as Paul McCartney's soft voice filled my ears. As the song played out, I did something I hadn't done for a while …

I smiled.

International Sex Machine
Age 28

Since the tsunami, Thailand hadn't felt like the right place for me. Jai had no work and our relationship got lost in translation. The language barrier meant I had run out of things to say, and the odd 'I love you' wasn't enough anymore. I craved something else, somewhere else. So I packed my bag.

'Good luck, Wic,' Jai said as he gave me a Thai-style sniff kiss on my cheek.

'Thanks, Jai. *Pok gan mai.*' It means 'see you soon', but I knew I wouldn't see him again.

*

I moved home. Back to England. It was all right for a short while, the familiarity comforted me, but that wore off, and I was itchy. I did try to do normal: get a job and integrate back into society. But Reading town centre on an overcast day was depressing. Trudging around recruitment agencies, handing in a crap CV to sneery women in stylish suits, was enough to make me want to run for the hills. Instead, I called my local doctor and topped up on malaria tablets.

After the adventure and self-imposed chaos of travelling, England felt grey and disenchanting. Being there meant confronting the fact I had no qualifications and no work experience in anything much whatsoever. All I could offer was the two best knots to use when hanging a hammock, how to wear a sarong in seven different styles, and how to say, 'One beer, please' in 15 languages.

My plan, within three weeks of being home, was to leave ASAP. Get the hell out before I started watching *Coronation Street* or moaned about the weather. England just didn't suit me. I was all love, peace and flip-flops, not rain, cuppas and chip shops. Home reminded me of feeling panic, and bad times at school. I never wanted to go back to either of those horrid places. Travelling liberated me. I loved slugging a bag over my shoulder and picking a random destination on a map. Heading to unknown destinations gave me a thrill. I wanted to live life differently, I wasn't ready to conform.

I think my family thought I was fleeing responsibility and shirking my chance at being a functional citizen by 'going off like that', but I was living life on my own terms – an endless adventure, free from expectation and anxiety.

I wasn't running, I was seeking. Finding my feet. (And maybe the tip of my finger.) When I first left England, I knew I would never live there again, and for the next ten years, I travelled.

Just me and my backpack.

*

Throughout my extensive travels, when I didn't have my head stuck in a good book, I was drinking. It was how I connected with others and how I chose to wind down each night.

I always started my nights alone, but people like me have a need for companionship, for people to laugh with, so as soon as a fellow nomad took my fancy, I necked my beer, went over and introduced myself.

'Hi, I'm Vic. Do you come here often?'

'No.'

'Do you have a job?'

'No.'

'Do you own a pair of shoes?'

'No.'

'Do you have half a brain?'

'No.'

'Okay, you've passed the test. Fancy being my boyfriend?'

If they had tattoos, nice eyes and a cheeky smile, I was satisfied. I developed a bad habit of picking up strays at nearly every port in the Southern Hemisphere. These lost souls were excellent company, though. We had lots in common, and rooms were cheaper if I shared a bed.

Since witnessing the devastation of the tsunami, I'd begun not to care very much about my safety. The realisation life was fragile, and could be snatched away at any moment, meant my behaviour became more reckless than ever before.

'You only live once,' I'd say to myself while being led down a pitch-black path to a stranger's beach bungalow. I didn't stop to question putting myself at risk. The amount of booze in my bloodstream soaked up any idea of self-care. Too drunk to care, too wasted to reflect.

My affairs were short (and tall, handsome and peculiar). I had one-night stands in hot, steamy cities, and two-week holiday romances. Sometimes, I travelled with a man for a few months ... until the jokes wore thin, or he got clingy, then I traded him in for a newer model. One who didn't snore or steal my shampoo.

I fell in love – not with one man but with being liked. My low self-esteem got a hit of adrenaline when I 'pulled' a mysterious, handsome stranger. Each empty bottle on the table represented my confidence increasing and the chance of going home alone ... decreasing. The more I drank, the less I cared about what lay ahead. Numbing out because I was bored, lonely and perhaps a little traumatised.

Every night of my travels was a quest, with me not knowing who I'd meet or sleep with. It excited me. Sex wasn't my goal, but someone being interested in me was. Chasing an attractive man, then him admitting, after five beers, two drags on a spliff and three vodka shots, that he liked me boosted my ego. So I was more than happy to have sex, it was the least I could do. Sex with strangers gave me a feeling of having done a good deed, like when I had an hour left on a parking ticket and gave it to a stressed stranger, tipping their handbag upside down for loose change. I unwittingly exchanged these moments of internal euphoria for sex. I should have given the men a box of chocolates or a firm handshake but instead I gave them ... me.

This promiscuous lifestyle was fun (I believed) and hardly ever pulled on my heartstrings. I thought of myself as a good-time girl, sexually free and in charge of my body. An empowered female using men to satisfy my needs ... when, really, I was a vulnerable female being used to satisfy the needs of others.

This destructive behaviour led to bizarre encounters and low self-worth.

Some of my lovers were funny, some were gorgeous, some had issues, and most were losers, but I simply did not care. The affairs gave me a story and a companion for a night (and, one time, a bout of chlamydia). So, no matter how dodgy or lovely they were, they became simply a part of my chaotic world tour.

There was the guitarist with a soft-rock mullet and a death-metal anger issue. A flat-capped Canadian with a quick wit and cheerful grin, who I wanted to marry. There was the camp French guy, who licked my face and told me I was 'exquisite'. Another one was a very sweet Japanese boy, who taught me to say shit in Japanese (*kooso*). Then there was the total moron from London who said to me, 'Your gut's getting smaller, but I didn't want to mention it, in case you started putting weight on.'

I had a night of heavy petting with a Romanian man whose teeth looked like a row of abandoned Clacton-on-Sea beach huts. 'I love you ... er ... Christina?' he said, looking adoringly into my eyes. I held hands with a beautiful pointy-bearded Swedish folk singer. I danced and smoked fat cigars with handsome Cuban boys, and slept in the bed of a fellow traveller's father, who reminded me of a young Robert Redford in *Barefoot in the Park*.

As a female travelling solo, I could *be* or *do* anything. I didn't have anyone to answer to. It was carte blanche to do whatever I liked, including my carnal escapades, humping my way across the globe. I was way too pissed to pause and consider if it was immoral or if a naughty downstairs disco would infect me with a nasty STD.

I regret being annihilated during so many of my sexual encounters, as I had little or no knowledge of what I did, where, when or with whom. There were a few encounters during which I wish I *had* blacked out, though. Like the man in a backpackers dorm room in Barcelona, sprawled on top of me, arms flanked by his sides, flapping like a dying goldfish who'd leaped out of a tank. Torso to torso, we battled like a couple of sausages fighting for space in a frying pan. He grunted, then slumped and said, 'Thanks for that,' as I scooted down the ladder of his top bunk. I wished I could have been the goldfish and forgotten the rendezvous as quickly as it had lasted.

Then there was the hippie in Vietnam who'd held on to his pink sausage when he ejaculated, and caught the sperm in this self-made compartment on the top of his dick (add vomit emoji here). There was the ski instructor in France who'd dropped his pants to reveal the biggest trouser snake I had ever seen. It looked like an anaconda swinging between his knees. I was impressed, but darted in the opposite direction, scared it might curl around my ankle, drag me backwards and eat me. Fleeing to my accommodation, I got lost in a snow blizzard, and cried out to my friends, as I burst through the door with icicles hanging off my nose, 'I've just seen the biggest willy in the world,' before passing out.

There was the wide-eyed, speed-dealing Londoner on Koh Samui – a proper geezer who reminded me of home. I beat him at pool, and he drove me to his bungalow, where we made nice love. Then he snorted white powder, and cried for six hours straight about having left his wife and kids back home. He punched walls and I had to comfort him until dawn.

Last, but not least, there was my favourite compliment of all time, from a gorgeous Dutch man: 'You're the first girl I've slept with who has an arse that's hairier than mine.'

Not much more to say about that one.

I also fell for a handsome surfer who, unbeknown to me, was sleeping with the whole of Indonesia. I had a disastrous few months with him, wondering why all the Balinese beauties in the quaint fishing village where he lived gave me odd looks. Children often ran over to us shouting, *'Pak Pak'*, which I thought was 'hello.' I did a runner the day I found out it meant 'Daddy'.

One of my long relationships was with a fantastic boy from Birmingham, who called me his 'Babby'. Together, we ran a café in Cambodia, where ex-Khmer Rouge demanded beer and never paid. Despite me having been sure I'd never live in England again, for a while we rented a flat near Wimbledon from a creepy landlord. We split up after I found another girl's face cream bottle in my bathroom. I was gutted that our romance ended, and even sadder when the landlord tried to keep our deposit of a thousand pounds. I got angry and sent the mean old bastard a text: *A body has washed up near the Thames in London with no brain and a very small penis. Text me back and let me know you're okay!*

I did fall head over heels with Jai, and also with a sweet Belgian, but I wasn't after long term. I broke the news in hostel cafés over banana pancakes, made sad calls from 7-Eleven phone boxes, or sent awkward emails that ended with 'I hope we can stay friends'.

Men came and went, quite literally. Most of the sex was messy, pissed-up and pointless, with no emotion involved. Just sloppy snogs and awkward fumbling with condom wrappers.

The few I liked I would tell my parents about in soppy postcards. *I've met someone*, I'd confess, with conviction.

Two weeks later, I'd admit it hadn't worked out: *Sorry, didn't mean to get your hopes up, Love you.*

P.S. You wouldn't have liked him anyway. Can you lend me fifty quid?

Mum and Dad were very welcoming to every barefooted hippie I brought home. They knew I was sieving out the lumps before I reached the finer stuff and weren't judgemental. The first two questions were always the same – 'Does he drink?' And 'Does he like fancy dress?'

Their garage was not just crammed with booze, it also housed boxes filled with silly hats, sparkly shoes, glasses with plastic noses attached and hundreds of crazy outfits. Dressing up in outrageous clothes *and* boozing were family traditions. All visitors were forced into participating in both. My dad often appeared for a garden party dressed in a curly wig, sequin bra and thigh high boots. Also, my array of boyfriends were good gossip fodder for my mum and her mates. They loved discussing each strange character who appeared at the airport with me, or trundled up the garden path with her ethnically robed, scraggy-haired daughter. After a few beers, a rummage in the fancy dress boxes, each fling (now wearing a fake moustache and a pair of comedy clown shoes) was welcomed into our family.

'He's nice,' Mum would say, with a nudge under the dinner table. 'We like him. Why hasn't he got a job? When are you going to settle down? Do you want to have children one day?'

'No, he hasn't got a job. He's a traveller like me. I don't want to settle down. I like my life, and I'm going to have children in a commune in India after I've visited every single country in the world,' I smirked. I was joking, but imagined myself getting up from the dinner table and sprinting to a travel agent to book my next ticket out of Dull Town.

I always made light of my love life, but no one saw me the morning after, once whatever man it was had scribbled a fake phone number on a beer mat. I never admitted to anyone that, as time went on, some of these encounters made me feel empty and uncomfortable, that I did things I shouldn't have done or that I was often scared. I would lay in bed afterwards, staring at the ceiling, holding a crumpled sheet to my chin, feeling regretful.

Is this all I'm worth?

I should have shown more restraint and weeded out the grubs. Drunk, my judgement was topsy-turvy. Alcohol affected my life the following day in more ways than a sore head, unexpected rashes, moments of cringing. Little mishaps snowballed into lasting failures, a long-term impact on my very short-term lifestyle. This solo sexual revolution perpetuated bad behaviour and I never caught on, never considered that what I was doing was causing me to need to numb out more and more.

I never stopped to think about my faults.

But then I had someone who pointed them out for me.

A Blue-Eyed Baby Girl

My pregnancy was a much-needed holiday from the mayhem I'd created. A break in the rain. The drinking stopped the moment I knew I was pregnant, and I had a beautiful window of sobriety where I was able to socialise without the risk of anxiety or shame. I loved it. Not having to consider being hungover was totally liberating and I promised myself that I'd halt my downward spiral. And, of course, my pregnancy meant the monster had vanished.

'This is it,' I said to John. 'I know drinking has been making me mentally unwell. I'm going to cut down.'

During my pregnancy, we both quit our jobs. I'd been selling jewellery at the markets, which made my feet sore, and John was done with city life – we wanted a change. We packed the car, and moved from Sydney to Queensland's Sunshine Coast, where we bought a house near the beach. A new life with new friends was what I needed. They didn't need to know about my party-girl reputation. Nobody needed to know. I could start anew, with no judgement. I'd had to weather the storm to really feel the sunshine. I was determined to be the mum I'd promised myself I would be, but I guess things don't always go to plan.

*

I had a baby girl. Nell. She was tiny with sky-blue eyes (not weird big ones, she did not resemble any rugby players). I called her TBH, for Tennis Ball Head, as her hair was all fluffy and yellow.

As Nell was so small, we had to feed her with a tube. I again stayed up all night to squeeze minute amounts of milk from grazed, cracked nipples. My days were long and hard, with a three-year-old and the demands of a baby. Some days, John came home to find me asleep on the sofa, a baby feeding on one boob, with my boy snoozing under my arm, all of us exhausted. He stepped up when I needed him to, but he worked full time.

Being new to the area meant I couldn't really call on anyone for support and, before I knew it, my old habit started to creep up on me. The pressure and tiredness that came with becoming a mum again made me hanker for relief.

'Fancy a night out?' asked one of the playgroup mums, as she squeezed a yogurt into a toddler's mouth.

One question was the only elbow twisting I needed.

'Yes, I'd love that.'

My girl was six weeks old.

I felt excited getting ready. I would be having a break from it all. A moment of me. I decided to drink no more than three glasses of wine. I couldn't risk the anxiety monster returning.

Just a few quiet drinks … then home.

At the local bar, the third drink was down the hatch within an hour of arriving. I swayed and danced around the room, with my mummy tummy flopping over the top of my trousers.

I deserve this. I deserve to drink, said my alcohol-sodden brain.

I chatted and downed beers. I tripped over and smoked cigarettes.

I told a man with a ZZ Top beard that I had a newborn baby. He looked at me with concern and said, 'What are you doing here then?'

I looked at my watch. It was past midnight.

I zigzagged home.

The next day, I sat in my big wooden rocking chair, holding Nell in my arms.

Fear. Self-hatred. Guilt.

The monster. Back again. Never dead. Always present. Waiting for me to fuck up.

I can't do this.

This has to stop!

I looked down at my baby, and then looked up to the ceiling and exhaled.

I knew then.

I just knew.

It was one hangover too far.

Something in my head flipped. Every drink I ever drank had led to this moment, this realisation.

I was failing as a parent, breaking my promises again.

Why can't I stop doing this to myself?

I knew if I kept on drinking, I would not survive. I'd either do something stupid to myself, lose everything or develop a more serious alcohol habit.

I picked up my baby girl and walked into the lounge room. John was watching the news. I put the baby in the crib, kissed George as he played with his train set on the floor, and switched off the TV. Then I burst into tears.

'I can't do this anymore,' I sobbed. 'I promised myself I wouldn't drink much and here I am with a hangover.'

'Yes, you were pretty hammered last night,' John said.

'I thought I'd slow down after the baby, but last night I couldn't stop. Why do I continue doing this to myself, to us?' He pulled me close, and I mumbled into his chest, 'What do you think about my drinking habits, really?'

I thought he'd say, *You're brilliant when you're drunk. Everyone loves you and you're an amazing dancer. Have a Pringle?*

But he didn't say that at all.

He said, 'You drink too much, too quickly, and I'm scared for you. I watch you when we're out, and you're not having a good time because you're so concerned about where your next drink is coming from. You gulp back wines fast and I feel like you're constantly holding your glass out for a refill. You don't do anything bad, you just go glazed and a bit wobbly.' He looked down at the floor as he kept opening up to me.

'It's not so much the pissed bit I'm worried about, it's the next day. You're unreachable when you're hungover, and no matter how hard I try to be positive, to talk you down from the anxiety, you can't hear me. I can see in your eyes that you feel mentally unwell. I don't like seeing you like that – I lose you. I definitely agree it's getting worse every time you drink.' He raised his head and his eyes locked on to mine.

'I just want you to be happy, be the Vicky I know. Not this scared girl hiding in our bedroom, thinking she's going to die of panic. Alcohol suppresses all the things I love about you. It sucks the joy and beauty from you. I'm scared.'

I was astounded.

'Oh God, I'm so sorry,' I said, twiddling my thumbs in my lap. 'I'm scared too. Scared for my health. Scared for my children. I don't want to be a chaotic mother, gagging for a wine on a Tuesday night. I'm scared of losing you and, to be honest, I'm scared of losing my sanity. I can feel it. I think I need help?'

John said he'd support me in whatever I decided to do. He hadn't judged me or told me off. He just loved me. I sobbed into his armpit, knowing everything was about to change.

This turning point had been a long time coming. Every pint I had ever downed and every bar I had ever been thrown out of had led me to my first step towards change.

I'd never considered giving up booze completely. It was always a matter of slowing down, or drinking in moderation. But it was obvious that the disco dirt was starting to stain. I wasn't getting away with it anymore. My playful social drinking had got serious and was turning me into a very rubbish parent. The guilt tipped me over the edge. The scream inside was too loud to ignore.

I had to get professional help.

Poor Drunken Choices
Age 30

What happened wasn't really my fault. By the time it transpired, I was in too deep to leave. (A bit like with booze.) Early on in our relationship, I did have an inkling he was bad. I should have listened to my gut. I knew things would end this way. My poor drunken choices meant I couldn't stop it.

*

After Jai and the international trail of broken hearts, I met a Brazilian guy in a beach bar on Koh Samui in Southern Thailand. The sun was setting. Deep rootsy reggae throbbed from speakers on wobbly shelves above rows of upside-down spirits. The bottles vibrated with the bassline. He came over and asked me for a light. As he leaned into the flame, his hand reached up and pushed back thick curls that had spiralled down over his forehead. He sucked in and the cigarette blazed. 'I'm Lucas,' he said as he looked up. When his gaze met mine, I nearly melted into the ground. His eyes were dark like coffee and flecked with copper like lightning in a black sky. I handed my heart over to him right then.

He was wearing a loose-fitting Hawaiian shirt and faded board shorts that sat low on his hips, a line of hair creeping down to his groin. He smelled of the ocean mixed with coconut sunscreen. He perched on a stool next to me, and we spent the evening chinking beers and sharing stories of our travels. He was charming, eccentric and smart. He made me laugh and, with every casual glance, he took another piece of me.

*

Lucas and I happened quickly. We kissed that night and lived in each other's pockets from then on. We travelled together, island hopping and trekking. He came home with me and met my parents. We planned together, hoped together. I was excited, optimistic that I had a rosy future with someone.

Some days, though, he awoke with a dark cloud hovering over him. He was angry, agitated for no reason, and at those times I lost sight of our potential. There was something so distant about him and the closer I got, the further away he became. He said he loved me, sometimes. His evasive manner made me frantic for approval. The storm in his eyes now scared me. There was a hurricane around every corner, a foreboding, and I was nervous about what would happen next.

*

Our car sped through the countryside. Trees rushed past me in a green smudge. He overtook everyone, swerving across the straight white line, shooting past a tractor piled with sheep. His palm pressed down hard on the horn as he pulled in front of a bus. I said nothing. Instead, I stared out of my window, taking in the Tunisian landscape, feeling the beat of this strange country.

Public transport was shabby: the rusty old buses bulged with people, cages were stuffed with chickens, and luggage spewed from roof racks as these dilapidated tin beasts swayed down the dusty roads, goats wedged in between passengers. Smiling children gave me happy waves from back windows. I waved back. Secretly. Everyone seemed to be in such a hurry here, weighed down with their bags, going somewhere far from home.

Broken-down vehicles lined the roads like bony carcasses, some sat abandoned, tipped at a jaunty angle on the grass verge and left there to die. We passed a bus with steam pouring from its engine. Sweating, heavily clothed women huddled under a tree, fanning themselves with tatty magazines as serious-faced men kneeled next to the flat tyre, while the driver bent over the open bonnet, scratching his head.

Lucas ignored the locals, the landscape and me. He just drove, his eyes firmly on the horizon.

I sat still. Frightened.

Hoping his mood would pass.

Up ahead, a man on a rickety old bike. I knew Lucas was trying to scare me, and it worked. My heart leaped as we missed hitting him by an inch. I looked in my wing mirror as the man wobbled and toppled to the ground. I turned my head around to look out of the rear window to get a clearer view, to check he was okay. I saw a dust cloud from where the wheels of the car had stirred the ground beneath. A beige mist danced behind us. I kept watching as the spirals twisted around like a mini tornado. My eyes stayed focused on the dust as it disappeared into the distance.

I wanted to be back there, where the dust was settling. To watch it fall onto the ground. To feel the silence as it landed. I closed my eyes and imagined being away from here, being within the calm that was left in our wake.

Lucas hadn't flinched. Sweat dripped from his brow. I wound the stiff handle of the window towards me. The glass panel slid into the door, and I placed my bent elbow on the open ledge and let the warm, filthy air flow over my body.

'Shut the window!' he shouted, his voice startling me.

'Sorry, it's just so hot in here.'

As I lowered my hand back onto the handle, I was trembling, and turned it fast in the opposite direction. *I must not upset him.* Trying to talk to him when he was like this was wasted breath.

I turned my attention to the stereo, hoping music might ease the atmosphere. I chose a playlist, 'Driving Songs'. The upbeat intro of 'Sweet Home Alabama' cut through my unease. I closed my eyes, sank into my seat, and pretended to be somewhere else.

In the darkness, I could think what I wanted. There were no apologies there. No placating him. No giving in to him. I was strong in my head, so could say what I liked without fear. I could win.

I remembered another time: when we fell in love. But any affection I had for him was a memory. Time had allowed me to see through his thick layer of bullshit and break down his fake persona. I knew there was nothing good left inside of him. He oozed manipulation and spite from every pore in his body. His light was out, and only shade seeped from beneath his smooth, dark skin.

I felt sad because I'd lost myself to him. Lost my cheerfulness, my joy. With tiny sips, he had sucked the life from me, and now, sitting in this boiling car, I felt hatred for him.

I knew it was over. I was waiting for the right time to leave. Thoughts rushed through my mind, like the trees that blurred in my window. Morbid images bounced against the corners of my brain. I envisaged a knife hidden under my seat, my hand plunging it into his stomach as he drove, and feeling happy as he begged for help.

Beads of sweat slid down the side of my face, and I wiped my temple with my t-shirt. I opened my eyes to take in the scenery. I didn't look at him, but I felt his anger surround me.

The song played, then another.

The lushness of the lower lands vanished as we climbed higher. The terrain turned desolate, and the sun was low in the sky and shone directly into the windscreen. The glare flashed in and out as the car swept around the steep curves.

We ascended high up into the mountains. The trip was supposed to be an adventure but, as always, things annoyed him. Minor irritations become big dramas and I was left trying to soothe him, trying not to awaken his anger.

*

That morning, before the long drive north towards the snow-covered peaks of Tunisia, we'd taken the wrong path on our trek. It meant we missed one of the more beautiful views in the region. I wasn't bothered because I'd enjoyed the route we'd gone. I didn't think anything of it. But he was unhappy. A pointless misunderstanding about directions caused the journey to become tense. My fault, I suppose.

I felt the rage in his driving, as it got more chaotic and more reckless by the minute. His foot got weighty on the accelerator; dust covered the bonnet, changing our red minivan to a dusky burnt orange. I swayed from side to side as we screeched around bends, getting too close to the cliffs. I was afraid the car would tumble off the road and hurtle down the mountainside, but there was nothing I could do but sit. My hands gripped each side of my seat.

I took a chance and flicked my eyes to look at Lucas. His body was hunched over, his chest almost touching the steering wheel. His knuckles were pale, and his pupils were as black as those of a great white shark. The muscles in his cheek contracted as his jaw clenched. I focused on him, wondering what he was thinking.

Then there was a jolt as the front wheel hit a rock. The car veered towards the drop.

He braked. I lurched forward, saving myself with my outstretched arms. I pushed back on the dashboard and the car came to a sudden halt. I took a deep breath.

Before I had time to consider the consequences, I said, 'Can you slow down? You're going to get us killed! Please, I'm scared.'

He unsettled me by turning the key, cutting the engine, and looking right at me.

'Are you okay?' I asked, eager for a gentle *I'm fine*.

'I wanted to do the other route,' he snapped.

'Oh, okay. Sorry. We can turn around and go back there, if you like. Do it again in the morning?'

'It's too late now! It's too fucking late!' he shouted.

'I don't mind going back. If you feel like we've missed out, we should go back,' I said.

'We can't go back. You've ruined this trip, you stupid bitch.'

Fear filled my body. I looked down at the hands clasped in my lap.

'I'm sorry,' I said in a weak voice.

'You're always fucking sorry.'

Being in the car, in that exact moment, felt lonely. I was thousands of miles from home, by the side of a road with a man I knew was about to hurt me.

His hand rose above his head and I saw madness in his eyes.

Then his fist slammed down. I felt the blow land on my cheek and heart.

I covered my face with my forearms. I pushed him back, but he was too strong.

He came at me, harder.

Curled downwards into a ball, my forehead touching my knees, I protected myself as best I could as he pounded my body. The thumps sounded dense, like when a book falls from a desk onto carpet. I felt no pain. Just numbness.

I left myself then and flew away into the mountains that surrounded us.

Giving into it. Accepting it. I let him finish.

I was angry at myself more than with him.

How had I got here?

But then it stopped. There was silence until I heard a door click open.

I waited and stayed still in the car for ages.

Then I looked up.

He was kicking the ground near the car, walking in circles, cursing.

I should have slammed the door, jumped into the driver's seat, and left him there. I didn't. I wasn't strong enough. He'd broken me. There was nothing left. I was incapable of leaving him. That's what he did. Made me feel worthless. It gave him power.

I flipped down the sun visor and looked in the little mirror. My face was swollen. I couldn't see out of one eye. I touched my cheek. It stung. I cried for a while.

The door clicked again.

The keys jingled and the engine started. I felt the car move.

We carried on as if nothing had changed, knowing that everything had changed.

I didn't look at him. I hid my face and looked forward to showing him the damage later. Somewhere safe.

I knew my beaten-up body was the door to freedom, but I bided my time.

I wound down my window and felt a sudden cool wind wash over me. Rain started pouring from the black sky and droplets of water disguised my tears.

And I watched … as the storm rolled in.

A Bit of Leprechaun Magic

Getting help meant I might never be able to drink again. How very fucking depressing. I envisaged being in a hospital bed with a monitor next to me, the arrow on the dial flicking from 'Fun' to 'Dead'. For me, there was no intermediate place. No place in between blotto and boring. I could almost hear the long, dull *beep* of the machine as I flatlined. I imagined nurses rushing to my bedside, saying, 'She's gone. Unable to face a world without bad robot dancing, vomit and karaoke, poor thing.'

I couldn't see a future for me beyond the bottle. I thought I might just as well bonk myself over the head with Captain Caveman's club and fall into an early grave. Life seemed pointless to me without the effervescence of a cheap champagne or the joyous twist of a beer-bottle top. No matter how much I was hating drinking, hating myself, I still couldn't imagine what it would be like to stop.

Could I really give this up? Forever?

*

I thought about my eldest sister, Louise. She'd been sober for 15 years, having been a socially acceptable binge drinker like me. I'd never thought of her as an alcoholic and, I hate to say, had never taken her sobriety seriously. I thought she was overreacting, being a bit of a party pooper, or just doing it to be different. I never stopped to consider her reasons why. All I thought was, *That's bloody boring!* Who the hell is going to dance on tabletops and sing the Na-na-na-na-na-na-na, na-na-na, na-na-na from 'Freed from Desire' with me now?

I couldn't imagine our relationship would thrive. Having long, meaningful chats over cups of Earl Grey was about as appealing as inhaling a stranger's fart.

A decade and a half later, she was still going strong. I witnessed her iron will at many family gatherings. She danced and laughed along with the rest of us, without seeming to have a twinge of jealousy or doubt. At the end of a night out on the town, as I was dumped in a taxi home, she ambled up the street with a big smile on her face and a glittery shawl wrapped around her shoulders.

How does she do it? I thought.

Maybe being sober is better than being drunk?

It was definitely better than being put in a taxi with a plastic Coles bag to puke in.

I had come to quietly admire my sister and recognise her power. Her abstinence gave her a kind of supremacy, an understated superiority. She was still doing what we were all doing, partying, but she did it without a sip of booze. Being able to socialise and not get a hangover afterwards looked utterly magical.

I need a bit of that leprechaun magic, I thought.

I wanted to look forward to events like my inspirational sister did. I wanted to tip my hat at passers-by on a Sunday and say, 'Top of the morning to ya!' Rather than pull a hood over my eyes to avoid comments from smug wankers. 'Oh, you looked like you were having a good time last night. I've just been for a run!' (Which translates as 'Oh, you were a mess last night and I'm better than you.')

I thought about giving Louise a call, but I was nervous. Telling her felt overwhelming, and then what if I failed? What if I didn't do as well as her?

*

I went into the kitchen, where John was scrambling eggs, and said, 'Don't tell anyone about this. It's something I need to do on my own.'

If no one knew, then I couldn't disappoint anyone. The pressure was off. I could tell friends and family once I'd done the work. Once I was better. I mean, no one knew I was struggling, so telling them might attract judgement and I didn't fancy a serving of that. Instead of calling my sister, I got a pen and a paper napkin and wrote:

What I Want and What I Don't Want.
1. I want to be able to drink alcohol well.
2. I don't want anxiety when hungover.

That was it. To be able to drink like a normal person, to be able to moderate it. I wanted to learn better ways of drinking. Be one of those smarmy angels who just has a couple.

To consider being a total non-drinker seemed way too far-fetched.

Maybe I could just drink at Christmas? Yes, a festive drinker in a Santa hat and a gaudy jumper. I could just drink when it was rude not to.

So, maybe birthdays too? Oh, and weddings, and funerals; you have to drink at funerals. And what about festivals? I couldn't sip fizzy water at a music festival. Sacrilege. I'd be punching a bug-eyed jester-hat-wearing reveller before anyone had peaked on their molly. I simply would not cope being at a festival sober. What if I got invited to a lock-in? That counted as a special occasion, didn't it?

Out of the corner of my eye, I saw my baby girl wiggle in her crib. She rolled onto her side and poked her head through the railing. She gave me a big, toothless smile. Gosh, I loved her so much. I picked her up and gave her a squeeze. Whatever lay ahead, my children were going to be my why.

The Shits and India

Age 31

Lucas begged me to meet him in India. I wasn't sure. I hated him. I hated me. I hated him for hurting me and for staying with me, but I hated myself for staying. I was so downtrodden, so manipulated, that it felt like I had no choice. So I went. I gave him another chance. I wanted him to learn from his mistake, to get better. I wanted to witness him change. My pain could be the reason he became a better person.

Maybe he does love me after all? I wondered.
Maybe I can save this relationship if I go?
God, I was deluded.

I threw in the (damp travel) towel and went into town to buy a plane ticket.

I was nervous about going, for obvious reasons. I'd heard awful stories about travelling in India. Apparently, the toilets were not quite up to western standards. (There were rumours about the 'pig toilets' that consisted of an outhouse mounted over a pigsty, which apparently proved to be a very efficient method of waste removal.) Also, there was no toilet paper, just the old left hander.

Travel buddies had spun me yarns of swamping themselves (shitting and puking at the same time) after too many oily vegie samosas. Imagine every orifice working in unison, or on the reverse, becoming so constipated the only way to get a stubborn turd out of its hidey hole was to snap it off and try again later, or flag down a passer-by who happened to have a shoehorn. Either way, in India my luxury western lavatory habits were destined to be challenged, and even a spattering of piss on a public toilet at Paddington station had me holding on to walls and hovering above the rim. I was all for confronting encounters on my travels, but could do with missing out on the opportunity for a shit-eating-swine diary entry.

I considered all this in the departure lounge, while stuffing a Pret A Manger sandwich in my face 45 minutes before take-off. I was going to Kolkata from Heathrow Airport. I didn't know what lay ahead for me. I sat on the flight with a knot in my tummy, wondering if I was flying into a disaster zone, just like after the tsunami.

*

I liked India, though. The countryside was gorgeous and lush. The towns, hectic and colourful. Moving my eyes from one side of my peripheral vision to the other revealed a diverse land. My gaze would alight on a beautiful sunset over the Ganges, then take in a decapitated head floating by. India was beautiful and threatening all in one glance.

Lucas was all smiles and no shoes for the first few days. It was strange being in that mystical place with him. I still hated him, but played along, fantasising everything was okay. When he was moody, I left him alone and went on walks in shady parks. I passed the time by writing in my bulging diaries and listened to the array of different bird songs coming from the palm trees that swayed above my head. I zoned out when he wasn't near me and tried to absorb my surroundings, taking in what India had to offer.

We managed to have some good days. I saw wild tigers at Ranthambore National Park. I sat on the same bench as Princess Di at the Taj Mahal. I trekked and picked tea leaves in the Himalayas and shat myself on a boat at sunrise in Varanasi.

But it wasn't long before the name-calling started again.
You're a bitch.
You're a liar.
You're fat.
His digs stung my sensitive heart and made me feel horrible about myself. He said these things so often, I started to believe they were true.
Maybe he's right?
Maybe I am a bad person. Maybe this is my fault?
His cruelty sank into my bones. His anger continued to be quick and sudden, and I could never predict what would set him off. My generally sunny disposition annoyed him. He thought I was too happy, too jovial. Everything I did was tapping at his emotions. It meant I was walking on eggshells all day, every day. Emu-sized ones.

I had never come across someone like him before, and didn't know how to handle him. He was good at goading forgiveness from me. He'd apologise, tell me he loved me, with his brown eyes peeking over a posy of hand-picked flowers. I was stupid, blinded. The more horrible he became, the less I felt I could leave. I was stuck in an abusive relationship – in India – with no one to help me.

He threatened me a few times, and once said he was going to kill me. He threw a handful of sand in my eyes when I beat him at Boggle. He blamed me if he tripped on a kerb. Every day, he became more irrational, and I was afraid.

I wrote a letter to myself in my diary one afternoon after an argument:

Dear Vicky,
You need to get out of this. You need to be strong.
This is not the life you are meant to be living. Leave.
Leave now.

I stared at the words as if they were about someone else's life.

It took far too long, but eventually I ran out of patience and clean underwear. I simply couldn't cope with him anymore. I craved something else: a new life. Going to India had felt like the right thing to do, the last hurrah, but I could hear the need for change whispering to my soul.

*

One morning, after Lucas had been rude to a nice waiter about his coffee not being hot enough, I packed my bags.

'I'm going home.'

He didn't care. Aside from getting angry, he never really seemed to care about anything. He saw caring about others as a weakness. Like it affected his power, broke his strength. I couldn't understand any of this and his lack of emotion made me feel worthless.

'Okay,' he said.

He dropped me off at the airport, then hugged me. 'See you soon. Love you.'

'Love you too,' I lied.

He wandered off into a moving crowd. As he walked away, I watched him until his head was a tiny prick (apt) in the distance. Then he disappeared ... and that was that.

I breathed a sigh of relief.

And I never saw him again.

It took me a while to get over Lucas. I couldn't believe I was a victim of physical abuse. It had sneaked up on me. I had been trapped and felt too low to consider leaving. It took a punch in the face and a disastrous trip to India to realise how toxic the situation was.

A combination of factors had led me to that point. One-night stands and short relationships made me question my ability to have a long-term boyfriend. I'd made a conscious decision to stand by my man, not just run away like I had from others.

That was a huge mistake. I should have left at the first sign of weird. But, as with everything that had ever gone wrong in my life, I drank the bad away. I numbed out his malice. If he was in a huff, I cracked open an extra bottle of wine, to drown out the bullshit. I drank throughout our entire relationship, nearly every single night. It made being with him easier and made me forget how truly unhappy I was. I'd always wake up with a fuzzy head and hope today would be better.

Sitting on the plane home, I felt a sense of freedom. I concluded my approach to relationships had to change. After being a battered girlfriend, I needed normal. I needed to be a square, and do what my parents had wanted, for once. To settle down.

I didn't want alcohol to have a lead role in any future partnerships. No more drunks, druggies or wasters. No more travel bums and unsatisfying shags. It was time to grow up. A simpler life was calling. I needed some kindness and stability, to find someone who truly loved me.

And I needed to start loving myself too.

*

My years of travel had been a wild ride that had taken me to India, Nepal, New Zealand, Cuba, Cambodia, Hull … and so many other weird and wonderful places. I'd trekked in the Himalayas and drank tea in Darjeeling. I'd seen an ancient Sadhu holy man tie his willy in a knot. I went on safari, and washed elephants in the fast-flowing river as rhinos watched on from the bank. I drove around North Africa, buying silk and jewellery to sell at French markets. I'd run bars in palm-lined Thai Islands and sold cold beers to Khmer Rouge in Phnom Penh. I'd eaten scorpions, drunk tea with monks and got dengue fever in a jungle. I even got bitten, on my finger stump, by a sea snake in Fiji. 'We must wait 30 minutes,' said the smiling man at the tiny island clinic. 'Maybe you die, maybe not.' (Note – I did not.) I'd hitched in Havana, salsa danced in moonlit cobbled streets. I slept next to a corpse on a train to Bangladesh. I'd had the Singapore shits, the Bali belly and the Polynesian ring of fire. A finger had been lost, as had a bit of my belief in human kindness. I had an interesting ten years, full of love and laughter, tears and heartbreak.

It was time to meet people who ate pizzas with friends on Friday nights, and set alarm clocks to wake up for work. I wanted a bank account and to talk knowingly about house prices. I wanted to get stuck in traffic, and queue up for stamps at the post office. I wanted to peek inside what made people happy. I needed to judge if it was for me. After all the ups and downs of travelling, I needed constancy and companionship. I'd been adrift too long, floating on an empty ocean on my bright yellow dingy of life, waiting to be hauled towards land, towards the safety of a well-rounded, happy man. Preferably, one who owned a pair of shoes, had no skull tattoos, spoke English, had a job, had a car, owned a house, was funny, put shopping trolleys back, wasn't an alcoholic or a murderer, and had a huge … heart. That wasn't too much to ask, was it? It was time to fire my flare into the sky and hope someone noticed me.

The night before I left India, I sat on the ancient stone stairs at the edge of the Ganges in Varanasi, and I made a wish.

'A kind man, please …

Oh, and some Imodium.'

I don't know who I was asking, but whoever it was, they listened.

Beneath Lies and Lager

I'd been to an Alcoholics Anonymous meeting many years before, when Louise first decided to get sober. My sister's car grumbled to a halt outside a shabby-looking hall in a sleepy hinterland village. The building reminded me of England; it was quaint and whitewashed, with flowers in baskets hanging by either side of the door. I envisaged local residents wandering around with damp umbrellas, eating humungous slices of Victoria sponge, beer being poured from kegs, and wine in feeble plastic cups. I was hoping a rosy-cheeked farmer would poke his head through the door to announce, 'Ian Pritchard is the winner of the "Barrow of Booze" raffle, and don't forget Des down at the Dog and Duck has promised a lock-in.'

But this wasn't a cosy village hall in England. We were in Bangalow, a quiet hinterland town in Northern New South Wales. My sister and I got out of the car and headed towards the light shining from a little doorway. It was dark by then and a summer storm was brewing in the distance.

I had imagined, like all snobs do, that lots of people in shabby clothes smoking rollies would be standing in the doorway, passing cans around. There weren't. Still, I walked through the entranceway expecting to step over a few mangy dogs tied to chairs. There weren't any of those either.

Instead, the small room was full of people who resembled those you would expect to see in a parents committee meeting. Everyone looked clean-cut and ordinary. They were smiling, chatting. One woman reached out and gently tucked a loose piece of hair behind another woman's ear. It was a gesture that showed kindness and care.

I'd had a picture in my head of what an alcoholic would look like. I imagined a downtrodden, sad soul with a deeply lined face, an emaciated body, yellowing skin, missing teeth. I was astonished they all looked so normal. They looked like me.

Maybe these people are here to do a presentation, I thought. *Maybe the real alcoholics are out the back, having a smoko?*

I found a chair and plonked myself down. After five minutes of low murmurs, a little bell rang, and everybody found a place to sit. A lady in a flowing kaftan stood in front and said, 'Hello everyone. Welcome. Is there anyone that has never been here before?'

A few raised their hands. I did not.

She went on, 'Alcoholics Anonymous is a fellowship of men and women who share their experience, strength and hope with each other. We hope that by being open about our individual journeys, we can solve our common problem and also help others to recover from alcoholism.'

She asked if anyone would like to go to the front and introduce themselves. There was an awkward moment when three people stood up at once. After some polite gesturing, a man made his way up there.

I leaned back in my flimsy plastic chair and listened with my arms crossed high on my chest, feeling a little bit defensive. *I hope he doesn't tell me that drinking is bad.*

The man's voice was quiet as he said his name. He stood with his hands on the lectern, staring down at his shoes. At AA, members' stories are kept private, so I won't repeat here what this man, or anyone, said that night, but all the stories were linked. Alcohol was causing these lives to be, well … a bit shitty. The man was brave and open, and I applauded him with vigour as he returned to his seat. I'd never experienced such raw vulnerability, such a willingness to reveal.

For two hours, I sat immersed in these stories. There was a fireman who'd been off the grog for five years. *Clap.* A mumsy lady in a floral dress. *Clap.* A broken young woman with scars on her arms. *Clap.* A teenage girl. *Clap.* A posh boy in a salmon shirt with the collar up. *Clap.* A man who was 50 and looked 90. *Clap.* A businessman, a cleaner, a teacher. On it went – *clap, clap, clap* – one sad, moving story after another.

Little AA chips jangled on keyrings as, one by one, they rose and sat. First with trepidation, then with pride. I nodded and gave the odd thumbs up. I had to get a hanky out at one point, so I could disguise a loud sobbing noise as a sneeze.

Beyond my applause and nods of respect, something was happening within me. My jaw clenched and my toes bent in my shoes. A pang of knowing gripped my gut as I recognised myself in their stories. It could have been me talking. These public confessions were so close to the bone and, shedding a thick, protective layer of lies and lager, I could relate to every single word. An uncomfortable feeling surfaced for me, like when you leave a tight hairband on your wrist all day and only notice as your hand is about to drop off. It wasn't because these people didn't resonate with me. It was because they did.

I swallowed hard and shoved this confronting fact so far down in my soul, there would be no chance I would deal with it for another 15 years. I separated myself from these brave people. *I'm different from them. My drinking is fun. I'm not like these people. I'm a happy drinker. These people have a problem, and I don't.*

I was about 25 at the time of this meeting, still in my honeymoon period, in love with getting bladdered. I didn't want alcohol bad-mouthed. I wasn't ready. No matter how moved I was and how enamoured with each courageous individual … I just wasn't ready to put myself in the same category as them. I nearly heckled from the back row, 'Oi! Don't slag off my best mate!' But I held back, knowing no one shared my opinion.

We had a cup of tea and a biscuit afterwards. I felt honoured to witness fellow humans at their most exposed and could see why AA worked. These people had love, understanding and support all over the country. An incredible network of kindred spirits who knew each other's stories and felt each other's pain. It was inspirational.

When I decided to seek help for my drinking, I went over this AA meeting in my head. Was I brave enough to stand up and tell people about the time I pissed in my friends' hallway or woke up with a pair of men's socks down the front of my knickers? (Don't ask.)

I thought my AA audience members would smile and nudge their neighbour. *What's this twit doing here? She's not an alcoholic, she's just a binge drinker.*

Their stories were raw and extreme, and mine seemed lame. I hadn't lost my kids or my home. I didn't have any liver issues or gout. I was happy, with a loving family. I didn't have any serious trauma. Yes, alcohol was affecting my life in a negative way, but I didn't feel like I was balancing on a skyscraper, with my life about to topple over the edge. I'd look like a privileged middle-class fraud, standing up there talking about how my mothers' group had some 'peerrritty kerrr-azy' nights out and how my hangovers were causing me to be a bit of a crap mum. Basically, I did not think my drinking was severe enough to warrant AA. And I still wasn't sure if I was an alcoholic.

Am I a drinker who doesn't get drunk enough to deserve help?

The other reason I thought I couldn't go to AA was that I am very rubbish at public speaking. I'd have sweat dripping down my forehead, and have to put on an exaggerated cockney accent, like Dick Van Dyke in *Mary Poppins*, to make me seem more down to earth. That's the sort of idiotic thing I did to try to fit in. Act like a tough East End gangster's moll if someone had a less posh accent than I did. *Ridiculous, innit.* I knew I'd also add dad jokes, a bit of comedy to make everyone in the room laugh. It just wouldn't work. My need to be liked would overtake the reason why I was there.

Also, I'm not a religious person; I would rather tell a prawn than a priest what I felt. When anyone referred to God, I had a terrible habit of ceasing all cranial operations. Aside from my flirtation with alternative therapies when trying to deal with the anxiety monster, I was the same with crystals, sound healing, aromatherapy oils, meditation, regression, reiki and star signs. I couldn't retain information on these topics if you paid me, or feign the slightest bit of interest in them.

At the AA meeting I'd gone to with Louise, every person who got up thanked God or acknowledged a higher power, and it annoyed me a bit. Handing myself over to AA's rumoured Godly presence wasn't something I thought I could ever do. It never occurred to me to ask why that was or how using the idea of God could help people in recovery. I just walked out of there with an excuse for why I wasn't going back: *Nah, I don't need to stop drinking. They're just a load of Bible-bashers.*

'I didn't know you were religious,' I said to my sister after the meeting.

'I'm not,' she replied. 'It's not a God as such. AA wants you to understand that your addiction is impossible to confront on your own, and that by trusting in a higher power, be it a man on a cloud or a coat hanger, you have support during your completion of the twelve steps. Believing in something more powerful than yourself can help restore your sanity and open up addicts to the idea of recovery. It's just about believing there is another force that will have your back.'

I wasn't convinced.

After considering a number of factors, I came to the conclusion that AA didn't suit me when I was 25 and didn't suit me at 40.

I wasn't ready to expose myself to the world. (I only did that when I was plastered.) And I wasn't ready for the whole 'I'm an alcoholic' thing. I was still a silly 'drinks cabinet binge drinker' in my eyes. Just a naughty party girl who didn't know how to slow down.

I looked online to see if there were any other ways I could be helped. As I sat at my computer, searching the internet for a lifeline, I sipped on a huge glass of pinot gris, with ice, to water it down a bit.

At least I was trying.

The first option that popped up on my screen was a retreat in Tibet. A few weeks of finding my inner truth and staring at an orange-clad monk was very appealing. Some time away from the family, and a vegan diet, no temptations – perfect.

I had an image of sitting in a wooden shack, with my palms resting on folded knees, looking composed and being at one with myself. The location, when I clicked on the little photo gallery, looked amazing and the devotees blazed with happiness. I read on. There were silent meditations for four hours per day and talking to any other attendees was prohibited. *I could do that.* You were given jobs, like cleaning the floors and cooking, and the rest of the time 'should be spent contemplating'. *I could contemplate*, I contemplated.

Then I had a look at the price. It was $5000 for two weeks, flights not included.

Five thousand bucks to clean and be quiet.

Even though I was an excellent peeler of potatoes and could make a mean vegie curry, I decided it wasn't for me. In reality, my room would probably have been a prison cell hanging off the side of a mountain, with a hole in the floor for a toilet. I'd have to share with an annoying, glazed-eyed roommate with body odour, spit in the corners of his mouth and a weird tuft of hair in the centre of his head. I'd be having arguments with Nordic yoga experts over pots of spoiled lentil dahl before the first sun had set. I'd get home with nothing but some infected mozzie bites and an unfriendly parasite living in my bottom.

Ayahuasca, perhaps? I loved the idea of heading to the Amazon to puke up my ego in a rainy, tarantula-infested jungle. Unravelling my boozy behaviours by ingesting muddy plant extract from coconut shells sounded illuminating but, unfortunately, drugs still scared me, ever since my E meltdown in my 20s. Even a dabble would have me banging on the doors of a psych ward. My time of licking toads, drinking strange concoctions and allowing witchdoctors to turn my genitals inside out had passed long ago, and taking a hallucinogenic drug to cure a drug problem didn't seem like a smart move. I'd also read that sometimes an Ayahuasca trip didn't end, and I couldn't risk forever being chased around by a spotty purple dragon called Trevor.

Anyway, leaving home wasn't an option. I had a baby and a nearly-four-year-old. I had responsibilities. So I kept searching, scrolling, until I tracked down a practical, nearby solution: a small local counselling service that was called Breaking Free. The title sounded good, and when I read further, this place felt like it was a perfect match for me.

It said:

Are you ready to start healing?

Join me. Heal Your Addictions and Compulsive Behaviours.

Are the things that originally helped you to avoid your pain and numb out now the very things that are contaminating your relationships, your health, your life?

Perfect. I needed healing, and the idea of someone listening to and helping me heal sounded appealing. The course took place over three months, and was 12 one-hour consultations with a therapist.

I picked up the phone and dialled the number before I'd have time to change my mind. A lady called Dianne answered. She was very sweet and asked me, 'What can I help you with?'

I paused as a million thoughts ran through my head, then blurted out, 'Hi, I'm a mum that binge drinks, but secretly I hate it and it makes me very ill. I want to stop but I don't know how.'

I thought she'd say, *Sorry, love, this course is for serious drinkers who are downing mouthwash for breakfast.*

But she didn't.

She said, 'This will be perfect for you. See you at 9 am on Monday.'

Holy shit!

I was really going to do this. I was going to get help. To talk about everything. Be honest for once. I ended the call and sat at the kitchen bench. I heard my baby murmuring from her cot and the sounds of my son tapping a spoon on his plate. This was for them. They had made me question my drinking. They were the wake-up call I needed.

As I thought about this, I couldn't help but wonder why I'd ignored the hundred other loud wake-up calls throughout my life.

Why hadn't I listened before?

Everything You See I Owe to Spaghetti

Age 33

After India, I went somewhere with flushing toilets. Sarah was still living in Sydney, so I flew there, hoping to find a place to call home. Not long after my arrival, an old friend, Kath, contacted me through Facebook and told me John, the guy with the gap in his teeth from Luton University, was living in Sydney. One day, I was bored and called him to arrange a meeting. Even though that very toxic relationship with Lucas had blindsided me and put me off dating for a while, I knew I couldn't avoid all humans with willies forever. So here I was, walking along the edge of the Pacific Ocean, about to reunite with this old friend.

I'd arranged to meet John at Circular Quay in Sydney. It was a beautiful day. The sun shone down over a harbour buzzing with people, ferries and water taxis. I found a spot on a sandstone wall near where the huge cruise ships docked.

I heard my name and squinted as I turned towards the sunlight.

'Hey, long time no see!' I said.

*

When John and I were at university, he was drunk all the time, wandering around the halls of residence in that Aran jumper, while I was busy studying for a degree in marketing and a Higher National Diploma in hangovers and recreational drug use. We lived two rooms away from one another, and most evenings met in the communal kitchen over a plate of fish fingers and deep-fried onion rings. We were mates, but our paths didn't intertwine much because I was usually awake dancing on a speaker somewhere when he was passed out in his dorm room. My memories of that time are, of course, a blur, and any social connections I made were either with drug dealers or the lady in Boots who sold me the morning-after pill once a week.

I liked John, but there was never anything romantic between us. He was a bit square. (Yes, he drank but it was basically standard uni-student drinking, and I thought anyone who didn't neck five Es and a gram of speed on a Tuesday night was a bit square.) That deep-fat-fryer was all we had in common, besides alcohol. We were on different pages then and it took 15 years for our chapters to align.

*

I held my hand up to block out the sun and it took a moment for him to come into focus. John strode towards me, surrounded by light. He was handsome and tanned, with a kind smile, looking much the same as he had all those years ago, but was holding an important-looking folder instead of a bottle of whisky.

I stood up. The bright sun shining in my eyes made my nose itch. I busted out a stupid sneeze, which sounded like a weasel being run over. I tried to do it in the opposite direction, so he didn't see me. I squeaked over my shoulder and into my hand, then managed to quickly wipe a palm of snotty spit onto my dress before I put my hand out to greet him. He pulled me in for a hug and pecked my cheek. I was surprised. His lips felt warm and soft.

He seemed pleased to see me. 'Right, where do you want to go, Vic? Lunch is on me.'

He linked his arm in mine and we strolled together along the promenade, in search of a restaurant. When I could, I turned to sneak an inquisitive peek, to take him in. He still had a gap in his front teeth and slight stubble. His jawline was strong, and his nose, aquiline like Hugh Jackman's, fitted his face well. Our eyes met briefly as I studied his features. Kindness was in his eyes as well as his smile. I saw they were deep sea-blue, and how they sparkled. He seemed different from the men I'd met before. Good different.

John chatted as we walked, seeming relaxed as he talked about his life in Australia. He was jolly. He told me about his family back in England and his job and, as he spoke, I looked down and noticed his polished black shoes. Real leather work shoes. For ten years, I hadn't had a boyfriend who owned shoes. All my exes tripped over dreadlocks while wearing flip-flops.

We found a little bistro on the edge of the water and sat at a table with a crisp white tablecloth. John pulled out a chair for me. I wasn't used to gentlemanly gestures, the nicest thing a guy had ever done for me before was passing me a spliff before he gave it to his mate. A waiter placed a napkin on my lap. It was that sort of place, with rows of cutlery and rock salt in a bowl.

I didn't ask John what was in his important-looking folder, but could bet it was something grown-up, about tax or mortgages. Opposite me, he was all smart in his crisp shirt. He reminded me of my dad, always dressed in a grey suit, carrying a leather briefcase. Either going to work or coming back from it. I used to wait at the front door for him as soon as I heard his car tyres crunch over the stones in the driveway. I'd jump up, clasp my arms around his neck and hang from him like a pendulum as he entered the house. He smelled of photocopiers.

I imagined John smelled the same, all officey. He reminded me of home.

I ordered spaghetti. That was a big mistake. The noodles were long, connected to the plate, and in my mouth was a never-ending cable line. I slurped while trying to nod politely along with what he was saying. In the end, I bit down, cut the cord and let the redundant strings drop onto the plate. I must have looked like the Creature from the Black Lagoon, with sauce on my chin, mangled pasta dripping from my mouth, and more flecks of Neapolitan on my forehead. John kindly pointed out the giant sprig of oregano sticking out from my front tooth. I found myself blushing as I wrangled the feisty branch and delicately placed it on the edge of my huge plate. I didn't order dessert.

As we chatted, John's leg bounced under the table. He was jiggling just like I do when nervous. I watched his agitation and wondered if I had missed out on a connection between us, all those years ago? His jumpy limb let me know he was nervous too, which relaxed me. I wiped my face on a napkin, grabbed the stem of my glass, kicked back, and enjoyed our lunch.

I realised very quickly John was a catch. He seemed stripped of bravado. He was confident but not in a showy-off way. His laugh was loud and endearing. I liked him.

I got back to Sarah's place and told her I'd had a lovely lunch with a nice man. She was intrigued, but I didn't give too much away, just in case it would turn out to be another total failure.

John texted me that afternoon: *Thanks for a gorgeous lunch, so great to catch up.*

I quickly wrote back: *Fancy going to see Ziggy Marley with me tomorrow night?*

*

Our first proper date was different from anything I'd experienced before. I knew his name, he spoke English, and I didn't sleep with him within an hour of us meeting.

That night, I dressed in a more feminine way, with a low-cut top and flowing skirt. I brushed my matted hair, licked the top of my fingers and bent back my eyelashes with my spit, to make them look like I was wearing mascara, and I turned my underwear inside out. (You learn a lot of tricks when you're a traveller.) I even plucked out the stray black hair that stuck out of my chin. I looked about as pretty as I could.

We went to the reggae gig, and I didn't fall over or use my body as a human podium. I didn't even smoke. I knew he hated it. I suppressed my crazy behaviour, allowing a more civilised person to creep out from within me, and the inebriated traveller girl stood in her shadow. I knew what I wanted. I wanted this man, and if I had to act like a prim idiot to snare him, then so be it.

The night was fun. It was easy, even with me modifying my behaviour, it felt genuine. John wasn't side-splittingly funny, and he wasn't the coolest cucumber (his favourite album of all time was the compilation, *Now That's What I Call Music!* '92) but he was everything else. Shallow traits – eyebrow piercings, cool sunglasses, tattoos, a Nick Drake album in the CD collection and a complete lack of employment – that had attracted me to a person in the past became insignificant. My superficial need for a punchline at the end of every sentence dried up and all that was left over was a barrelful of squishy loveliness.

We danced with the deep bassline reverberating around our already tingling bodies. He spun me around under his arm in an old-fashioned twirl. It was very cheesy, but I loved every minute of it. After the gig, we found a bar and sat on high stools with our toes nearly touching.

I'd never been so open or so natural with anyone. I told him about past disastrous relationships, and he shared a sad story of his ex-partner leaving him. As we revealed ourselves over a few pitchers of lager, there was no judgement, just warmth and understanding. I felt the heat of his hand on mine and didn't look away when he stared into my eyes. Eventually, we sank into comfy chairs and drank huge glasses of red wine. Our hands reached out to be held as we walked home and then he cornered me in a doorway, going in for a kiss.

It was a nice kiss. One I wanted to remember.

We fell in love that night; not an obsessive bunny-boiler kind of love. It was comfortable, more like a slow-roasted-ferret kind of love.

After we parted ways, I lay awake for hours, partly because my fold-up bed was like sleeping on the point of a pyramid, and partly because I had girlie fantasies about wedding dresses and writing my signature using his surname.

We spent the next five weeks in a perfect love bubble. John accepted me, my faults and weirdness. He saw the good in me and I continued to let my true self shine out. He was the first person to see me. The true me, not the party girl.

Until we met, I'd been running through life without a partner, jogging along with no one at my side. Now, someone was running next to me and my pace slowed to a contented stroll, which was wonderful. We were in sync, walking towards a future together.

The few weeks until my visa ran out zipped by, and we went our separate ways. John dropped me off at the airport and we said goodbye. It didn't feel right leaving him. We hugged and I promised I'd be back after the summer. I stood in the duty-free shop and did some ugly crying over a tin of travel sweets, then boarded a plane.

*

I touched down in the Land of Smiles, and then spent my days trudging around Chatuchak market, slurping on freshly squeezed orange juices in the sweltering heat, picking out silver to buy and sell at the markets. I was speechless when John called to say he was flying to Bangkok to meet me for two nights. No one had ever made such a bold statement of their feelings for me.

He arrived, all handsome and enthusiastic. It was his first trip to Asia, and I was thrilled to show him around. We spent a wonderful 48 hours exploring the city on tuk-tuks and on the back of motorbikes, weaving in and out of the traffic. We visited the Grand Palace, bought tailored suits, and climbed ancient steps to crumbling temples. John soaked up my cherished city, loving every minute, taking it all in. At nightfall, we ended up sitting on a kerb on Khao San Road for well-deserved cold Chang beers.

On our last evening together, we boarded a boat that cruised down the Chao Phraya River at sunset. John ordered a bottle of champagne and everything on the menu. 'A treat,' he said. We were entertained by a traditional Thai dancer in a golden crown. She contorted her body to the music, splayed her fingers out like they were a blossoming lotus flower, and stood as still as a statue, balanced on one leg, only moving her dark eyes, from side to side, to the relentless beat of the drum. We watched her in awe as we feasted on an incredible banquet, the hustle and bustle of the city passing us by. As the orange sun dropped behind a golden temple, John dropped down onto one knee.

'I think I want to marry you.'

'Are you sure?' I asked.

'I'm sure.'

'Okay.'

I couldn't believe my luck. We'd met six weeks before, and here he was, his kind blue eyes staring up at me, proposing. This new demeanour had worked, the mature lady/me, got her man. I gave myself a mental pat on the back as all the crew and diners on the boat clapped. They sang a funny song to the tune of 'We Wish You a Merry Christmas', making it 'We Wish You Happy Mawidge'. I reached over the table, took hold of John's hand and squeezed it as hard as I could.

We got tipsy and wandered back to our hotel with a warm breeze flowing over us. I was getting married! *I deserve this. After everything I've been through, I deserve love.*

Am I a Weirdo?

I waited until John and the children were asleep, got a little notebook out of the top drawer and sat at my desk. I wanted to be prepared for my first therapy session, but had no idea where to begin. I stared at a blank page. My thumb clicked the end of my biro. Up and down, up and down, *click, click, click, click* the only sound I heard.

I wondered if I should cancel, forget the whole thing. I knew that going through with it meant I might not be able to have another beer, ever.

Maybe I should reschedule?

Maybe I should have a beer now?

I poured out the hot liquorice tea from my orange teapot. As the steam rose into the air, I breathed in its sweet aroma and began to write: *Why do I continue to drink alcohol when it makes me so unwell?*

If I could get to the bottom of this one simple question, I would have a chance of understanding myself and a chance of getting better.

What else? I held my pen to my lip and thought hard.

Why can't I say no?

What am I scared of? Being sober? Being boring?

Why do people's opinions of me matter?

Is being sober possible?

Will I hate it?
Will I be frowned upon by my family as a party pooper?
Will I miss out?
Will I change?
Will I fail?
Is it okay to fail?
Will I run out of fabulous stories?
Will my friends think I'm a weirdo?
Am I a weirdo?
What does waking up on a Sunday with a clear head feel like?
Who on earth am I?
And ...
What the hell am I going to do with myself if I don't drink?

That last one was too much to consider. What would the weekend entail? I'd be a non-drinker in the land of lushes. An island of boring in a sea of frivolity. I'd become one of those dreary dullards that I often berated in pubs.

'Come on, get a drink inside you. What's wrong with you?'

'I don't drink.'

'WHAT? You don't drink?' I'd reply with a disgusted look. 'WHAT THE FUCK IS WRONG WITH YOU?'

I was angry when non-drinkers sipped on pints of orange juice and lemonade. I couldn't imagine being one of those smarmy losers who went home early to have a hot chocolate in their special chair, with their favourite paisley blanket draped over their knobbly knees.

Oh, what time is Escape to the Country *on, darling?*

Seven-thirty, sweety pops. We've got time for a quick crossword.

Kill me now! I thought.

By stopping drinking, am I going to become someone I hate?

Will my friends go on at me to drink when I don't want to? Like I did?

How will I ever say no to them?

It all seemed unfathomable.

I was guilty, terribly guilty, of always making people drink when they didn't want to. I penalised them for it, taunted them with accusations of being spoilsports or goody-two-shoes. Even if they, and I, were unwell, I prattled on: 'Just drink through it,' or 'Just have a couple. Come on, it will make you feel better. Shall I make you a hot toddy?'

If they refused, I turned on them, appalled by their unwillingness to join in. I suppose I wanted people to be on the same ride as me, have the same vibe. Then the consequences and shame were shared. The humiliating stories from a night out would be about 'What we did' rather than 'What you did'. I preferred to practise group embarrassment, rather than sinking underneath individual blame.

I had never trusted people who didn't drink, because I thought they were weird, mysterious and smug. Who were these tedious sober warriors with their arrogant dispositions and glasses of Orangina? Their judgemental eyes upon me made me feel too exposed. If I wasn't going to remember my awful behaviour, I didn't want anyone else to either. I found it easier to fob off the righteous bastards, rather than consider why they were making the choice not to drink. I pretended to hate sober people because I wasn't strong enough to be one.

My pen paused on the paper as I considered the enormity of this.

Hmmm. By shunning people who don't drink, I've been creating a more secure drinking community for myself.

I'd always wanted to feel my friends understood me, and drinking together was that confirmation. *We're here, staggering around the dancefloor, spilling cheap wine, and we love you. Now, let's hook arms, do the hokey-pokey and neck a shot of absinthe. Let's drink away the seriousness of life and then fall over.*

Brilliant.

But was it brilliant or was I convincing myself it was brilliant because I couldn't stop doing it? Was that why sober people were so annoying? Because they were achieving something that was out of my grasp?

As I wrote all of this down, I realised my attitude towards drinking stank. It was loutish and unintelligent.

Drink! Or you're out of the tribe. Excommunicated if under-inebriated!

There was no middle ground.

I sat with my pen poised over my notebook and had a mini epiphany. I wrote down: *Sober people are not my enemy. They are my goal people.*

It was true. I'd shunned them because I wanted to be them. Deep down, I was desperate to be an abstemious, fizzy-watered soldier. These people were my goddamned heroes. My jealousy made their sobriety too confronting for me, though, so I ridiculed them like a spotty teenage bully: *I don't understand you, so I hate you.*

I definitely needed help.

I sat there at my desk until I heard birds tweeting outside the window. As the sun pierced through the blinds and a new day began, I felt something within me shift.

I had hope.

I slid my notebook in the side pocket of my handbag and prepared to get a few hours' kip before my appointment with Dianne. Before I climbed into bed, I peered around the door to check on my sleeping baby. She was on her front with her bum in the air. Her thumb had dropped out of her mouth, but her lips were moving, like she was still sucking. She looked perfect.

'New beginnings,' I whispered as I switched off her owl night-light. 'I'm going to be the best mum I can, just like I promised.'

I sneaked into bed and snuggled up to my furry husband (whose bum is much hairier than mine). I tucked my knees into the back of his legs, like I always did, and gave him a kiss that he wouldn't remember. I was so grateful to have his support. He deserved a healthy, happy wife. Even though I loved him and the kids more than anything in the world, I knew what I was doing was for me. If I could get myself in shipshape, then the rest of the crew would join in.

As I drifted off to sleep, floating somewhere between dreams and darkness, I felt a zap of fear and jolted upright.

Once the wine had soaked out of my skin, would I like what was left over?

I hope I don't turn into a total wanker, I thought.

Camembert and Warm Beer
Age 34

After John's proposal, I headed to France alone, to spend the tourist season selling silver jewellery at the markets of the Dordogne region. I wanted to move Down Under with some money of my own. I wanted to be responsible.

I spent the summer driving from one quaint medieval village to another, in an old converted ambulance I picked up online. It was army green, smelled of burning oil and broke down about once a week, but I loved it. Its unpredictability was part of my adventure. On hot days, steam pumped out of the engine, and I had to pull over and sleep by the side of the road until it cooled down. I would fling open the double doors and watch sunsets over lavender fields, while drinking warm beer from small green bottles. John was always in my thoughts, and we exchanged sweet text messages every night before bed.

It won't be long. I miss you x
I miss you too x
I can't wait for us to start our lives together. Night x
Night, night wife.

I lay on my back on a mattress and hung my head out of the double doors. I breathed in the warm air and watched as a spray of stars filled the night sky.

I knew this trip would be my last for a while. I was engaged, there was a chance this might be my last hurrah before I settled down to have kids, so I wanted to inhale the feeling of freedom and independence so deeply into my lungs that I would never forget it.

Each morning, with a fuddled, crapulous head, I grabbed a towel and a bar of soap, and made my way through the fields until my feet met water. I dunked my naked body under the cold, fast-moving water of the Dordogne River. Pebbles underfoot, I pushed against the flow and allowed the water to rinse away the soap from my hair. Back in my van, I dried off and warmed spicy, milky tea on a little gas stove.

When I arrived at the market, I followed *Le Placier* (the market boss, who was on a power trip) to wherever he was going to put me. Your position was based on looks and how much money you were slipping into his old-fashioned bum bag. It didn't take me long to understand I had to pretend to fancy him (yuck) and pass him an extra twenty euros to get on the main drag, where the bulk of the money was made. I set up my stall and displayed the jewellery in lines on a soft velvet tablecloth. Most days, at 6 am I had a hot chocolate with the Olive Man (a tall, gangling man with a little ponytail and one hooped earring, who displayed his green and black olives in big white barrels); the Cheese Lady (a serious short-haired Dutch woman, who wore a mumsy apron and ripped off tourists with overpriced Gouda and camembert); and the Wine Guy (you can work that out yourself). He stood behind a huge rack that displayed dusty, dark bottles of red nestled in straw. He had a small moustache that sat on his top lip like a dead slug, and with each sip of his morning coffee, it filled with frothy milk. After a morning catch-up, I allowed myself 20 minutes to get back to my stall, during which I would be inundated with cheek kisses from various acquaintances. By the time I started work, this traditional French greeting meant I had the saliva of everyone '*dans le Sud-est de la France*' dripping from my cheek.

'Victorria! *Viens ici.*'

The Wine Guy dragged me to his stall and demanded I taste his freshest Beaujolais before the town clock had even chimed 8 am.

'*Pour réchauffer la tête*,' he said as he filled a little plastic cup.

Needless to say, 'warming up my head' became a daily necessity that kept me rosy cheeked for the entire four months I was there.

I met people from all over the world at the busy morning markets. Italian tourists who never spent a penny, and generous Brits who loved that there was an English girl who knew what time Super U closed and where to get the best tinned *confit du canard*. Most evenings, I set up a chair and table next to my van, and tucked into bread, local cheese and saucisson, which I hacked off in big, thick chunks. I threw back cheap red wine by the gallon; I was in France, after all, it was a national offence not to. I made some friends: lots of techno-loving hippies who travelled to Asia to get stock in the winter, and worked hard enough during the summer to pay for a bag of weed, the site fees, and the plane ticket for their next adventure. Kind-hearted souls who took care of this lonesome English girl.

I was able to save money quickly and, after one summer of market life, moved to Sydney to be with my man.

*

I pushed my metal trolley piled with bags into arrivals. I saw a hand frantically waving over the top of some men who held handwritten signs with surnames. His smile shone through the crowd like a ray of sunshine.

Even though I had been eating cheese and *dauphinoise* potatoes for four months, John picked me up in the air and planted a big, wet kiss on my lips.

'G'day, mate!'

'Gudday, indeed.'

We rented a house at Lovett Bay, near Scotland Island: a small enclave that boasted a lovely ferry ride from the mainland. Our house was boat access only, so we bought a tinny, and I spent six months planning our wedding while on a big wooden deck that overlooked Pittwater. I loved living in this 'Oh so very Australian' environment. We had goannas skulking around the garden, big cockatoos that squawked outside the kitchen window, kangaroos bounding among the bottlebrush and giant huntsman spiders hiding in dark crannies. I took John over to the mainland every day in our little boat, so he could catch the bus to work, and spent my days walking in the bush and having wines with the neighbours. Even with everywhere I'd travelled, I had never been in a place surrounded with such beauty. I saw white sandy beaches from my bedroom window, and watched boats dart across the twinkling water as the sun dipped behind the gum trees.

My drinking slowed a little while we were living offshore. Boat rides after big nights were risky – you needed your wits about you when crossing the water in the dark. Instead, John and I practised safe drinking, just the two of us polishing off a couple of bottles of wine on the deck each night.

Three months before the wedding, I decided it was time to have a big night out. I had a few new friends and wanted to celebrate the fact I was off the market, so I organised a mini hens' night. I arranged to sleep at one of their houses and booked a table in a nice Thai restaurant.

It started well. My friends and I ate a meal, sat in a bar in Manly, chatted about the wedding. But people bought me drinks and I lost count of how many I had.

That was the night I got blotto and smashed a tray of shots on the floor, then became a human podium and got thrown out of the pub. I puked on my shoes and was lugged down the main street, with my feet dragging along the ground. It was also the night of falling off the bed and getting wedged, like a doorstop, between it and a wardrobe. I stayed there groaning until my friends found me in the morning.

I called John and asked him to pick me up from the jetty. As the ferry chugged towards me, I leaned over and vomited into the bay. A man walking past stared as I wiped my mouth with my jumper, and pulled his dog away from me.

'Jeez, you look a bit rough around the edges,' John said as he switched off the engine.

'It was a big night,' I answered. Unwell, I fell into bed for the rest of the day.

This time, it wasn't the alcohol that made the hangover so awful.

It was George.

The tiny baby growing inside me.

Rainy Days and Mondays with Dianne

I stopped at some red lights and pulled up the handbrake. I considered doing a U-turn when they turned green, heading back home towards a hot bubble bath and a massive glass of white wine. I could forget all this and go on as normal. I was nervous about facing the truth. Again, my mind was tricking me, telling me that my problem wasn't serious enough to warrant therapy, and Dianne would think I was a twitty, exaggerating mother, whose hardships were insignificant compared with those of her other patients.

But normal isn't working, I thought as the lights changed.

Normal had become complicated. In the week since the night I'd told the man with a ZZ Top beard that I had a newborn baby, and the awful hangover afterwards, I'd become uncomfortable around alcohol. If I opened the fridge and saw a six-pack, I'd slam it closed. If I saw anyone sipping a glass of red, I felt scared. Even the mention of booze made me feel tense. The previous morning, an invite to a birthday party had popped up in my notifications, and I'd instantly clicked *not going*, knowing I was incapable of having just one glass, and fearing my children wouldn't see me the next day. The thought of that made me accelerate in the direction of help.

I parked outside a grey building and sat in the car. I had no idea where to start or how this was going to finish. I looked at myself in the rear-view mirror, put on a bit of mascara and locked eyes with my reflection.

'You can do this,' I said in a firm voice. Then I stepped out of the car.

Dianne was a pretty, middle-aged lady with bobbed hair. Her unrushed, warm handshake comforted me, and I sensed an understanding between us. Underneath her sharp suit and kind smile, she had a story too.

She asked me to take a seat. Without warning, I burst into tears. Dianne handed me a box of tissues and asked, 'What's going on?'

'Where do I start? I'm failing as a mother and I need to change, but I don't know how,' I snivelled from under the snotty tissue. 'I'm having anxiety every time I get drunk, and I feel like booze is causing my life to spiral downwards. I'm frightened.'

There was silence as Dianne considered what I'd said.

'Let's identify the problem and go from there. What is the problem, Vicky?'

Drum roll ...

'I drink too much.'

'You mean you have a problem with alcohol?'

'Er, um, maybe? I have a problem with alcohol.'

'Sorry, what? I can't hear you?'

'I have a problem with alcohol.'

'I still can't hear you, Vicky.'

'I have a problem with alcohol.'

'Louder,' she persisted.

'I HAVE A PROBLEM WITH ALCOHOL, DIANNE!'

There – I said it.

(And the crowd went wild.)

I sat up straight, wiped a tear from my eye and said 'fuck' a few times under my breath. Even though I had only stated what should have been obvious, it had never been so clear to me as in that moment. I felt like I'd been slapped round the face with a wet fish and had finally woken up.

'I have a problem with alcohol' was one sentence I'd never said.

That's why I was here. That's why I was breaking promises.

No matter how big or how small, I had a problem.

I sighed. Acknowledging my problem to Dianne alleviated a heavy unease on my shoulders.

'Tell me about your relationship with alcohol, Vicky,' she asked, once my startled expression slackened.

I started talking and didn't stop for around 57 minutes.

Dianne's office space was small. We sat close together and she faced me, our knees almost touching, her eyes looking directly into mine. She reminded me of Ruth, the lady that had given me a pebble all those years ago.

There was an A4 notepad and a biro on the table in front of me, and the cup of tea Dianne had made me sat untouched, I was so busy nattering away. Occasionally, as I talked, she got up and wrote notes on the whiteboard. When she moved around the room, the smell of her perfume wafted over me. The scent was soothing. In fact, her entire presence was soothing.

Her total acceptance of me and my story made her easy to trust. The only words she spoke were encouraging: 'Yes, don't worry. That's very common,' and 'It's okay. You're doing really well.'

I told her I felt like I'd lost control of my drinking and no matter how hard I tried to moderate it, I failed. I told her I wanted to be a better mum, and that when I was hungover in the bedroom all day, my children weren't feeling any love from me and that made me feel terribly guilty.

'This is very normal, Vicky. Having children has given your drinking a consequence. All we need to do now is understand some things from your past to know your reasons why,' she said.

'I've just always been a big drinker. I don't think there really are any reasons why, Dianne. It's just who I am.'

'I think over the next few weeks, we are going to have to go deeper than you just being a binge drinker. We're going to have to dig up your truth.'

As she spoke, I felt myself dismiss her words. This wasn't about my past. This was about addressing my current problem. I didn't need to go over all that again, surely. My heart sank as I imagined weeks of dredging up old feelings from a life gone by. I couldn't grasp it. How on earth were silly things like getting a bit bullied at school, sleeping with a few random menfolk, and spending most weekends dribbling in a nightclub toilet, affecting my life now?

'We have to heal the past in order to move forward, Vicky.'

'Okay, but I can't remember much. I've been in a blackout for most of it.'

'Well, next week we will try and piece it all together, and see what we come up with. Is that okay?'

I thought about saying no, I couldn't be bothered. *What's done is done.* Then I could just march out of the office and head to the pub for a pint. But I didn't. I sat in my chair and looked at Dianne's notes written on the whiteboard:

Alcohol
Anxiety
Fear

Doubt

Guilt

These words represented me. They perfectly summed up my current situation and were impossible to ignore. I couldn't fix what those words represented myself, so I handed over my trust. Unpacking everything from my past was going to be hard, but Dianne's kind eyes assured me I should give the process a chance.

'Okay, Dianne, let's do this,' I said as I hooked my handbag over my shoulder. 'Is it okay if I take that biscuit to eat in the car?'

Lady Lumps and Prune Juice
Age 34

Putain de merde! My stomach was doing somersaults. The big day was here. Time to get hitched.

We had decided to get married in France, in the garden of my parents' house. Surrounded by fields filled with swaying sunflowers, and huge pine trees that dropped sweet-smelling needles onto the stone driveway. Being so close to England meant our whole families could be there to raise a glass on this special day.

John's parents headed up the tree-lined driveway and we saw his elderly grandparents squeezed into the back seat of the car, smiling. We all stood waving, and my parents appeared from the house, holding chilled beers and cold glasses of wine.

After hugs and hellos, my future husband's parents politely refused the alcohol, asked for a hot cuppa and we all headed inside. Like me, my parents found it odd when people refused a drink; they just couldn't understand why someone would choose to abstain when booze was an option. It was like choosing to eat a brussels sprout when you could have a Lindt ball. But they never hassled John's parents, never tried to talk them into it. Mum just went to the kitchen and turned the kettle on, and we all sat in the dining room as they told us about the traffic on the *autoroute*. Everyone's unquestioning acceptance of one another made me proud of them.

*

I was relieved on my wedding day. First, after two days of rain, the sun streamed into the windows of the caravan we were staying in and, second, I was relieved in a literal sense. I'd successfully been to the toilet. Stress and baguettes had caused a backup of traffic at the Arc de Triomphe. The day before, I'd been lying with my legs spread, a French doctor's index finger up my derrière.

'*Il y a un problème avec mon caca, Monsieur,*' I said to the doctor. '*Trop de merde.* Too much shit. I'm blocked!' I finished in English.

He had a feel and agreed that I was certainly '*très constipée*'.

I explained I was getting married the following day and needed to go '*immédiatement*'. On retrieval of his digit, he printed out a document, signed it as only a doctor could, handed me a small white paper bag with a plastic tube, and asked me if he could fondle my breasts.

'*Pour nodules,*' he said.

I'd been warned this dapper doctor was a pervert. If a local lady patient had stubbed a toe or suffered from an earache, he'd whip off her bra and run his dry hands over her nipples, checking for lumps. The suave Frenchman was the best-looking male in this *petite* village, though. The local women all fancied his pants off and were, I was told, offended if he didn't ask them in for an annual nodule check. No one ever reported him. The village had a high density of decrepit pig farmers who resembled their livestock, and the doctor, a film star by comparison, got away with his deviant indiscretions.

Alas, I was about to marry the man of my dreams, so I declined his intimate inspection of my lady lumps and opted for some strong stool-extracting medication instead. I necked the pills with a litre of prune juice. When I got home, I lay on the stone floor of the bathroom with my legs akimbo, and inserted a suppository and the plastic pipe '*dans mon petit passage*'. ('*Petit passage*' is not a medical term, so please don't use it in any French pharmacies.)

*

On the morning of my nuptials, my parents' house was alive with excited friends and family, all rushing about with trays of glasses and suits on hangers. Some set up the marquees, some carried tables and others strung lights between the huge willow trees. People kept coming over and offering me champagne to 'calm my nerves'. They knew I was pregnant but 'Just one won't hurt' had me pretending to sip at a small flute as my make-up was applied. In my family, pretending to drink was usually easier than saying no.

Once my hair and make-up were finished, my girlfriends helped me into the dress. It slipped over my body, the weight of the fabric smoothing out the creases. There was some tucking and a forceful boob lift, then I was ready. I looked into the wooden free-standing mirror in the centre of Mum's bedroom.

My friends watched as I turned around for the head-to-toe view. For a moment, I didn't recognise myself. My hair was pulled back from my face and, as I turned slightly, I could see a row of little white flowers tucked into it. The back of the dress was decorated with golden embroidery, which tapered off at the start of the long train that gathered in a pile at my feet. The only jewellery I wore was a simple silver band: the engagement ring John had bought me in Bangkok.

I could see I was pregnant. Neither my massive knickers, nor the swathes of heavy silk, could hide my small bump. The material pulled taut across my stomach.

I cradled my tummy and whispered to my baby, 'Mummy's getting married.'

I slipped on my best sparkly flip-flops, and was handed a bunch of beautiful wildflowers picked from the garden. As Dad grabbed my hand, I swallowed a bit of pungent fruit-flavoured hurl. He squeezed me hard, in a 'You'll be fine' kind of way, and led me down the stone steps towards the awaiting congregation.

When John turned around to see me, his eyes crinkled as a huge smile spread across his face. His grin was infectious. I smiled back. Everyone turned around in their seats as I approached and, despite how hard I tried to keep it together, tears trailed white lines down my face, dissolving my cheap fake tan.

After the ceremony, I took a seat and watched everyone I love get completely shitfaced. It was weird not being smashed for once. It was like watching a merry-go-round spinning too fast and everyone onboard getting flung around inside the mayhem. Friends cheered and sang songs, aunties fell down stairs and gatecrashers helped themselves to canopies. People got too close and bad breath hung around after incoherent conversations. I didn't mind. I knew drunk people. I was drunk people.

I'd enjoyed my wedding day from a different perspective: a sober point of view. No blackouts, no falling over and no vomit. A miracle. Instead of my ponytail being held while I regurgitated chunks of cupcake into an ice bucket, I laughed through speeches, stuffed my face with amazing food and danced like a zombie to 'Thriller' in the warm moonlight.

I remembered every perfect moment, every kiss and every slow dance. I was sitting on a bench under one of the willow trees with my adorable new husband. All the people I loved twirled around the dancefloor. I was captivated by the love that surrounded me.

Being pregnant at my wedding gave me a brief insight into what life would be like as a non-drinker. A window into a different lifestyle. I liked it. Not enough to stop, but I liked it. That feeling stayed with me and sat dormant in my brain for a long time. It was proof life could happen without alcohol.

At midnight, with my flip-flops dangling from one hand and the hand of my new husband in the other, I strolled down a quiet country road, feeling full of love, hope and prune juice.

Irresponsibly Responsible

Exactly one week after our first meeting, I sat in Dianne's office again. I didn't feel great. It was cold and I hadn't slept well. The baby was up all night crying and my son wet the bed. John and I crossed paths in the hallway a few times, like ships passing in the night, holding damp sheets and bottles of warm milk.

I still wasn't ready to release my inner feelings or go over any sticky situations from my past. But maybe tiredness made me more vulnerable, because that morning it all poured out.

As I took my seat, Dianne handed me a scruffy teddy bear wearing a little blue jacket. I held it, knowing its presence meant I was in for an emotional ride.

'Let's begin at the beginning, Vic. How did this all start?' Dianne asked.

'Well, good question,' I said.

I thought back to those first whiffs of wine that seeped from the black nozzle of the silver space-age wine bag, guzzling liquor from tall bottles in the drinks cabinet, the first sips at the park and leaning back on the swing with my hair dragging along the ground, the feeling of being free.

'I've been wanting to drink heavily ever since I can remember. Being a binge drinker was my destiny, Dianne.

When I was little, I watched my parents be the life and soul of the party. It looked like a great way to fit in and be liked, so I drank to feel accepted. I think it's become so ingrained in me that I can't see a way out. It's all I've ever known. It's who I am.'

It was true that drinking was the only way I knew how to have fun, to be me. I had loved the parties, the preparation, the accolades my family got for being so bloody cheerful. Parties and drinking had given me purpose. I was honoured to be the kid with the outrageous family. It was my pleasure to be the reliable supplier of fun. My family squished me into shape. What popped out the other side of my teens was the perfect cookie-cutter party girl. A disco biscuit; someone who had drugs, one-liners, VIP passes, and the stamina to keep most of Brighton entertained until the sun rose over the West Pier.

As I spoke, I began to understand. Revealing felt healing. Emotion and honesty heaved their way up through my oesophagus and out through my mouth, all over Dianne.

'It's been fun, I think? I've enjoyed the traits passed on to me. I've made my parents proud and carried the flaming party mantle proudly above my head. I've fulfilled my role as an excellent merrymaker and good daughter.'

I looked into Dianne's blue eyes. She was squinting.

'Vic, fulfilling this role has been detrimental to your health. Your drinking is causing you anxiety and you're suffering because of alcohol. Can you see that now?'

She was right. After all, I *was* getting therapy. Perhaps being a party girl wasn't that cool?

Party girls are just addicts with backstage passes, I thought. I realised then I didn't need loud music and pumping basslines anymore. I just needed a cuddle and a cup of cocoa.

'I think I'm starting to understand,' I said. Rolling around on dancefloors, sleeping with strangers and barfing up Buckfast in kebab shops was not as 'rad' as I had once imagined.

In fact, none of it was ...

I squeezed the teddy bear as I coughed up all my past indiscretions. I spewed out the promiscuity, the drugs, the anxiety, the accidents, the drink driving and the feeling of never fitting in. I was strangely numb as I talked about the tsunami, and sobbed as I recalled the moment I sat on a kerb in the Tunisian mountains, with a black eye and a broken heart.

I have no idea how long I talked, but when the torrent stopped, I felt different.

'There we have it, Dianne! All my fuckuppery in one hit.'

She made some notes on her A4 pad. All I could hear was her fountain pen scratching the paper. When she stopped writing, Dianne squeezed her chin between her thumb and index finger, and pursed her lips in deep thought.

'It's sad,' she said.

Sad? I thought.

I'd never thought any of it was sad. Pathetic, perhaps. Stupid; insane, maybe?

As I sat there, I suddenly felt sad too. Maybe what had happened to me deserved attention, rather than being drowned out by a pint of Stella and a gag.

A girl sitting on the side of the road, alone, nursing a black eye was sad. Being abandoned by friends I loved, who were my world, was also sad.

In that flimsy chair in Dianne's pokey office with the rain battering the window, I really began to see the seriousness of my problems. Alcohol had covered up the sadness she could sense. It was a shock to realise how I'd allowed myself to be treated and how I had leaned on booze to cope.

Even though I never admitted it, I *was* sitting somewhere on that vast scale of alcoholism. I wasn't at the far end, about to lose everything, I wasn't at rock bottom, but for the first time I saw I fitted within the gamut.

'I guess I'm using alcohol to forget, to ease my pain, and that means I'm some sort of alcoholic, Dianne?'

The room went quiet. She reached out, put her hand on my knee and gave it a little squeeze as my words floated around her tiny office, like ghosts from my past.

'These moments don't have to define you, Vicky.'

'What do you mean?'

'You don't need to give yourself a label or give space in your head to the events from your past. They are gone. Over. We can heal those situations, rectify them. Then you can clean the slate and start again.'

'But I thought everything that happens in life makes you who you are?'

'Yes, but you can become a new version of you,' she said. 'You can change.'

Her tone was very guru-ish, so I believed her.

'Why do you think you started drinking heavily as a teenager?'

'I drank because everyone drank. I didn't know there was another option. I guess things really shifted when I was around fourteen and my friends decided they didn't like me. It broke my heart.'

Being rejected isn't the worst situation a 14-year-old can experience, and many teenage girls experience rejection of this kind, but for me it triggered major feelings of insecurity.

I thought I wasn't good enough, and from that point, I went off the rails.

Sad, drink; lonely, drink; stressed, drink; confused, drink; happy, drink.

I commiserated and celebrated.

Alcohol was always the answer.

It washed my pain away until the tide came back in.

The realisation was enormous and I started sobbing as all the emotions passed through me. By the end of the session I felt I had closed a chapter in the past and let go of the pain I had been numbing for years.

*

The following week, I rolled up at Dianne's office, ready. As soon as I entered the room, she grabbed a box of tissues and placed it beside me on a little stool.

'You might need these today.'

She placed her chair closer to mine and anchored herself beside me. I inhaled through my nose and looked up at the flickering light above my head. The office smelled sweet, like a Victoria sponge was rising in the oven. I exhaled and looked at Dianne.

'Tell me about your family.'

This was the chat I had hoped to avoid. It was going to destabilise a mansion of emotions. Talking about my family in therapy felt disloyal, like I was breaking an unspecified code.

I held on to the sides of my chair and put myself back in the family home, sitting on my beanbag in the corner of the lounge room, flicking through records. My home was filled with love, the warmth of heated rooms, the support of strong foundations.

'I'm from a very happy home, Dianne.'

'Did anyone in your family over-drink?'

Her question unsteadied me.

'Everyone. We're a drinking family. It's what we do.'

A house of full-throttle drinkers with no off switches within reach. People you could trust to supply a good time, some competitive banter and a dusty hangover. No half-measures in this family home. Our drinking and vulgar humour came with a dash of piss-taking and an extra serving of strong language. No *I'm having an early night* or *Let's save the rest of the bottle for tomorrow*. An open bottle would be drunk, appreciated briefly, then another one would be popped open.

'I can't remember ever putting a half-empty bottle of wine back in the fridge, Dianne.'

One Christmas, Mum was given a bottle stopper to keep the open fizz bubbly. 'What am I supposed to do with that?' she asked, holding it in the air. The stopper remained in the pull-out present drawer under her bed, among the smelly soaps and potpourri.

My parents were at their happiest when organising a gathering or an event. They planned ahead, prepping for the festivities. Cars left at home, lifts organised, pints of water placed on bedside tables, the mini karaoke machine plugged in, with 'Dancing Queen' on standby. And enough booze for a hundred people, even if only ten were coming.

Growing up around Mum and Dad was exciting. The ultimate partiers, they had a fantastic ability to make a room full of people laugh in a single bound, turn an empty glass full faster than a speeding bullet, and become more powerful than a locomotive in lifting the spirits of even the grumpiest town mayor. It was an amazing superpower, and I adored them for it.

Drinking connected us, with friends, with each other, with humanity.

'We love drinking,' I said to Dianne.

'If you asked anyone in your family to stop drinking, do you think they could?'

'If I asked them to stop, I'd get a red stiletto in my eyeball and a glare so scathing it would turn me to stone.'

'Do you think there may have been alcoholism within your family for generations?' Dianne asked.

I wasn't sure. My dad's side of the family were not heavy drinkers at all. The sort of people who had a tiny glass of sherry on Christmas Day. My granddad, William, was teetotal, having signed 'The Pledge' – a religious agreement never to imbibe alcohol – as a young man.

Mum's father, I heard, had been unkind, including being verbally abusive, when she was growing up. If he didn't get his fish supper on a Friday, or Nan chatted with the nice man at number 29 too much, he got angry and shut them out of the house. As an old man, he sat in a rocking chair in front of a gas fire, smoking roll-up ciggies and sipping from a stubby glass containing an inch of whisky. He did spend a lot of time at 'the club', a smoke-filled drinking establishment over the road from the estate in Woking where they lived. He died when I was young, so I never saw if his 'work hard/drink hard' lifestyle disrupted the Stubbs family unit. Also, I think alcohol use in those days was so ingrained that even if he did have a problem, he probably just got a pat on the back as he bought one for the road.

My memories of all my other relatives were nothing but good. Big-hearted people with a barrelful of jokes. They were cheek pinchers and knee bobbers, who smothered me with love. No trauma handed down from them. The worst that happened was the neighbours complaining they couldn't bear another rendition of 'Knees Up Mother Brown' and could Nan please remove the man wearing a Union Jack thong from their front lawn. Anyway, it wasn't right to blame long-gone people because of stories I'd heard.

'I'm not sure, Dianne, I don't think there is a history of alcohol abuse … They all drank for fun.'

As the words formed in my mouth, I suddenly felt uneasy in my chair. Was their drinking more dysfunctional than I originally thought?

As for my immediate family – every Christmas, birthday, funeral, and all other family gatherings – drinking was the main plotline. No one stood out as having a drinking 'problem'. How could there be a problem if everyone else did the same? We were just like every other family we knew. People who let their hair down after a long working week. We were normal drinkers.

Your average British family of pub-dwelling over-doers.

Banter, party tricks and punchlines.

Happy drinking, social drinking, is the type of drinking that would never be questioned, so it never was. My drinking was so much a part of this nonchalant attitude that it got absorbed by the crowd, diluted into the culture. It was never out of the ordinary to be passed out in a bush or to wake up dressed as a member of the Village People, even doing a nudie run around the garden was considered pretty normal. Such incidents added to our rich history of amusing stories and made me feel accepted within my family. The more extrovert, the better. Our home wasn't scary or out of control. It was welcoming, and it lit up every Saturday night. In a street full of darkness, our house twinkled like a disco ball.

At gatherings, there wasn't any 'out of the comfort zone' drinking. And there was no alone drinking. No morning drinking, no drowning-your-sorrows drinking. It was joyful, communal. No one was singled out as having an issue. Not even Louise, who ended up in AA. We were all considered smart enough to know what was okay and when to stop.

I looked at Dianne.

'No one ever said to me, "You look like you've had enough." I was never told to slow down.'

Having 'had enough' revealed itself through waking up with an eyebrow missing, or an accidental snog with someone's husband. There was no half pissed or tipsy. All or nothing. It was never explained that drinking until you fall over wasn't the best. So, I drank until I fell over.

'If you can't remember a night out, then it's been a success,' my mum used to say.

The only gauge that we drank more than most families was the endless trips to the recycling depot and the number of times we headed across the channel on booze runs to France. The old Citroën's exhaust used to scrape along the road as we pulled up in the ferry line at Calais port, where the *gendarme* gave us a squinty once-over.

Dianne prodded me into recalling my feelings growing up in this comical, fancy-dress-filled environment. I flipped through the archive in my brain and found hardly any negative memories of my upbringing. My heart swelled with pride at the thought of my eccentric parents. I wanted to be just like them – a glamorous host with a quick wit and a streetful of friends. My mum was strict occasionally, but I didn't feel traumatised by it. There were times we'd fallen out and not spoken for a while, but we always forgave each other. We always said, 'I love you', even if it was through gritted teeth.

'Even if my mum did throw the entire contents of my bedroom out of the window, she was a great parent.'

Dianne looked concerned.

'Do you think your family's practice of consistently entertaining has had a bigger influence over you than you realise?'

'Maybe? Do you?'

'Yes. I do.'

She told me I had probably learned to be a party girl from watching them as a kid. My automatic, almost subliminal, reaction to my family's tradition of partying and necking booze until blacking out was to copy it. I never questioned if drinking alcohol was good or bad for me, my legacy of being legless.

As I sat there, I realised *not* drinking had never really been a possibility.

'Not drinking was never an option for you, Victoria, but stopping drinking is. Your parents didn't know you were absorbing their behaviours. There is no need to be angry with them. This isn't about blame, it's about doing something different. Breaking the cycle.'

She was right. Blaming my parents for my problem was pointless. Blaming anyone but myself would stir up a cesspit of negativity and the hearts of those dear to me would get wounded.

When my parents weren't partying? They were there for me. Tucking me up in bed, reading me stories. They supported me when I was bullied, they didn't judge when I had anxiety, and they bailed me out when I needed them (one time, literally). They took me on amazing holidays: to

America, where we ate hot dogs for breakfast, and Kenya, where big spiders jumped on our heads and sea urchins' spikes got stuck in our toes. I had wonderful memories of driving through France with Billy Ocean on the tape player. We snaked around mountains, waved at serious-looking strangers through the back window, and played a game in which we held our breath as the car accelerated through long tunnels on the motorway. We had running races in our slippers around big pine trees at sandy campsites. Happy Christmases with cheeky cousins; birthdays where we had trick candles that we never managed to blow out and ate yummy Victoria sponge off flimsy paper plates.

'Do your parents know you are here, getting help, Victoria?'

'No,' I said. 'This has nothing to do with them. This is something I have to do on my own. Also, they'd think I'm a wet blanket for getting counselling and they'd probably be disappointed in me if I quit drinking.'

'That's their problem, not yours,' Dianne said. 'Think about yourself now. You're a grown woman, not a child. You're doing what is best for you and your family. Now, look at the clock! We've run out of time.'

She flipped her notepad shut and I let out a sigh.

I decided not to tell my parents about sad meetings in dark rooms where I admitted to having 'issues'. In no way did I want to be the person to put an abrupt end to their conga line of celebration. All I wanted was for them to carry on being the perfect hosts, serving cheap sparkling wine in plastic flutes and handing out chicken liver pâté on toast to the masses forever more.

I had nothing but love for them. My mum and dad instilled a sense of independence in me by simply allowing me to be me. I now realised what had resulted from their parenting was a confident woman, brave enough to admit she had a drinking problem. Their good parenting had ensured I followed this through to the bitter end (not that sort of bitter).

I felt better, glad to be thinking outside of blaming. My drinking, for various reasons, had morphed into something serious; sinister, almost. It wasn't fun anymore. I was numbing out the stresses of being a mum. I didn't know another way of dealing with the ups and downs of being me. I abused alcohol to skip some of the harsh realities of life, and not face the fact I was lonely, unhappy with boyfriends, with my choices, with becoming a parent, and a billion and one other things.

All that combined led me to misuse alcohol in a way my parents never had. I didn't know until that day I was using it to drown out my stuff from the past.

I stood up, grabbed my handbag and headed to the door.

Something simmered in me, though.

I turned to Dianne as I stood in the doorway. 'I feel like I've been tricked, conditioned to believe that drinking was okay. I never pressed pause to ask why I needed to make myself "more happy".'

It was true. I'd latched on to alcohol's jolly reputation and followed it devotedly, just like I did with that charismatic American cult leader. Brainwashed by booze. Subtly, slowly indoctrinated until I was too soaked to protest. Alcohol had made me believe I wanted more of it. That I couldn't live without it. That addictive drug did exactly what it was designed to do and I couldn't believe I had fallen for it.

'I'm not annoyed with my parents at all, Dianne. I'm angry and pissed off with alcohol.'

'Feeling angry won't get you anywhere, Victoria; this has to be about you. Focus on the role you played in this story. Now, go home and see your lovely kids.'

As usual she was right – hatching a cunning plan to bring down the big alcohol corporations would have to wait. I had to look at the role I played in all this. I'd taken this merry style of social drinking and turned it up a notch. It wasn't anyone else's doing, and I had to take responsibility for the problem. Otherwise, who would?

When I thought about it, I realised that my arm was always stretching out for a refill, my hand reaching into the fridge for a second bottle, my twenty-dollar note being waved at the barman for a second round of shots; me heading to the lock-in, playing a drinking game …

It was me.

All me.

And the only way I was going to move forward was to face the fact I was the problem!

Not my parents, my environment or the culture of drinking.

It was little old me.

*

That night, I went home, put the dinner on, kissed my family and went to have a long soak in a hot bath. I lay back as rubber duckies and squirty toys floated around me.

I listened to my children play on the landing outside the bathroom door. Nell giggled as George blew raspberries on her tummy. It was a perfect sound.

Taking responsibility meant sobriety was going to be my choice. My choice for them and for me.

I got out of the bath, grabbed a towel, rubbed the condensation from the mirror above the sink, and looked at my reflection.

There's no need to drown, Vicky – there isn't any water pushing you under.

After I dried off, I went into the living room. Nell had flung a packet of rice around the room and John, red faced, was leaning down, picking grains from deep within the carpet. I kneeled down and helped. George then slipped on a Hot Wheels car and banged his head hard on the coffee table. There was blood, and golf-ball-sized swelling. When I touched it, he screamed so loudly I thought the windows might shatter. Nell, seemingly just for a laugh, then joined in the cacophony and started to cry too. Total chaos. I rushed around in search of bandaids, an ice-cold compress, and Dobby, the saggy sloth. All of which I distributed between each bawling child. When our little house calmed down, I did what I always do when I'm overwhelmed, bored, tired, stressed, or angry.

I got two fishbowl-sized glasses out of the cupboard, opened the fridge, reached in for the bottle of white banging around in the door, and clasped the cold neck. As I was about to slam the fridge shut, a series of thoughts crossed my mind.

Take responsibility.
You don't need it.
Change.
You can do it.
Just try.

My hand paused. I slid the bottle back into its cosy space next to the milk.

It was a simple move. A non-strenuous undertaking that didn't involve any screaming or being held down. I just put the wine back where I'd got it from. It was life changing.

Pregnancies aside, it was the first time I had ever decided not to have a drink.

I moved to the opposite side of the kitchen and switched on the kettle. I got a mug out from the cupboard and stood waiting for the jug to boil, in a state of utter disbelief.

Could it be this un-dramatic? So silent? *Don't I need to be wearing a black dress, like a grieving Greek widow, bent over a casket of wine, wailing to the sky?* I thought I'd have to walk through a tunnel of raised trumpets as people clapped me down the street, or that there would at least be a few fireworks.

But there was just me and a kettle.

I poured myself some tea and made my way out onto our veranda. I sat with the warm mug in my cupped hands, staring at the ocean.

'What are you doing out here?' John asked when he saw me.

'I'm having a cup of tea.'

'A cup of tea, eh?'

'Yes, a cup of peppermint tea.'

He didn't say anything else. He smiled, pulled up a chair next to me and took my hand. We sat there together and watched the sky turn from orange to black. I squeezed John's hand and stared at the horizon. I'd never felt so proud of myself as in that moment.

This first step felt like the beginning of something exciting.

Can I Have My Toothbrush and Dignity Back, Please?

Age 39

Life without a liquid lunch?

I imagined waving a white handkerchief like one of the Railway Children. Goodbye, G&Ts at the beach; *adieu*, Margarita Mondays; so long, Tequila Tuesdays; farewell, Friday-night Fireballs.

I was like Gollum holding onto my precious ring. I knew my hobbit – sorry, habit – was harmful, yet I couldn't imagine breaking free from it, cutting off my festering limb with one thwack of the guillotine. I'd heard myself use the term 'my drinking' to Dianne, like 'my arm' or 'my leg'; like it was part of me, or a valuable possession I clutched close to my chest and couldn't let go of.

Sitting on our verandah that night had felt great, but I was still stuck in a mindset that labelled sober people as total dullards. Fun cancellers with sad faces and no friends. What did they do apart from moan, knit and do Wordle? Where were they when I was in a pub? What were they doing when

I danced on podiums and ran naked along Brighton Beach with a traffic cone on my head?

Watching *Friends* re-runs, for God's sake?

Fuck. Sober. What a drag.

What would I do all the time if I wasn't drinking and being social? Where would I go? To milk bars? Roller skating rinks? Graveyards?

Did it mean I wouldn't be able to go to pubs?

How very un-British.

I thought of Sunday country walks growing up in England. Strolling down a winding, hedge-lined bridle path. A perfect whitewashed Tudor building with low door frames and dark wooden beams. The opening of a creaky door that led you into a musty bar area ... a rosy-cheeked landlord holding a jar of ale to the light ... leaning on damp beer mats as I ordered the drinks ... carrying them to the garden on a slippery round tin tray ... then arguing over whose round it was. Everything about it made my mouth water. I really couldn't imagine not being part of that. And in Australia everyone I knew met at hotels or bars. Friends had dinners at breweries or turned up for barbecues with heavy Eskies crammed with grog. Every social occasion was based around getting 'blind'.

Where would I meet my friends?

No one had ever phoned me and asked, 'Fancy going to a medieval loom-weaving workshop tonight, Vicky?'

It was always, 'Will I be seeing you down the boozer later?'

And what about girls' nights and weddings?

'It's not the venue, Vicky. It's not the environment. It's you. You need to redefine what you think of as fun,' Dianne had said.

My booze-soaked brain was telling me life without booze would be boring. But I'd been carrying the party pile around with me for so long, the load was hard to put down. I was used to creating a drinking environment anywhere, pub or no pub, and I had a continual excuse on hand to get messy. Anything from a bad day at work to the weather.

I used wanting to stay out of the rain to keep me in the pub for an extra round, or enjoying a warm summer's day to extend my stay in a beer garden. I pretended to be interested in skiing, so I could spend my holiday at a bar drinking mulled wine, from lunchtime until the snow melted. The rising of the sun, the sharing of food, or the fact my new fridge was delivered on time all gave me a reason to start drinking. Plane journeys were an excuse to get boozing in the morning, and camping trips enabled all-dayers. I could turn a mound of mud into a drinking environment. Just chuck some fairy lights up, pass the bottle opener, and let the good times roll. All I needed was a drinking partner (drinking alone was for alcoholics), a bottle and a justification.

I had never been out with people who didn't drink, except for Louise. I mean, why would I?

I didn't go to knitting classes or join a Morris dancing club, because those environments would have exposed me. Other people would have noticed when I vomited into a yarn basket or got my feet tangled up when jigging in the Adderbury 'balls and cock' dance-off.

But could I put an end to my longest-lasting relationship?

Look here, booze. This isn't working. I think it's time we went our separate ways. I hope we can still be friends. Now, can I have my toothbrush and dignity back, please?

I flashed back to that terrible scenario with Lucas, where I'd felt trapped. This was the same. I couldn't live with booze, and I couldn't live without it. I was in the battered-wife situation again, but alcohol was the offender.

Yet, the day I put the bottle back in the fridge and had a cuppa, I had made a healthier decision. I defended myself against the abuser.

'You did leave him. You got out of it, and you were free. It's the same with alcohol, Vicky, you can stop,' Dianne said.

She gave me the tools, the knowledge I needed, to break free. Yes, it was going to be hard to bid farewell to my longest-ever love, but there'd been too many ups and downs, too much heartache, anxiety and vomit. Booze and I were only staying together because I'd been too scared to leave.

I had to keep fighting back.

After weeks of therapy, and coming to understand my reasons for drinking and to heal stuff from the past, another option revealed itself to me. Giving up drinking didn't mean the end of my life. It meant a new life – stepping out of my comfort zone, trying something fresh, living a happier, sober existence.

Not hiding the person I truly was.

'I need to end it. "Take the L out of Lover", Dianne. This relationship is well and truly OVER!' I declared, and slipped my biro behind my ear. It was time to say goodbye to the old me.

Hello, spandangly-new, sober me.

Dianne took her spot near the whiteboard and began writing.

'Let's start again, Victoria. Now you know the reasons why you drank to excess, and you've taken responsibility, and you've decided to leave alcohol in your past. Let's start working on what you want from here on in.'

It was time to start building the life I craved, become the mother I knew I could be, and fix those broken promises.

'Imagine your life as a thing, Vic. A touchable object that can be manipulated and re-formed. Altered,' Dianne said.

I closed my eyes and imagined being a dilapidated old house that needed a revamp. Something with good bones but that required some work.

'Can you knock down the old thing and start again?' Dianne asked.

'Er, yes, I suppose I can,' I said.

I imagined driving a big, ugly bulldozer straight through the old building and smashing the place to smithereens.

'Now, build the house you've always dreamed of.'

This simple analogy pushed me into envisaging a different future. Yes, my roof was falling in, and I had some shit graffiti on the walls and a few cracks in my paint, but I had bones, solid structure and character. I was ready to flip this old hovel and get a fantastic new makeover.

Those pesky holes in my heart, where horrible boyfriends and failed friendships resided, would be excavated. I had unearthed every single wiggly worm from my past, and dug them up to give me room to grow. The soil beneath the house was fertile and I was ready to get building upwards. I would rebuild the foundations. I would search through the rubble, take out the good bits, leave the crap behind for the skip, then build a castle with a hundred bedrooms, bum-cleaning hoses, and a big pointless chandelier hanging in the stairwell.

Fabulous, darling.

Over my last two weeks of therapy, I made plans. I pinpointed what was important to me and rebuilt my house accordingly. When I got home, I made teas instead of wines, without hesitation. I sat with the cravings, remembered all the reasons why I had chosen this path and, slowly, began to feel myself be reconstructed. My brain felt like it was repairing and getting stronger. I read books about sobriety, including Louise's copy of *Twelve Steps and Twelve Traditions*. I read first-hand accounts by severe alcoholics and watched documentaries about addiction. I saw myself in every person; I recognised my problem, and developed an understanding and sympathy for the struggles of others. I wasn't dismissing alcoholism as being something separate from me, like I had at that AA meeting all those years ago. I was accepting that these people were just like me. I didn't like the term 'alcoholic', but I was learning more and more that I sat somewhere on the alcoholic spectrum. And, more importantly, I didn't mind sitting there. It was comfy.

With each passing day, I saw the truth about booze. Had I really enjoyed it that much? And what had I been getting out of being the drunkest person in the room for the past 26 years?

As the weeks passed, I started to hate alcohol.

I couldn't believe I wasted so much of my life being drunk.

So blotto I couldn't remember anything.

Why did I pour this substance down my throat? It seemed like total madness!

'I wish I had worked this all out sooner,' I said to John.

'Don't worry,' he said. 'You're doing it now and that's all that matters.'

He was right. (He is always right, but don't tell him that.)

For the first time in my life, I began to like myself. I could see my good points, and discovered people liked me for being me: a loyal friend, a listener, and someone who cheered them up (without being pissed).

I learned to put myself first, and no longer cared what other people thought, and that made me not want to drink. It was a circle of positivity, with each change supporting the next, like elephants holding on to each other's tails. All my deep feelings of insecurity dwindled. I didn't feel the need to impress or outdo.

Having therapy had allowed me to grow up, to see what and who was important. My check-up from the neck up was really working.

I read in one of my sobriety books that people stop maturing from the day they start drinking alcohol and, for me, that rang true. Emotionally, I was still 11 when I started therapy.

'I feel like I've aged twenty-six years in twelve weeks,' I said to Dianne.

'Well, luckily, you don't look like you have!'

When I finished a session with her, I got home and squeezed my family so tight their eyes nearly popped out of their heads. They didn't know why I was hugging them like a crazy person. They just hugged back. They were the reason I was learning so much, and they were the reason I was changing. If I didn't have them, I'd be propped up in a bar in Thailand, drinking my life away with some other lonely expats. I was so glad to have them.

Slowly, my need to escape motherhood disappeared. I was happy at home with my kids and husband. Having realised alcohol was not the disco ball of joy I once thought it was, its light was dimming, as was the constant negative chatter from the 'itty bitty shitty committee' in my head. As each week passed, my mood lifted. I didn't get angry as quickly.

When the house was a mess, or there were wet towels on the floor, or glitter up a nostril, or a poo in the bath, I wasn't as annoyed. I was still shouting like a rabid howler monkey every now and again, but not as much. It was progress.

*

'Bloody hell!' I said to my mate Bogfish on FaceTime one night. 'I think I've been doing life all wrong! I've been passed out for years and been missing all the good stuff!'

'What?' She looked confused, 'You mean waking up most Sundays with one shoe missing, twigs in your hair and the haul from *Deadliest Catch* multiplying in your underwear isn't normal?'

'Apparently not!'

'Geez,' she said with a smirk. 'Can I have the phone number of that therapist?'

To Me, with Love

I went out. To a party. I held a full-strength beer but didn't take a sip all night. Just stood there, clutching it like it was my lifeline to fun.

I accepted the invitation to the party towards the end of my 12 weeks of therapy. I decided it was time to test myself, to see if socialising without my liquid lover was even possible. I hadn't told any of my friends what I was doing. In fact, no one noticed anything different about me. I still managed to do the limbo, laugh and stay out past midnight.

The morning after, we met some friends for breakfast who all complained of bad headaches while munching on bacon sandwiches.

'What a night! But who bought that "Crazy Uncle" Moonshine rum?'

'Yeah, that ruined me!'

'And who was the streaker?'

I managed to sidestep these conversations and internally beamed about having a hangover-free day.

I can do this.

This party was proof I was changing.

All this growth had stirred up some things I had never asked myself before, that I guess were too confronting or I was just too immature to tackle. I wanted to see myself from another angle, outside of my drunken bubble. What did I look like when I was smashing pint glasses, drunkenly grinding against bar stools in grimy drum-and-bass clubs? Was I cool and funny? Or was I a mess?

That evening, I cosied up in the corner of the sofa with a pen and piece of paper, writing down all the times I had put myself at risk. I delved into my drunkest moments to see if I could step outside and have an opinion of them. A grown-up opinion, instead of laughing at myself like a teenager.

The list I made was worse than Santa's Naughty List. It included the sexual exploits I numbly participated in, injuries I suffered, and all my risky decisions. I held the piece of paper in front of me and read it aloud. I imagined the list was about someone else. What would I think of that person?

This whacked-out, pie-eyed lunatic was not the real me. It was an insane version of me, a nutter! Someone who was disrespecting herself every weekend. A girl who was displaying all the signs of being a raging booze bag.

When I returned to see Dianne, I showed her my 'naughty list'. She read it and asked, 'Do you think treating yourself in this way is okay?'

'No, it's not okay,' I said, a little ashamed. 'None of it is.'

I stared at my list and again questioned every single drunken deed. Then I grabbed Dianne's fountain pen and scribbled two words after each point.

Sleeping with random blokes: Not okay.
Blowing my finger off: Not okay.
Blacking out: Not okay.
Taking drugs: Not okay.
Being a human podium: Not okay.
Doing sickies from jobs: Not okay.

Telling lies: Not okay.
Drinking to impress my peers: Not okay.
Ignoring my children when hungover: Not okay.
Getting arrested: Not okay.
Having weird boyfriends with no shoes: Not okay.
Pissing my pants, often: Not okay.
Shitting my bed on my birthday ... [Did I not tell you that one?!]: Not okay.
Making dumb decisions: Not okay.
Vomiting on myself and others: Not okay.
Falling over: Not okay.
Drink driving: Not okay.
Drug driving: Not okay.
Flashing various parts of my body at strangers: Sometimes okay.
Starting long-term relationships after a drunken shag: Not okay.
Getting refused entry into pubs for being too intoxicated: Not okay.
Being hammered all the time: Not okay.
Getting beaten up by Lucas: Not okay.
Not being there for my kids: NOT OKAY!
What a list and what a waste of time it represented.
Stop doing stupid things, you total utter tit-head!
I sat there, looking at the piece of paper, bemused. How had I never examined the consequences of my binge drinking?

The list proved I had never cared about myself. The realisation stung my heart a bit. I wanted to leave a positive impression on the world, and not be remembered as that wild woman with various venereal problems, red-wine teeth and corn chunder splattered down her cargo pants.

None of this kind of thing was funny. (Apart from the time my friend woke up with a guy's business card stuck in her arse cheeks, with *call me* written on it. That was slightly amusing.)

There was not one 'funny' story from my past in which I did something brilliant, or helped someone or walked away with pride from a situation. My head was always hung low in shame. That shame penetrated so deep that I couldn't get it out. Hating myself, sleeping around, and not caring about my health were normal for me. Booze hid the real me behind this shit-faced idiot. It really was time to push her aside and step into the limelight.

I folded my list and put it in my back pocket.

I then read it every time I wanted to have a drink.

*

After testing the waters at the party, and one more session with Dianne on the topic of change, I slowly felt a weight I lumbered around under for over 26 years vanish. It was time to show the world I was stronger than booze: a brave woman, with a stumpy finger, capable of evolving. A tea-drinking rebel who could party until sunset. A proud H_2O slurper who elbowed shame in the ribs to get to the front of life's long queue. I had a VIP backstage pass to everything I had missed out on. The red velvet rope was unclipped.

At last, never drinking again didn't seem like a chore, it felt like a total relief. I would never, ever have the booze blues again. There was a cure for hangovers after all – it was me!

John noticed what was happening too. When we went out, his concerned gaze was replaced by one of pride. I wasn't making promises I couldn't keep, going to afterparties, or having to be hosed down in the bath like a muddy elephant.

The clear head from my newfound sobriety meant I understood so many aspects of my personality, my behaviour and what the old shrew at the brown school called comportment.

Since I was little, I'd always enjoyed witnessing stability, or order, get destroyed. Civility turned to carnage. Good to evil. I loved watching The Hulk transform from man to monster, seeing muscles ripple beneath his shirt and burst out, tearing the cloth. I rewound the video recorder when man became beast in *An American Werewolf in London*, so I could watch his body pulsate, distort and change, with claws breaking through the skin, and thick hair growing on his back. Dad called me down from my bedroom when footage appeared on TV of old water towers being detonated or chimneys being bulldozed. The times I bonded with him most were when we smashed plate glass windows at the dump. I watched in awe the Guinness World Records attempts by geeky Americans, in thick spectacles, as dominoes – incredible structures, thousands of pieces, which had taken weeks to erect – toppled over.

Blomp. Gone.

I was like this with drugs and alcohol. I liked the organisational aspect of it – setting up the night to watch it disappear around me. I started this pattern young, and it continued. Pouring liquor from the mahogany drinks cabinet down my throat, only to vomit straight after. Racking up perfect lines of cocaine – long, thick, white symmetrical bars – only to hoover them up my nose. I spent time making slick, well-packed joints, only to burn them down to ash. I mixed extravagant cocktails, adding fruit and ornate plastic sticks, to gulp them down in one swig.

Seeing girls who had started nights off all done up with perfect make-up fall over drunk or argue in the street made me happy. Watching eyes change from normal to glazed. Seeing bodies slumped on nightclub floors, and drunkards thrown out of clubs and sitting on kerbs, dishevelled remnants of their former selves. I imagined people, ready for a night out, looking good in the mirror before leaving the house, then getting home hours later, looking as if they'd had a fight with a lawnmower. I enjoyed it when friends got off their tits on drugs, with eyeballs rolling, teeth chattering, head in a toilet. Their total destruction made me feel like the night was a success.

Deep down, I knew I was doing the same, and destroying myself. Other people's bad habits took attention away from mine. Being around dysfunctional behaviours made light of my own darkness.

Drinking and drugging were types of public self-harm I laughed about as I ordered another round of drinks or necked another half a pill. It was acceptable to be a tad mashed up mentally in those ravy dazes, so self-reflection wasn't necessary. It was the nineties. If I hadn't been snorting a line of coke off a Filofax or barfing raspberry alcopops in an alleyway, I would have been considered odd. I was bred in a booze-worshipping culture, which meant I was preordained to be an unsteady piss-wreck, and once the party started ... it did not stop. I tested my limits more than most. Pushing, always pushing myself to the edge, my sadness smothered in booze.

Every weekend, as a young woman, a traveller, a partner, and even as a mother, I picked away at my petals:

I love me.

I love me not.

I love me.

I love me not.

I was tearing myself down, like those water towers, but brick by brick rather than in one giant explosion, so it went unnoticed for years. A slow dismantling of my mental equilibrium. My outwardly content demeanour was shadowed by low self-esteem and addiction.

Yet, if none of this had happened, I wouldn't have sought help.

My anxiety was my body screaming out for intervention.

It was my reason to change and my reason never to go back.

My children meant I acted on answering the questions that spun around in my head every Sunday.

Forced to seek out Dianne, she taught me not to be defined by my past and to have hope for a brighter future.

At our final meeting, I stopped picking the petals from that daisy.

A Thousand Wasted Sundays
Age 40

I stood at the kitchen benchtop, slicing a carrot into half-moons on a thick wooden chopping board. My baby girl was in her high chair, banging a red plastic spoon on the tray. John was picking up toys from the playmat and chucking them into a wicker basket in the corner of the lounge room. My little boy watched a cartoon as he peeled the skin off a tangerine.

It was a very normal evening, and I was looking forward to having dinner, putting the kids to bed, and snuggling up on the sofa to watch a grim British murder mystery series.

I scraped the edge of the knife down the board to add the carrots to our stir-fry. They fizzled as they hit the oil. I poured in the other ingredients and stood there stirring our dinner with a wooden spoon.

Without thinking, I said, 'What do you fancy doing tomorrow? Maybe we could go down to the park and cook breakfast on the barbecues?'

John, who was still crawling on his hands and knees collecting toys, turned his head. He looked surprised.

'Why are you looking at me funny?' I asked.

'Why do you think?' he replied.

I kept standing in the middle of the kitchen with wooden spoon in hand, while the wok sizzled behind me.

What do you fancy doing tomorrow?

It was something I'd never said on a Saturday night. For as long as I could remember, I'd always planned for a headache and a day in bed every Sunday.

A smile covered my face, and a rush of pride pierced my heart, as I realised the significance of my question.

I'm making a plan for Sunday morning!

Without even thinking ...

I'd chosen my family.

John got to his feet, strode over, and took me in his arms.

'I've done it.' I sobbed into his shoulder. 'I've changed.'

'You have! And we love you so much!'

I fought my way out of our tight embrace, leaned over to pull the baby from her chair and sandwiched her in the middle of us. My son understood it was time for a family cuddle, and weaved his way in between our knees and hugged my shins.

And, with our dinner burning in the pan, John and I stood, holding our children.

*

In all my years of drinking, I wasted over a thousand Sundays in bed hungover. If I add the days after the cheeky Tuesdays and the two-for-one Thursdays, that's probably another 2000 days lying in my lonely pit of discontentment. Three thousand days of my life hungover. Over eight years of my life spent in bed feeling like shit.

But if I hadn't been a drinker, I wouldn't have appreciated the kind man who accepted me and changed my life, and I wouldn't have my children. It was a journey that led me to now and every step had purpose. I'm five-and-a-half years alcohol free. My Sundays are normal. In fact, and I never thought it was possible, I've befriended Sundays.

The shame, regret, and the odd visit to the STD clinic after a blotto bonk with an electrician called 'Party Pete', have all dissolved into my past. Being a party-pooping teetotaller is wonderful. I do pottery now: I sculpt giant monkey heads out of lumps of mud and make coffee cups that leak like watering cans. I wake early too. I'm up with the birds for boxing class (I pound a bag instead of a box of wine), and go for ocean dips as the sun pops over the horizon (chunky dunks over skinny dips). I write, I podcast, I comment and I post. I talk with pride about my sobriety to whoever will listen.

I eat better, I sleep better, I'm not grumpy (as much), I recycle more, I care more, I feel more – and, most of all, I don't get kicked out of nightclubs by tetchy bouncers, dribble on strangers or worry that others think I'm boring. I embrace the boring now. Boring brings peace, boring brings calm; boring brings tea, crosswords and chocolate. Life's humble indulgences beat panic-ridden hangovers hands down.

*

Here I am, sitting at my computer with a big cup of fruity tea to my right and my smelly dog, Sandy, staring up at me on my left. I'm content and I'm writing a book. It's been a shock and a beautiful surprise to find life, alcohol free, is better in every single way.

Until getting sober, I'd lived life as if I was holding my breath, like when I'd travelled through long motorway tunnels in France as a kid. Finding sobriety is letting out a huge exhale and bursting into sunshine.

I have empathy for the girl in the scuffed Adidas shell toes with Sporty Spice hair, who danced till dawn and abandoned her body most weekends. I know she was looking for love in all the wrong places. In a bottle, a line of coke, a random man or a different country.

I've learned I was wrong about a lot of things. I thought sobriety was just about giving up alcohol, but I have found it is much more than that. It wasn't about taking something away, it was learning who I am without it.

I have no idea where my story would have ended up if I had not had my kids. They gave me two important windows into a different life, and I took heed of what they showed. I had to.

Even though my children don't know it, they now have a better person for a parent. I'm present to witness my life, including its failures and successes. I understand my children don't need a perfect mum; they just need a happy one.

Becoming a mother, with or without wine, was a big adjustment. I went from gulping strong cocktails from coconuts on far-flung beaches and standing on stages downing pints of warm ale, to blowing noses, pulling out splinters and endlessly wiping bum cracks. The transition was more difficult than I could have ever imagined. Parenting was a struggle and, to be honest, it still is. Being a mum takes time to get used to. Some days, I feel like marching out the front door and never coming back, especially after one too many 'lost-shoe' and 'whose-toy-is-that?' arguments. Some days, I just need space, and other days, I will admit, the image of a frothy cold beer slips into my mind.

But that's fleeting. I've learned how to deal with cravings: I sit with feelings, let them pass through me. I play the tape forward and remember why I no longer drink – then I go and put the kettle on.

Chaos averted.

My gift of sobriety means I will never waste a Sunday, or any day, again.

My goal with all of this is to be the cycle breaker, an inspiration for my children, rather than an embarrassment. I don't want them to learn bad habits from me and I don't want them to think drinking is how all humans have fun. I realise now that I was subliminally sending the message 'Mummy needs wine to be a parent' or 'Mummy has to drink to deal with your behaviour'. Mummy wine culture means we're taught to anaesthetise ourselves against our kids when times get tough.

I want to show them how much better it is to be the one who says no, who goes against the societal norm. I will show them that just being themselves is enough, and that life is about facing challenges and not hiding under a big, thick layer of alcohol. Lean into life instead of backing out of it. Grab it by the balls and remember each day.

My children will never know me drunk. They will never have to carry me to bed. Never have to clean up my vomit, bring me paracetamol, or talk me down from a panic attack. There will be no staggering around, no slurring, no demanding 'Club Tropicana' at 3 am and no boozy dog breath as I kiss them goodnight.

Life goes on, sober or not. The kids are busy getting beads stuck up their noses, spitting fish fingers at me, demanding they need a poo as we get into the car, choking on watermelon, eating bogies, leaving wet towels on the floor, dragging pens along newly painted walls, scoffing all the worming tablets, smearing bum cream on the dog, getting high temperatures on the first day of holidays, biting each other and hating anything green. It's a loud and crazy household, which drives me loony, yet fills me with love.

It will be Christmas soon – my favourite time of the year. I bought some mince pies at the supermarket (the cheapest ones are the best). When I was a drinker, I would never have eaten a mince pie without a huge ice-brimming glass of Baileys. Drinking made me create customs, like how it was impossible to eat white fish without white wine, or go to a girls' night without guzzling shots. They were unbreakable correlations that became so normal, changing them would be a crime. Therapy taught me to think beyond these stereotypical habits and change this stunted, dead-end way of thinking.

I stare long and hard at the Baileys bottle on the shelf at the shop, imagine swilling the ice around in the thick tumbler, making the edge of the glass go a creamy beige colour. But, with many years of practice under my belt, I really know myself now and understand my past behaviour. I would have had two, three tumblers, then cracked open Nan's ageing port, tripped over the turkey, and been sick on my new Christmas jumper. There was no sitting back in a big, cosy armchair, sipping on one glass while we played Trivial Pursuit. It's not how me and booze worked. It was all or nothing. Now it's just nothing.

I scoff my sugary mince pies, and hope no one catches me as I hold the squirty cream nozzle in my mouth and squeeze the trigger. Luckily, overdosing on cream and mince pies doesn't give me anxiety or cause me to flash my knickers at policemen, it only gives me heartburn and tighter trousers. I'm weighing up the damage here.

Perhaps one day, I will get wired up to a research scientist's magic noggin machine (otherwise known as a magnetic resonance imager) to see if there's neurological damage from my drug taking and binge drinking. I guess there is. It shows itself to me in various forms, like when I'm putting the dustpan and brush in the oven and forgetting to put bananas in the banana bread. Little F-ups that go unnoticed by everyone but me.

Every day, my choice to no longer get wasted throws a few curveballs my way. There are social hurdles for me to clumsily leap over, situations I have to navigate alcohol free, and boundaries I have to put in place, so I feel safe. Sobriety is not all glitter unicorns and never-ending squishy marshmallow rainbows. Life still hurts sometimes, but instead of numbing myself, I process my pain. It's raw and real, but breaking through unaided to the other side of sadness is so damn satisfying.

The main lessons I learned in therapy were that all people are capable of change and that I don't have to sink to the bottom of the keg to be deserving of healing. Even when habits are lifelong and deeply ingrained, everyone can choose to reframe and rebuild. That house is worthy of a makeover.

I'm sure there will be testing times ahead, unexpected moments when I will want to reach for a drink. Death, illness and disappointments that will lead me to dark places in my mind. That's life, but I will deal with each event as it unfurls. I can't worry about the future; all I can do is hope to make wise decisions when these challenges arise. I have a stronger frame of mind now and I don't think I'll break as easily.

I check in with my little 'Done Drinking' App. It shows over two thousand days sober. I think about adding it as my Facebook profile picture, but chicken out. There are enough smug, righteous cunts on there already.

Sober means the world to me. I hold it close. It's the secret to living a more joyful life, and a secret I simply cannot keep, even as I refrain daily from tapping the shoulders of random people at bus stops and sounding off about sober life, like an evangelical preacher. I am so desperate for the world to catch on. Of course, I hold it in, so I don't find myself on the end of a restraining order or get a reputation for being a total fruit-loop (I might be 80,000-plus words too late for that?).

Being sober is something I once never imagined possible. Now that I am, I trust myself, I have *my* back. I feel no weight upon me. No shame. No fear. No apprehension. I'm ready to race down a sand dune and leap into the ocean, hand in hand with the only people who matter: me, John and my two snotty little darlings.

'Wait. Slow down you lot!' I shout, a little out of breath as I watch them running into the distance.

I can't keep up and plonk my bottom on the sand as my family meet the water.

Bloody hell. Why am I so tired?

My pulse is racing, and small beads of sweat are dripping down my temple.

I put my hand inside my vest top and feel my left boob. It is tender. The only time my boobs ever felt like this was after I shot, headfirst, down a cement slide at Wet'n'Wild … oh and when I was pregnant with George.

What?
I can't be, I'm 41.
Wait?
The night away in the posh hotel?

*

Holy shit baskets ... here we go again.

Epilogue

If you're considering going alcohol free, then remember – this is not a journey about booze, it's a journey about you, of understanding the person who existed before alcohol and learning to love the person who is revealed after you quit.

Whether you're drinking because you're socially awkward, masking trauma, numbing out a bad relationship, escaping motherhood, depression, anxiety, addiction, or it's simply a bad habit, finding out why you drink will be the key to your sober door. It's not about frequency or the amount you consume. It's about your own mental relationship with alcohol. There is a vast spectrum of alcohol-use disorder, you don't have to be at the extreme – at death's door, or at rock bottom – to reach out, you can start now. If alcohol is having a negative impact on your life and you are questioning it, then it's time to act.

I believe the only way to unravel your relationship with alcohol is to seek professional support. Find the help you deserve and allow someone to guide you along your path.

Start talking about alcohol. Put it out there to the ones you love. Talk to a friend, a doctor, or a therapist, do whatever works for you. Tell someone booze isn't working for you anymore. Communicating your struggle to others, no matter how big or small the problem, will be a stepping stone into a new life.

It's not easy to stop doing what you have always done, to change ingrained behaviour, or perhaps even to imagine being a person who no longer drinks. But it is possible. You have to get stuck into sobriety. Read the books, walk the walk, talk the talk, and do the work. Give sober life as much attention as you gave alcohol. Pour sober down your throat, until it seeps out of your soul.

In time, sobriety will reveal the person you truly are. The perfectly, imperfect authentic you. (And, like me, could be an introvert, who likes pottery, long walks, is obsessed with tea, enjoys rescuing dying ants from puddles, watches brain-dead TV, eats chocolate and is in bed at 8 pm.) Your positive choices will turn chaos into peace, and self-loathing into contentment.

It's a simple life for this ex-party girl, free of expectations, headaches and wasted weekends. I'm no longer responsible for getting the last laugh, like Snarf from ThunderCats. Being sober means I'm free to live the life I choose, without shame and without anxiety. I have left any regret in the past, along with some ridiculous dance moves and dodgy boyfriends. I am happy to tell my story here, in these pages, because the old me, the party girl, does not represent the person I am now. She was a lost soul, under the influence, and unable to say no to a drink or, mostly, yes to a shrink. But, in the end, after many years, a hundred red flags flicking me in the face, I took my power back.

And you can too …

Now it's time for me to stop droning on. I hope my funny little book makes you think. Nudges you to 'reconsider alcohol', question the role it plays in your life and our society.

I also hope you give sober life a go. I promise (without wanting to sound like Mrs Knobby McKnobhead) it will be the best thing you ever do!

Then, once you're sober ... start talking about it and don't ever stop! Shout about sobriety from a frikkin' rooftop. Tell the world your story ... so others don't hide behind theirs.

*

Fred was born by C-section on 7 December 2018.

A Note to those Reconsidering Alcohol

For more information on being sober, head to my website www.soberawkward.com and listen to my comedy podcast *Sober Awkward* on Spotify, iTunes or wherever you find your podcasts. Discover what it's really like being sober in this booze-drenched society, and learn how to feel the awkward and do it anyway!

On there, you can also find Cuppa, the sober awkward community, where together we can normalise meeting for a lovely cup of tea, rather than a cringy boob-flash-making beer. It's a place to meet other sober people, and those who are questioning their relationship with alcohol, just like you. You can create sober events and groups, and share your sobriety journey. Put the kettle on and come for a cuppa!

Follow me (in an un-stalky way)
@soberawkward
@drunkmummysobermummy

You can also contact these amazing organisations, to get some extra support and advice.

lifeline.org.au
soberinthecountry.org
fare.org.au
beyondblue.org.au
aa.org.au
untoxicated.com.au
healthdirect.gov.au
diannespencer.com.au/sundays
(Say Vic sent you!)

Thanks

I started writing this book on the day I gave up drinking. It wasn't easy to get here. I wrote as I stirred spaghetti sauce, shuffled chapters around in between breast feeds and edited in bed with a sidelight while the rest of the house snored their little heads off.

I wrote the first round of 'Thanks' on the day before Fred's birth. It read:

> *I'm creating human life tomorrow; I'm booked in to have this giant baby cut from my big belly. It will be my third C-section, so the operation has some risk. I'm older now, being 42. I'm more worried about this birth than I was about the other two. It's probably irrational, but I thought I should write something down, finish this book, in case anything weird happens. Like death.*

Well, the good news is I didn't die, and now have three snot-faced barbarians interrupting my serenity. Being a mum of three is really rather awful sometimes, so hiding in my office, in a café or on the toilet with my laptop balanced on my knees, has been a life saver. (Their lives and mine!)

It's a dream come true to see my story come to life, and I could not have done it without the help of some amazing humans.

First, I would like to thank Dianne. She gently guided me to sobriety. I needed her so badly that first day in her tiny office. Together, armed with tissues, tea, biscuits and pens, we unravelled. I didn't reveal everything here – 12 weeks of therapy would not have fitted inside these pages – but what I will say is, everything she taught me, worked. Each Monday, she made me feel hopeful and dug out the answers. I will never forget that. Thank you, Dianne.

I also want to give a shout-out to my family: my lovely sister Sarah and her husband, Dan, my newly sober sister-in-law, Clare, my brother Neale, and all my nieces and nephews, all of whom had no idea I was over-drinking or that I was writing a book about it. I want to thank John's family for their unwavering support, and to congratulate my sister Louise for being sober for 24 years. I never gave her the credit she deserves. I'm sorry it's taken so long. Well done. You're amazing.

To my parents, who, at 85 and 80, can throw a better party than anyone I know. Thank you for understanding my reasons why, and I'm sorry you had to read so much about the adventures of my vagina. I love you very much.

Most importantly, I want to thank John, who has honourably and quietly supported me throughout this entire time. He has sat back and watched my story unfold without judgement. He is the only person who saw how fun nights out crippled me the next day, but he never told me I needed help, he just held my hand when I decided to change. His love for me and our children is unwavering – without him, I would probably be standing on a roadside, thumbing a lift to nowhere.

THANKS

I've realised it's not the good moments that make a marriage successful, it's enduring the bad bits. It's the times he got up in the night to a crying child, it's the forgiving me when I call him a prick, it's the investigating of rashes in dark orifices with an iPhone torch, it's the never seeing each other, the accepting of pecks on cheeks in hallways, it's the taking over if I'm tired, it's the cleaning of fridges, the washing of dogs' bums, the hosing out of bins, the picking at nits, the scrubbing of the stove, the removal of spiders, the hanging out the washing, the unblocking the toilet, it's the smile on his face when my mum gives him a horrible t-shirt for his birthday, it's the dealing with the everyday shit that makes him a winner. It's knowing he will be there, next to me every night when we collapse, exhausted. Thank you, John, I will try to have sex with you more often.

I also want to thank my three lovely kids in a way that's not going to make me, or them, stab forks into our eyeballs. I promise not to say 'blessed', because I hate that more than I hate people in yoga poses at sunset on Facebook. All I will say is, cheers to them. My beautifully annoying little brats have no idea what I, or they, have done. Them showering me with glory in their appreciation of my being a better mum will have to wait, probably until they're 40. But I will say this, strangers (that is, nosey ladies at the supermarket) warned me that my life would change for the worse after having kids, always giving me negative predictions: 'Have fun while you can.' 'It's downhill from here on in.'

No one ever mentioned how enriched my life would be, how worthwhile it would be.

I often hear 'How fast they grow up' or 'Blink and you'll miss it', but I feel like I've absorbed every moment. I've soaked up their joy and tears since they were born, a love that's stored safely away in my brimming heart. So, thanks for being cute enough for me to always like you. Thanks for cuddling me and making me laugh. I love you.

To my friends old and new, the bootcampers, the potters, the boxers, the antenatal girls, the mothers' group, my Sunny Coast buddies, the Sober breakfast crew, the travellers, the Cuppa crew and all my old mates from home. Your unswerving support means the world. To Shauna, for telling me to start my blog. A special flap of my wings to 'The Flies', for providing good stories and everlasting friendship.

My two friends from school reached out and apologised to me in recent years. They said they were not sure why they rejected me so long ago. It was healing to know it was never my fault. Just kids being kids I guess. I wish them well.

To Lucy and Hamish, my sober partners in crime, thanks for making our brilliant podcast *Sober Awkward* so relatable and allowing your dirty laundry to be aired in public for the sake of all humankind. Oh, and thanks to Alan, the sound guy, for technical support, emotional support, and allowing us to take the piss on a weekly basis.

And to everybody who has sent me encouraging emails, either via my blog or on social media. And a huge thanks to the online sober community who have shared my story and 'liked' my silliness. Virtual high fives! To all the failed exes and the shoeless drifters – if it wasn't for you, it wouldn't have been so interesting (or itchy).

Finally, an awkward long hug to Katherine and the team at Pantera Press, for believing in my story. Thank you Gina, my editor, for bringing my book together with supportive hints and incredible skill. I'm not the spiritual type, but meeting you was meant to be. And to Sarah, my agent, for pushing me forward and never giving up on me. You amazing ladies made this happen and for that I am forever grateful.

Oh, and thank *you* for reading this book. I hope it helps. I love you all. Now, can you turn the volume down?

I'm going to bed.

Australia's favourite drag queen tells all

CAUGHT IN THE ACT

'Glorious'
Osher Günsberg

'Funny and moving'
Dannii Minogue

'Fearless'
Benjamin Law

SHANE JENEK AKA COURTNEY ACT

PANTERA PRESS | SPARKING IMAGINATION, CONVERSATION & CHANGE